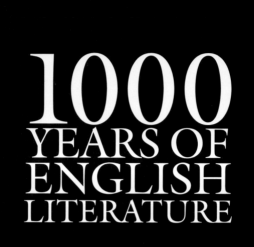

1000
YEARS OF
ENGLISH
LITERATURE

*A Treasury of
Literary Manuscripts*

HWÆT WE GARDE[N

Hna ingear dagum. þeod cynning[e

þrym ge frunon huða æþelingas ell[

fre medon. oft scyld sceefing sceaþe[

hreatum monegū mægþum meodo se[

of teah egsode eorl syððan ærest þ[

fea sceaft funden he þær frofre ge[

Act. II

Act Two.   Scene First.

Curtain discloses Prof. sitting alone before small table, ~~uuuuuu~~

~~uuuuuu~~ *red and white* cloth, before glass mug of beer.   Another unoccupied little

table, match stand on it.   Through narrow archway one or two heads o[

customers in main part are seen.   Mechani~~c~~ed piano, not visible finishe[

valse tune.

Large round spectacles.

Prof.   Small, frail, sallow, thin whisker, fair. Clothes very ill

fitting, extremely shabby.   Deplorable, heavy boots, ~~uuuuuu~~

visible under table.   Arms far through sleeves, no trace of

cuffs.   General aspect of inferior physique and poverty *contra*

~~xxxxxxxxxxxxxxxxxxxxxxxx~~ ~~um~~ through~~uu~~t the scene speech and de[*with*

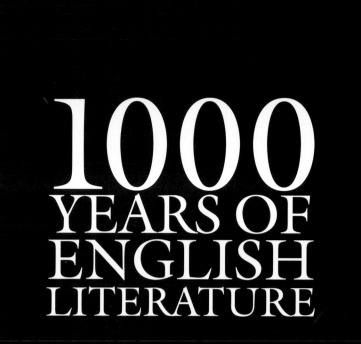

1000 YEARS OF ENGLISH LITERATURE

A Treasury of Literary Manuscripts

Chris Fletcher

with Roger Evans and Sally Brown

HARRY N. ABRAMS, INC., PUBLISHERS

Flagstaff Public Library
Flagstaff. Arizona

Contents

320.8
F6120

The Eighteenth Century   80

The Nineteenth Century   106

The Twentieth Century   156

What's so fascinating about literary manuscripts? An answer might well be found by looking at three remarkable discoveries made in 1934.

Colonel W. Butler Bowden, frantically searching in a cupboard at his home near Chesterfield for table-tennis equipment, unwittingly turned up (among a pile of old books which he at first vowed to toss on the bonfire 'so we may be able to find Ping Pong balls & bats when we want them') the 'Book of Margery Kempe', the earliest surviving autobiography in the English language and probably the earliest 'literary' work by an English woman. A safe in the bedroom of the warden of Winchester College disclosed, to the astonished scholar W. K. Oakeshott, the only manuscript of Malory's *Le Morte D'Arthur*, hitherto known solely from an edition printed in 1485 by William Caxton, through whose studio the manuscript is thought to have passed. Until the manuscript for Coleridge's verse *Kubla Khan* came to light, the only clear authority for it, and the famous story of its remarkable inspiration, was the author's 'preface' in *Christabel and Other Poems*, where it was first published in 1816. Those familiar with the poem and its evocative associations were intrigued to see not only that the carefully written out 'fair copy' (or finished text) seemed absurdly far removed from a 'fragment' snatched from the flux of drug-induced visions, but also that the attached explanation of its composition painted a far less romantic picture than Coleridge supplied in print. Not even a mention of the infamous 'man from Porlock'.

Such dramatic discoveries do not happen often, let alone grouped together in a single year. Yet any library founded with three extraordinary collections in 1753, to which it has added ever since, might be expected to be able to boast equally important items with which the remarkable class of 1934 could share its shelves. This is indeed the case with The British Library, the custodian of every manuscript featured in the pages that follow. It is a testimony to the breadth and depth of the Library's collections that a well-plotted story of the English literary tradition can be told entirely from its own holdings.

In some cases an embarrassment of riches presented itself in the compiling of this book. Which George Eliot manuscript to choose from the almost complete holdings of her novels? Byron's earliest manuscript drafts, or his very last? A poem by Hopkins, or one by Clare? William Blake's well-

known 'Tyger' or the more obscure and recently discovered poem 'The Phoenix to Mrs Butts'? Which of the major Oscar Wilde plays? Or his tear-stained 'De Profundis' instead? A draft of which poem from the entire manuscript of William Wordsworth's 1807 *Poems, in Two Volumes*?

There are, of course, omissions. Although it has plenty of his letters, the library holds no significant poetic manuscripts by T. S. Eliot (his draft of *The Waste Land*, covered with Ezra Pound's annotations, is in the New York Public Library); nor, apart from annotated proofs and a number of letters, is there much of note by Yeats. For the earlier period it would be desirable to be able to boast not just the largest number of copies of *The Canterbury Tales*, but the most important among them (the Ellesmere manuscript, in the Henry Huntington Library, California). The Vercelli Manuscript (in the cathedral near Milan from which it takes its name), with its important Anglo-Saxon poems would find a place on any curator's list of *desiderata*.

As, indeed, would any literary manuscript in the hand of John Donne. Yet only three poems actually penned by him are recorded (at the Bodleian, Harvard and in private hands). Even less has come down to us from Marlowe, while of Philip Sidney and Edmund Spenser, the world has precious little. In truth, very few writings survive in autograph (written in the hand of the author) before the Restoration. This fact played a significant part in determining the present selection. For the early and medieval period it was a choice (with one remarkable exception) of drawing upon significant copies or making do with nothing. The ever-so-slow but steady increase of the autograph record after about 1500 allowed for the inclusion of only those manuscripts actually produced by their authors. Thus while any number of contemporary copies of poems by the famous Dr Donne might have featured, it was felt more important to devote the space available to occasionally less august figures, such as George Peele, whose manuscripts provide a direct link, through, as Keats put it, 'this warm hand, my scribe', to the actual creative force behind the work.

Many remarkable individual stories of manuscript survival (such as witnessed in the year 1934) will be told throughout this book, but it is worth sketching out here the general provenance and shape of the collections to which they now belong. The British Library, an integral part of the British Museum until 1972, was effectively established in 1753 with three great

collections which had already been accumulated by men of great vision and dedication. The library of the writer and antiquary Sir Robert Cotton (1571–1631), badly damaged in a fire of 1731 in Ashburnham House, Westminster, preserves a wealth of early material, much saved from the monasteries dissolved by King Henry VIII after his split from the religious authority of Rome. Thanks to Cotton we have the unique tenth-century manuscript of 'Beowulf', the longest surviving and most important early literary work in the English language and, among the treasures of the medieval period, the poems 'Sir Gawain and the Green Knight', 'Pearl', 'Cleanness and Patience', all preserved in a single manuscript volume. The latter is still known as Cotton Nero A x, an example of the classification given by Cotton himself to record the fact that, in his library, this particular volume could be found the tenth along on shelf A in the book case surmounted by the bust of the Emperor Nero.

The Harleian collection gathered by Robert and Edward Harley, Earls of Oxford, contains a rich vein of literary material. One verse anthology, known as the 'Harley Lyrics', comprises more than half the known secular lyrics to have come down to us from the Middle Ages, while Harley manuscript 7368 contains three pages of Elizabethan secretary hand (a difficult, heavily abbreviated style of writing) thought, almost certainly, to be the only example of Shakespeare at work. Sir Hans Sloane, Lord of the Manor of Chelsea and a wealthy and influential physician, was another important collector of manuscripts. In addition to the many tracts on alchemy, medical recipes (or 'receits') and works on anatomy he collected (partly for his professional enlightenment) a significant body of literary material. Included here are the beautiful and strange prose reflections of fellow physician Sir Thomas Browne, and a volume containing the bawdy song 'I have a gentil Cock', thought to have been variously owned by a professional minstrel and the Benedictine monastery of Bury St Edmunds.

Among other important complete (often referred to as 'closed') single collections acquired by the Library after its foundation was that of the Royal Manuscripts, formed by successive sovereigns of England. Before being given to the nation by the authority of George II in 1757, the collection of some 2000 volumes was stored in an old dormitory in Westminster School. Among them was Jonson's 'The Masque of Queens', composed for the New

Year festivities at Whitehall Palace in 1609 and subsequently presented to Henry, Prince of Wales, thus escaping the fire of 1623 which broke out in the author's lodgings, to claim a great many of his papers.

T. J. Wise, bibliographer and, as it turned out, sometime forger of printed documents, was responsible for creating a fine collection of literary manuscripts. The richness, in his Ashley Collection, of the works of major authors of the nineteenth century is witnessed in these pages by drafts of works by Byron, Percy Bysshe Shelley, the Brontës and Christina Rossetti, while his enthusiasm for the manuscripts of living authors is plain to see in the draft dramatization of *The Secret Agent* sold to him by the ever-needy Joseph Conrad. By far the largest collection of manuscripts held at The British Library, however, and that most represented within the pages of this volume, is the Additional series. As the name suggests, this is a growing (open) collection upon whose shelves might be found for example, Lawrence Durrell's draft of *Justine*, which came to the Library by bequest in 1995. Of the single volumes of material forming part of this series (which might mean a single notebook or a bound gathering of some two hundred originally loose leaves), it represents number 73, 099, part C.

Having touched upon the sense of excitement they can generate, and the routes by which they have in one way or another come down to us, it is perhaps time to introduce the issue of what, exactly, defines a literary manuscript. The answer is not a simple one. In the most general of terms, it represents the work of an author which has come to us in a written form. But each component of this definition can be broken down into an array of more specific characteristics.

What is meant by the term 'work'? The earliest work represented here is a poem written in an elevated heroic style, in alliterative verse expressed through a West Saxon idiom impossible to understand unless the language has been studied. Among the most recent is a play, by Harold Pinter, in a naturalistic style and written in language which succeeds precisely through its immediately recognizable qualities. In between these two works (or worlds), separated by 1000 years, we have allegorical poems, didactic poems, verse romances, nonsense verse, secular lyrics, elegies, tales, short stories, novels, prose tracts, 'histories', masques – the list could go on. The term 'work' does not here exclude the genre of the literary letter (as for example,

T. S. Eliot's reflections from the Margate seafront or Jonathan Swift's letter to 'Vanessa'), or the diary (such as Dr Johnson's, kept while touring north Wales). Adding to the complexity of the issue is the fact that some works exist in the process of creation or, to put it more crudely, 'draft' state, while others represent a perfect 'fair copy', as immaculate and immutable as the printed page.

What then is meant by the 'author' of a work? For at least half of British literary history the very concept of authorship is problematic. 'Beowulf' may have had no one single identifiable master, with the text gradually shaped through the course of an oral tradition until caught for posterity upon vellum by a scribe. Margery Kempe could neither read nor write and the final version of her book, initially dictated to a priest, survives in a version copied down shortly afterwards by a scribe named Salthows – possibly under her direction, possibly not. The 'Harley Lyrics' are entirely anonymous, no one is certain whether the English poems in the copy of Charles d'Orléans's 'Prison Book' are by Charles or not, and scholars have devoted considerable energy to the task of feeding all the varying copies of *The Canterbury Tales* into a computer to try to get as close as possible to the text intended by Chaucer. Of course, the problem would be at least partially solved if a copy of the *Tales* had come down to us in Chaucer's hand but, as has been discussed earlier, in an age of professional scriveners the autograph manuscript was rare indeed. And would the problem of the author's intention necessarily be solved by the scrutiny of a manuscript written in his or her own hand? Of the numerous versions of the same poem in Auden's notebook, which is the most authoritative? The author himself had problems deciding.

The phrase 'written form', hinting at the actual physical constitution of a manuscript, demands closer attention. 'Beowulf', the earliest form of English literary manuscript, is to be found in a parchment codex (a bound book containing leaves fashioned from animal skins), written out in an English minuscule (or lower case) script with a quill. It wasn't until around 1495 that paper was actually manufactured in England, although its earliest domestic use can be traced to the early fourteenth century. Between those dates occurred the gradual replacement of parchment (usually sheep skin) or vellum (actually calf skin, but frequently used as a generic term for all soft parchment) by paper. The 'Sloane Lyrics' represents a manuscript compiled

using scraps of both material and is written in the Gothic hand typical of a medieval scribe, in many ways easier to read than the secretary hand which developed in the late fifteenth century and would appear to have been the style favoured by Shakespeare. He might well, however, have chosen the far clearer italic hand which became an alternative script from the mid sixteenth century. Some writers employed both styles and occasionally within one text, as demonstrated by Ben Jonson. The legible, elegant English round hand developed throughout the seventeenth century (perhaps best exemplified here by Katherine Philips) and can be seen as the proper precursor of our modern style which in turn owes a good deal to the speedy scrawl favoured throughout the eighteenth and nineteenth centuries. The use of loose sheets of paper was clearly established by the time Robert Herrick wrote out his fair copy elegy in 1620, while today's writers (or indeed compilers of shopping lists) would immediately recognize Alexander Pope's habit of seizing whatever scraps – particularly old letters – fell to hand.

But what of the future? We hear more and more how today's authors eschew the notepad and the typewriter in favour of the word processor; of their neglect of the postbox in favour of the email account. Yet the history of literary transmission, from the grandest of narratives to the slightest of couplets, has always been a history of change, from tales told round the fire, to vellum, to paper, to printing, to the typewriter, telex, telegram, telephone and even text message. The challenges facing the modern curator are not insurmountable. In fact, libraries are already beginning to find ways to preserve the burgeoning riches of the gloriously indiscreet and, in some ways, wonderfully old-fashioned correspondence of the digital in and out box and are determined to gather, as diligently as anything else, the numerous annotated print-outs encouraged by the word processor.

As twilight fell upon the outreaches of the Roman Empire at the beginning of the fifth century, pagan Germanic tribes began to move into Britain. Was it a dark age that followed? For what has come to be known as English Literature, it represented a dawn. The swift conversion to Christianity of the Anglo-Saxon invaders, and their consequent devotion to the importance of the written (rather than remembered) word, produced a culture in which writings could be formally set down, shared, preserved, passed on and developed; in other words, a culture with its own literary tradition.

Many of the earliest texts which have come down to us are of a religious, administrative or political nature: the first written specimen of Old English (or Anglo-Saxon) is a set of constitutional instructions; King Alfred's great programme of translations from Latin into Old English in the latter part of the ninth century, intended to reassert a sense of cultural cohesion in the face of Viking threats, included Bede's *Ecclesiastical History of the English People*, completed in 731; it was Alfred again who began the Anglo-Saxon Chronicle, a record of events which was continued through to the middle of the twelfth century and represents the first history of a western country in its own language; among the most outstanding sacred texts is the Lindisfarne Gospels, written down in an uncial script in about 715, illuminated to a quality unparalleled in early English art and given, some 250 years later, an interlinear translation in a Northumbrian dialect.

The political and religious significance attached to the written word contributed to the survival of works written as much for enjoyment as for edification. Without Alfred's insistence upon the importance of setting down texts in the vernacular, 'Beowulf', whose origins as a recited (or sung) text may date back as far as the sixth or seventh centuries, might never have been captured for posterity in the West Saxon dialect by a scribe around the year 1000. Similarly, the 'Hymn of Caedmon' (Caedmon sometimes being named as the first English poet) is known to us thanks to the account Bede gives in his *History* (several copies of which translate Bede's Latin translation back into Old English).

Few Anglo-Saxon literary manuscripts survive. Among those that do, the Exeter Book, preserved at Exeter Cathedral, contains numerous verses, including unique copies of the 'Seafarer' and the elegiac masterpiece, 'The Wanderer'. The Vercelli manuscript, in northern Italy, contains the 'Dream

of the Rood' and, as with the Exeter Book, a number of poems thought to be the work of the ninth-century poet Cynewulf. Sir Robert Cotton owned the manuscript of the heroic poem, the 'Battle of Maldon', but this was all but destroyed in the notorious fire which wreaked havoc upon much of his library in 1731.

The two earliest manuscripts chosen here escaped destruction in the same fire, before being transferred to the British Museum Library in 1753. Most would agree that 'Beowulf' is the most important extant Old English literary text and it can justly take pride of place at the beginning of this book. Wulfstan's 'Sermon to the English' cannot, perhaps, be described as a literary text in the strict sense of the word, yet its strong theme, vivid language and rhetorical skill mark it out as a carefully considered, powerful piece of writing. Perhaps more than this it is represented here because, whereas the vast majority of manuscripts from the period are scribal copies which may have no immediate geographical or even temporal connection with their original authors, this remarkable document, dating from 1014, bears annotations by Wulfstan himself – surely one of the earliest examples of drafting in the vernacular.

Over half the known English secular lyrics which survive from the period between the Norman Conquest in 1066 and Chaucer's death in 1400 are to be found in just one anthology compiled by an assiduous scribe (the 'Harley Lyrics' or Harley 2253). This quite astonishing fact reflects both the predominance of religious writing in the period – the apotheosis of which might well be represented by William Langland's 'Piers Plowman' – and the abandonment of the vernacular for some considerable time after the conquest, in favour of Latin or Anglo-Norman. When the language started to return to literary use, as for example with the verse chronicle 'Brut', written by Lazamon around 1200, it did so in a way which partly carried forward the alliterative force of Anglo Saxon lines (revived again even later by the 'Gawain Poet' and William Langland), but also introduced new idioms (particularly from the French) and techniques such as the syllabic rhymed verse. By 1390 English was sufficiently re-established as a literary language for the court poet and friend of Chaucer, John Gower, to choose it over and above French or Latin, in which he was equally gifted, for his most successful work 'Confessio Amantis'.

In addition to its new forms, what has come to be known as 'Middle English' differs markedly in theme from the older Anglo-Saxon tradition. Less elevated, solemn and altogether on a more domestic scale, its loss of an earlier heroic grandeur was compensated for in a new psychological and emotional intensity. Nowhere is this better exemplified than in the candid, confessional 'Book of Margery Kempe', the first truly autobiographical piece of writing in the English literary tradition. Even in complicated allegorical works, intended to instruct the reader on the finer points of theology, a human heart beats. This is the case with the anonymous 'Gawain Poet', whose long poem 'Pearl' would seem to suggest the author's trying to come to terms with a loss actually experienced in its detailed, wrought, questioning account of the death of an infant daughter.

The Romance was undoubtedly the most popular form in the medieval period, from the early, anonymous, 'Sir Orfeo', a jaunty reworking of the classical myth, complete with Celtic setting and happy ending, to Sir Thomas Malory's late great compendium of Arthurian tales, *Le Morte D'Arthur*. The rumbustious tradition, with its tales of courtly love, fighting knights, the supernatural and numerous challenges (to keep an audience gripped), derived from an earlier and generally much more refined body of French literature – an irony not missed by those with a shrewd sense of the follies of the age and a taste for wit, such as Charles d'Orléans and Geoffrey Chaucer.

Chaucer, according to his friend, pupil and fellow poet, Thomas Hoccleve, was 'the first finder of our fair language'. Certainly the regional dialect of the British Midlands in which he wrote is more recognizable to a modern reader than that of, for example, Langland's west England idiom or that of the 'Gawain' poet, from the north-west. But Hoccleve's opinion is perhaps true in a broader sense. Chaucer's technical brilliance, the scope and humanity of his vision and the sheer ambition of his literary effort (*The Canterbury Tales* remained unfinished at his death), led many to claim him as the first poetic genius of the English language.

The survival of some eighty-eight manuscripts of *The Canterbury Tales* testifies to Chaucer's great importance, popularity and influence. It also illustrates the increasing demand throughout the period for professionally produced copies of literary works – a demand leading William Caxton to

issue the first English printed books (which, to the untrained eye, might be mistaken for the professionally inscribed and decorated manuscripts whose form they at first imitated). One such early book was Malory's *Le Morte D'Arthur* (1485), which stood as the authoritative text until the discovery in 1934 of the unique manuscript which, as scholars more recently established, almost certainly passed through Caxton's own printing studio in Westminster.

'Beowulf'

The origins of the work which stands at the very beginning of the English literary tradition remain shrouded in mystery. It has been conjectured that 'Beowulf' emerged from an oral tradition as early as the seventh century and that it was most probably composed in the eighth, but it is known to us only from the miraculous survival of a vellum manuscript written out in Old English by an anonymous scribe around the year 1000. The long alliterative poem, written in a West Saxon dialect and possibly intended for recitation to the accompaniment of a harp, tells the story of Beowulf, a fifth- or sixth-century Scandinavian warrior hero, who rids the Danish kingdom of a terrible monster, Grendel, and his vengeful mother. His prowess is rewarded with a gift of lands, which he rules in peace for fifty years. A dragon, revenging the theft of a goblet from its hoard, attacks Beowulf's people and he once again goes into battle, a much older man. Although the dragon is killed, with the help of a loyal subject, Beowulf is mortally wounded. His funeral pyre and a prophecy of disaster for the kingdom provides a magnificent conclusion to a poem which, besides offering a compelling narrative, provides a richly allegorical exploration of the emergence of the new Christian faith set against the deeply rooted paganism of the past.

If other copies of 'Beowulf' were ever made, none has come to light. This manuscript, showing the opening of the poem, narrowly escaped destruction in 1731 when the library of its owner, Sir Robert Cotton, caught fire at Ashburnham House in Westminster. The damage is clearly visible around the ragged edges of the vellum pages, which were subsequently set into a modern mount and binding. In 1753 Sir Robert Cotton's library, together with those of Robert and Edward Harley, Earls of Oxford, and Sir Hans Sloane, formed the foundation collections of The British Library (then the British Museum Library), where the manuscript became available for study. It is hard to imagine, given the poem's pre-eminence today, that it was not until 1815, when it was published in Copenhagen by Grimur Jonsson Thorkelin, that it became known at all. An Oxford Professor of Anglo-Saxon, John Josias Conybeare, next turned his attention to the poem between 1817–20, collating Thorkelin's work with the manuscript and preparing the ground for the various subsequent editions and translations which have helped to make it justly famous.

BELOW:

Seamus Heaney published his award-winning translation of 'Beowulf' in 1999. He began his task in 1980, abandoned it and started again in 1995. This heavily annotated, word-processed draft, dating from the latter period, is one of several versions of the poem's opening presented to The British Library by the poet.

OPPOSITE:

The manuscript containing 'Beowulf' is known to this day as Cotton Vitellius A XV, a vestige of Robert Cotton's cataloguing system, in which his precious volumes were stored in book cases surmounted by the busts of Roman Emperors; thus the 'Beowulf' manuscript was the fifteenth volume to be found on shelf A in the bookcase supporting the head of Vitellius. The script is known as English minuscule (or lower case) and would have been written out with a quill pen – an instrument which only started to lose favour from the second quarter of the nineteenth century, with the development of the steel nib. Shown opposite is the opening of the poem.

HWÆT WE GARDE

na ingear dagum. þeod cyninga
þrym ge frunon huða æþelingas elle
fremedon. oft scyld scefing sceaþe
na þreatum moneȝu mæȝþum meodo setl
of teah egsode eorl syððan ærest wear
feasceaft funden he þæs frofre geba
weox under wolcnum weorð myndum þah
oð þ him æȝhwylc þara ymb sittendra
ofer hron rade hyran scolde gomban
gyldan þ wæs god cyning. ðæm eafera wæs
æfter cenned geong in geardum þone god
sende folce to frofre fyren ðearfe on
geat þ hie ær drugon aldor ase lange
hwile him þæs lif frea wuldres wealden
worold are for geaf beowulf wæs bren
blæd wide sprang scyldes eafera scede
landum in. Swa sceal geong guma gode
ge wyrcean fromum feoh giftum on fæder

Wulfstan d. 1023

Wulfstan, or 'The Wolf' as he was known in his writings, was brought into the world in the late tenth century after a difficult birth which resulted in the death of his mother. Of his younger years very little is known, although he probably entered holy orders at the important religious centre of Ely in Cambridgeshire. He was appointed Bishop of London from 996 to 1002, when he was advanced to the Archbishopric of York and also given care of the see of Worcester. The veneration in which he was held is indicated by the fact that he came to be regarded as a saint at Ely, in which Cathedral he was buried at his own request.

Wulfstan's political importance is clear from his role as a prominent royal counsellor, responsible among other things for drawing up legislation on behalf of Kings Ethelred II and Canute. These sacred and secular skills are both seamlessly and subtly joined in the most famous of Wulfstan's many writings, 'Sermo Lupi ad Anglos' (The Sermon of the Wolf to the English), which he first delivered in 1014. In attributing various unwelcome affairs of state to divine retribution, Wulfstan is able to launch a cleverly camouflaged critique of unjust laws, burdensome taxes and other political issues of the day.

BELOW:

In this volume of Anglo-Saxon documents (which includes the will of King Alfred), King Cnut (or Canute) and his Queen, Aelfgyu, are shown presenting a cross upon the altar of Newminster and Hyde Abbey, Winchester. Records show that Cnut, who was accepted by the English as their King in 1016, was present with Wulfstan at the consecration of the church of Assandun in 1020, a likely approximate date for this fine drawing.

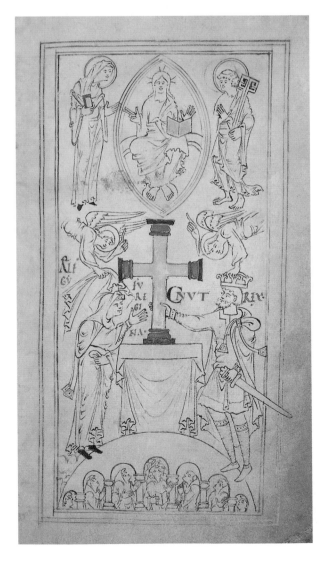

OPPOSITE:

The text of Wulfstan's sermon is found in just five manuscripts. That which is in The British Library is particularly significant in that the scribal text includes what are thought to be Wulfstan's own annotations, allowing us to make an extremely rare direct association between a document of this age and its original author.

A translation of the opening of Wulfstan's Sermon as shown opposite. The introductory passage is in Latin:

The sermon of the Wolf to the English, when the Danes were greatly persecuting them, which was in the year 1014 after the Incarnation of our Lord Jesus Christ: Beloved men, know that which is true: this world is in haste and it nears the end. And therefore things in this world go ever the longer the worse, and so it must needs be that things quickly worsen, on account of people's sinning from day to day, before the coming of Antichrist. And indeed it will then be awful and grim widely throughout the world. Understand also well that the Devil has now led this nation astray for very many years, and that little loyalty has remained among men, though they spoke well. And too many crimes reigned in the land, and there were never many of men who deliberated about the remedy as eagerly as one should, but daily they piled one evil upon another, and committed injustices and many violations of law all too widely throughout this entire land.

SERMO LUPI AD ANGLOS · QUANDO DANI
MAXIME · PERSECUTI SUNT EOS QUOD FUIT·
ANNO · MILLESIMO · XIIII · AB INCARNATIONE DOMINI
NOSTRI · IESU CRISTI ·

Leofan men geornað þ soð is · Ðeos worold
is on ofste · 7 hit nealæcð þam ende · 7 þi hit is
on worolde · aa swa leng swa wyrse · 7 swa hit sceal
nyde · for folces synnan · ær antecristes tocyme·
yfelian swyþe · 7 huru hit wyrð þænne ·
egeslic 7 grimlic · wide on worolde · Understandað
eac georne · þ deoful þas þeode nu fela geara·
dwelode to swyþe · 7 þ lytle getreowþa wæran·
mid mannum · þeah hy wel spæcan · 7 unrihta
to fela ricsode on lande · 7 næs a fela manna
þe ymbe þa bote · smeagorne ·
swa man scolde · ac dæghwamlice man ihte
yfel · æfter oðrum · 7 unriht rærde · 7 un-
laga manege · ealles to wide · 7 inde ealle
þas þeode · 7 we eac forþam habbað fela byrsta
7 bysmara gebiden · 7 gif we ænige bote gebidan
sculan · þon mote we þæt to gode earnian · bet
þon we ær þyssan dydan · forþam mid miclan
earnungan we geearnedan þa yrmða þe us on
sittað · 7 mid swyþe micelan earnungan þa bote motan æt gode geræcan·

The 'Harley Lyrics'

Although songs of love and high living were undoubtedly popular in the Middle Ages, the vast majority of surviving manuscripts from the period address theological matters. This reflects, perhaps, not only the concerns of a more sacred age but the fact that the transmission and preservation of the written word fell mainly to the religious houses. We must therefore celebrate the fact that over half the known secular lyrics which have come down to us from before 1400 survive in this one manuscript, known as the 'Harley Lyrics' (after its owner Sir Robert Harley). Despite its great literary significance, the vellum volume is fairly unexceptional in appearance and contains, in addition to its remarkable collection of non-didactic material, a diverse range of often very conventional prose and verse writings. The lyrics are written in a hand of around 1330, suggested to be that of a professional Shropshire scribe (another, earlier, scribe being responsible for an initial sequence of Anglo-Norman religious pieces). The original compiler of the manuscript, as is predictably the case with such early texts, should not be identified as the author of the verses; indeed, the identification of different dialects suggests that neither should the verses be attributed to any one poet.

ABOVE:

A portrait of Robert Harley, 1st Earl of Oxford, painted in 1714 by Sir Godfrey Keller.

BELOW:

Love lyrics were popular throughout the Middle Ages. This famous example survives in a rare musical setting dating from around 1500, although its origins are undoubtedly older. It reads:

Westron Wynde when Wylt thow blow
The smalle rayne downe can rayne
Cryst yf my love Were in my Armys
And I yn my bed Agayne

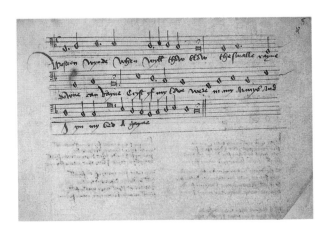

OPPOSITE:

Perhaps the most famous among the thirty-two 'Harley Lyrics' is 'Spring'. Its ebullient images of the world reawakening after winter contrast with the doleful mood of the disappointed lover, who threatens to forego the season's 'bright wealth' of joys and hide himself away in the forests. In the first verse, transcribed below, new love is associated with spring's perpetual return.

Lenten ys come with love to toune
With blosmen and with briddes roune, (blossom, bird song)
That all this blisse bringeth.
Dayeseyes in this dales, (Daisies)
Notes swete of nyghtegales,
Ech fowel hire song singeth.
The threstelcock him threteth oo, (thrush chides on)
Away is here wynter wo
When woderove springeth (woodrush)
This foules singen ferly fele, (vast numbers of birds)
And wlyten on here wynne wele, (warble in their great joy)
That al the wode ringeth

he chynþe ant honde cheyns ase dogge þat lyne
þat me were leuere of hire hen to fynte hire
to lare of al my kynne
atte constorie heo kenneþ vs care
ant Whisseþ vs euele & Worse to fare
a pynest proud ase a po
lesse Weddeþ vs bo
Kyd he heo Worcheþ vs Wo
for Wymmene Oue

Lenten ys come with loue to toune
Wiþ blosmen & wiþ briddes roune
Þat al þis blisse bryngeþ
Daýeseýes in þis dales
Notes suete of nyhtegales
Vch foul song singeþ
Þe þrestelcoc him þreteþ oo
Away is huere Wynter Wo
When Woderoue springeþ
Þis foules singeþ ferly fele
Ant Whyteþ on huere Wynne Wele
Þat al þe Wode ryngeþ

Þe rose rayleþ hire rode
Þe leues on þe lyhte Wode
Waxen al wiþ Wille
Þe mone mandeþ hire bleo
Þe lilie is lossom to seo
Þe fenyl & þe fille
Wowes þis Wilde drakes
Miles murgeþ huere makes
Ase strem þat strikeþ stille
Mody meneþ so doþ mo
Ichot ycham on of þo
For loue þat likes ille

Þe mone mandeþ hire lyht
So doþ þe semly sonne bryht
When briddes singeþ breme
Deawes donkeþ þe dounes
Deores Wiþ huere derne rounes
Domes forte deme
Wormes Woweþ under cloude
Wymmen Waxeþ Wounder proude
So Wel hit Wol hem seme
Ȝef me shal Wonte Wille of on
þis Wunne Weole y Wole forgon
Ant Wyht in Wode be fleme

In may hit murgeþ When hit dawes
In dounes Wiþ þis dueres plawes
Ant lef is lyht on lynde
Blosmes bredeþ on þe bowes
Al þis Wylde Wyhtes Wowes
So Wel ys Wel under fynde
Þat not non so freoly flour
Ase ledies þat beþ bryht in bour
Wiþ loue Who mihte hem bynde
So Worly Wymmen are by West
One of hem ich herie best
From Irlond in to ynde

Wymmen Were þe beste þing
Þat shup oure heȝe heuene kyng
Ȝef feole false nere
Heo beoþ to rad upon huere red
To loue þer me hem lastes bed
When heo shule fenge fere
Lut in londe are to leue
Þah me hem trewe trouþe ȝeue
For trecherie to ȝere
When trichour haþ is trouþe yplyht
Byswykeþ he þat suete Wyht
Þah he hire ofter fere
Wymmen Wan þe Wiþ þe sterte
Þat sew ant þeoly þt to fote
As fare is o to founde
So Wyde in World þat Wiere Won
in such a toune un to þe ist on
from Weyrestre to Wounde
Ȝef ȝenye nis þe trichour naht
bote he habbe is Wille ybrocht
at steuenyng umbe stounde
Ah faire leuedis be on Wau
to lare comeþ þe ȝeyn char
When loue on haþ yboumde

'Sir Orfeo'

BELOW:

The fear of strange abductions evidently extended a powerful influence upon the medieval imagination. A narrative series of marginal illustrations found in the magnificent Taymouth Hours of 1325–35 here depicts the legend of the 'wild man' seizing and ravishing a lady out walking in the woods.

The genre of the Breton Lay (or song) can be traced to the French poet, Marie de France (fl.1160–90), who composed twelve lyrics dedicated to Henry II of England. The tradition probably stretches much further back, however, into the ancient days of Celtic minstrelsy. Although such an early provenance is thought unlikely in the case of 'Sir Orfeo', it is perhaps the most famous example of the form in Middle English, with its familiar theme of love set in the mysterious 'otherworld' of fairyland. The poem, probably written in the early fourteenth century, takes its inspiration from the well-known classical legend of Orpheus but neatly transforms the sad ending of disobedience and loss of the earlier narrative into a happy vision of fidelity and order. Just below the middle of the page displayed, Sir Orfeo declares that he would rather lose his life 'than to lese the quene my wyfe'. On realising that his queen has indeed been lost – to a fairy

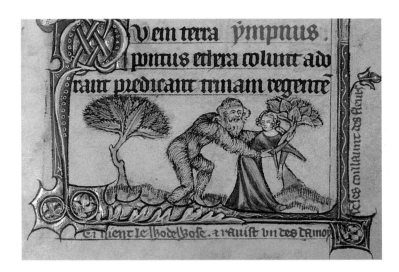

king, no less – he visits the 'otherworld' in disguise. He charms the king with his musical skills, wins back his wife, and returns home to prove the loyalty of his subjects.

Just three copies of the poem survive. This one is written out in an early fifteenth-century hand, with a sixteenth-century note suggesting an association with a curate of Baddesley Clinton in Warwickshire. The text differs in many respects from the other extant sources (in the National Library of Scotland and the Bodleian Library, Oxford). This suggests a wide oral transmission of the poem by minstrels, resulting in much variation when the texts came to be set down.

OPPOSITE:

In the following slightly modernised transcription, the queen describes to Orfeo the terrifying appointment she is obliged to keep, under threat of death, with the fairy king. The text begins on the second line down in the manuscript:

And then he brought [me] again home
Into our owne orcharde,
& sayde to me this afterwarde,
"Loke to-morew that thou be
Here under this ympe-tre;
& yif thou makest ony lette,
Wher-euer thou be, thou shalt be fet, [fetched]
& to-tor thy lymes alle, [torn apart]
That nothing thee help schalle;
& though thou be ever so torn
Yet shall thou away be born."
When the Kyng herd this case,
'Out!' he seyde, & Alase!
Me wer leuer to lese my lyfe

Than to lese the quene my wyfe!'
He axed consel of many a man,
But non of hem help hym can.
On the morewe, when tyme came,
The kyng his armes, forsoth, he name,
& two hundred knytes with hym,
Wele y-armed, stout and grym;
With the quene went he
Into the orchard, under the tre.
Ther made they watche on every syde,
& cast them there fir ti byde
& suffre deth every-chon,
Er sche schulde from hem gon;

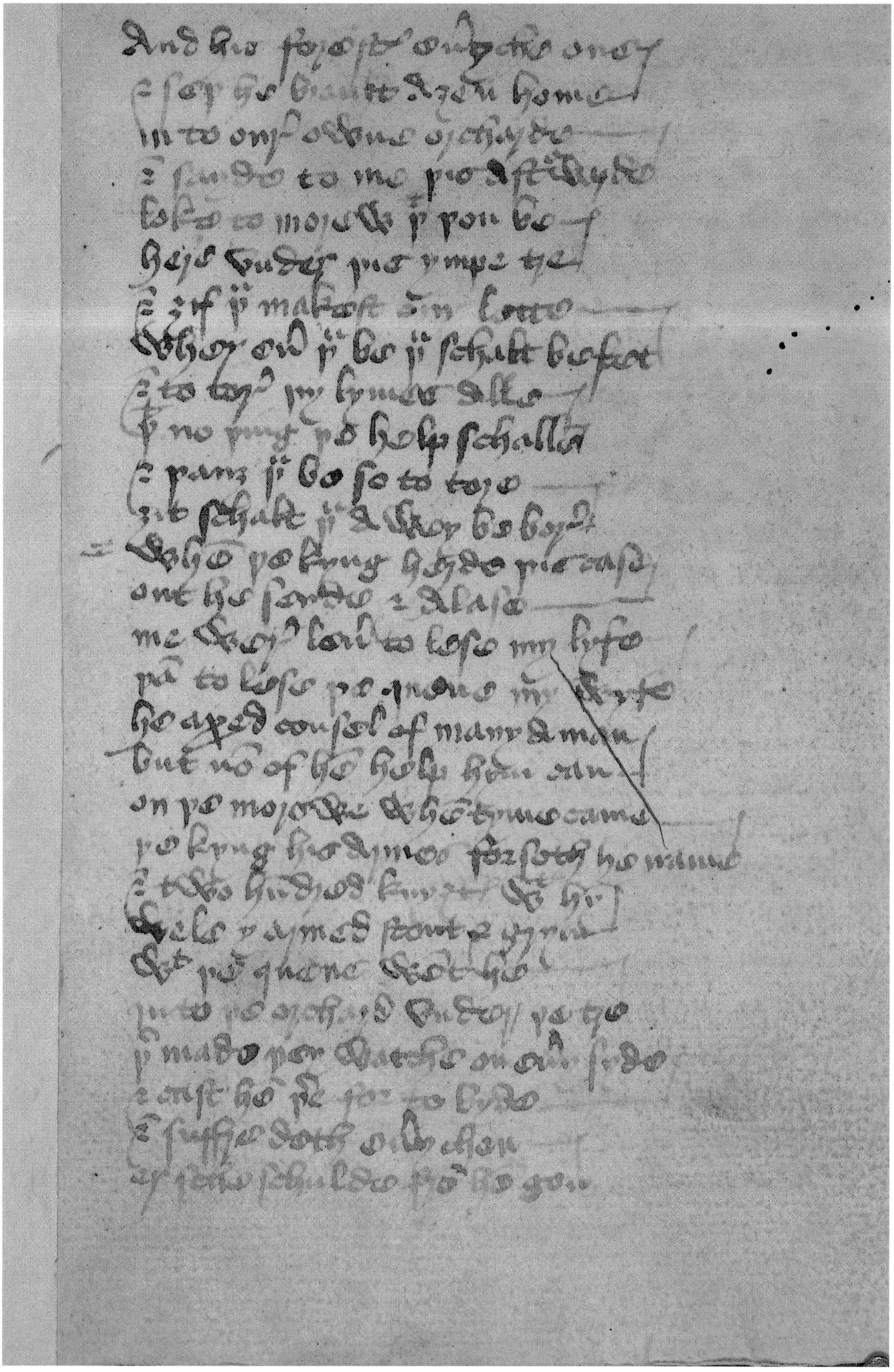

William Langland fl. 1360–1387

OPPOSITE:

Shown opposite is the latest version of the poem, the 'C'-text, in a manuscript volume written out by a scribe probably just before the end of the fourteenth century. The poet describes a 'loveli ladi' who explains three truly necessary things: meat, clothes ('vesture') and drink. A stern warning is issued about the last, and a later owner of the manuscript has marked a passage relating to the Biblical story of Lot, noting in the margin that 'thorow dronkkynnis all myschf ys wrott' (through drunkenness all mischief is wrought).

William Langland was born in the West Midlands around 1332, was well educated, took minor orders and most likely lived a life of modest means in London with his wife and daughter. Little else is known of him – other than that he wrote one of the masterpieces of medieval literature. 'Piers Plowman' opens 'in a somer seson' on the Malvern Hills and proceeds to portray the corruption rife in contemporary society, famously represented by a 'Fair Feeld ful of Folk'. The poem's narrative, which slips between dreaming and waking states, is shared by a character referred to as 'Long Will', who is often associated with Langland himself, and an honest ploughman, Piers, who displays Christ-like attributes. Although the long poem is a complicated allegorical work, intended first and foremost for the edification of its readers, its sheer imaginative power and poetic brilliance raise it far beyond the level of theological dogma.

About fifty manuscripts of the poem survive, in various locations. There are three versions, the earliest of which, the 'A-text', has been dated to around 1362. It is quite probable that Langland himself spent at least the last twenty years of his life trying to perfect the work, with each new version embodying his own additions and revisions. Another theory suggests a number of different authors may have had a hand in the poem's development.

RIGHT:

This fine-printing of the poem, published in New York in 1901, portrays the 'loveli lady'.

he wolde þat ȝe wrouȝten · as his wille were
ffor he is fader of faith · and former of alle — *...ty ye father to fayth*
To be faithful to him · he gaf ȝou fiue wittis
To worschepe him þer wiþ · while ȝe liuen here

¶ Wher fore he het þe elementes · helpe ȝou alle times
and bringe forþ ȝoure biliue · boþe linnen and willen
In mesure þaȝ hit muche were · to make ȝou at ease

¶ He comaunded of his curtasize · in comune þree þinges
ben none so nedful as þo · and nemene hem i rewle
And ȝiwene hem bi ȝelwe · ȝeliȝse hem wher þe likeþ

¶ þe firste of hem is fode · and nesture þe secounde — *mo þre þinge in comune*
and drinke þat do þe good · but do hit nouȝt out of tune

¶ Loke how loth in his lijf · porȝ likerous drinke — *...or or drunkynnes*
wrouȝte he wrouȝte · and wreyes god almiȝti   *all myschefe he wrott*
In his dronkenesse a dai · his douȝter þe dirte
and lai bi hem boþe · as þe bok telleþ
In his glotenize he gat · gyles þat we cheples
and al he witte hit þe win · his wickede dede

Inebriemus eum uino ⁊ dormiamus cū eo ut semaȝ possimꝰ

¶ ȝow and ȝour wommau · was loth þei encombred
for win ored delitable drinke · boþe dawes and niȝtes
Mesure is medicine · þouȝ þou michel wille — *...fure ye medycyne*
al is nouȝt good to þe goste · þat þe gut asket   *agaynst all...*
Ne liflose to þe likame · þat lef is to þe soule

¶ Loue nouȝt þi likame · for a liȝer him techeþ
þat is þis wrecchede world · wolde þe bi gile
ffor þe feud and þi flech · folewen to gidere
and þat sleþ þi soule · and þou sette hem in þin herte
I wisse þe þat þou be i war · leste þei þe disseiue

¶ A madame mercy · quod i · some likey wel ȝoure wordes
But þe moneie on þis molde · þat men so faste bi holden
telleþ me nolþ to wham · þat tresour apendeþ

¶ Go to þe gospel quod sche · and seo what god seide
whan þe peple apofede him · of a peni in þe temple
And he askede of hem · whose was þe coigne
Cesares þei seiden · soþliche we knowen
Reddite cesari · quod god · þat to cesar bi longeþ
Et que sunt dei deo · or elles ȝe don ille — *Ryghtfull reson*

¶ ffor riȝtful reson · schulde ȝelwe ȝou alle   *kynd witt schall*
and kyndewit · be waȝdeyn ȝoure soules to kepe   *will all...*
and tutur of ȝoure tresour · to take hit at ȝoure nede

The 'Gawain Poet' fl. c. 1380

ABOVE:

This homely illustration from the manuscript shows the father's amazed reaction on finding his lost 'pearl'. His daughter's white costume is at variance with the poet's description and represents the sort of dress familiar from the times of Richard II or Henry IV. The episode is translated from the text of the poem by J. R. R. Tolkien:

'O Pearl!' said I, 'in pearls arrayed,
Are you my pearl whose loss I mourn?
Lament alone by night I made,
Much longing I have hid for thee forlorn,
Since to the grass you from me strayed.'

The 'Gawain Poet' remains one of the most mysterious figures in English literature. We know almost nothing about him, other than that he was associated with a noble house in the late fourteenth century, and that he wrote the four untitled poems which survive in just one manuscript and have come to be known as 'Pearl', 'Sir Gawain and the Green Knight', 'Patience' and 'Cleanness'. The poet was a contemporary of Chaucer, but as J.R.R Tolkien has pointed out, the two could hardly have written in more different styles. Whereas Chaucer's works are often characterised by their immediacy and use of an increasingly dominant southern idiom, his anonymous counterpart, from the more sparsely populated West Midlands, created a didactic and richly complex body of work composed, not in the language of the everyday, but in the powerful alliterative forms of the earliest Anglo-Saxon poets. His polished use of this highly literary and elevated style places the poet at the forefront of what has been termed the alliterative revival of the late fourteenth century.

Of the four poems, 'Sir Gawain' and 'Pearl' are the most celebrated. The latter may well reflect the author's own experiences in its moving depiction of a father's anger, sorrow and incomprehension at the death of his infant daughter, or 'Pearl'. Dreaming upon her grave, he sees her on the other side of a river, grown up and radiantly dressed. She reproaches him for his sorrow but, overcome with longing, he plunges in to join her. Although he immediately awakes, still a grieving man in the mortal world, he is able to find some consolation in the thought that his daughter is now a 'queen of heaven'. 'Sir Gawain' has an enduring folkloric quality and the story is familiar to many who have never read the original poem. During a great New Year's Feast at Camelot, a mighty horseman attired all in green offers his neck to the sword of anyone who will promise to yield his own in return, one year hence. Gawain accepts the challenge, embarking upon an adventure in which his fidelity and courage are tested to the full. The poem achieves a great thematic richness from its fluent, instructive and entertaining assimilation of pagan, romance and Christian elements.

LEFT:

In this illustration from 'Gawain and the Green Knight', divided into two scenes, King Arthur and the nervous Guinevere sit at the trestled high table, with Gawain represented to the left. Underneath is portrayed the moment of his short-lived triumph.

OPPOSITE:

This small and naively decorated vellum manuscript of around 1400, written in the tight, angular hand of a copyist, escaped destruction in the Cotton fire of 1731. It remained largely hidden from the world until the palaeographer and Keeper of Manuscripts, Sir Frederic Madden, published it in 1839. It provides the unique source for the four known poems of the 'Gawain Poet'. Shown here is the opening of 'Pearl'.

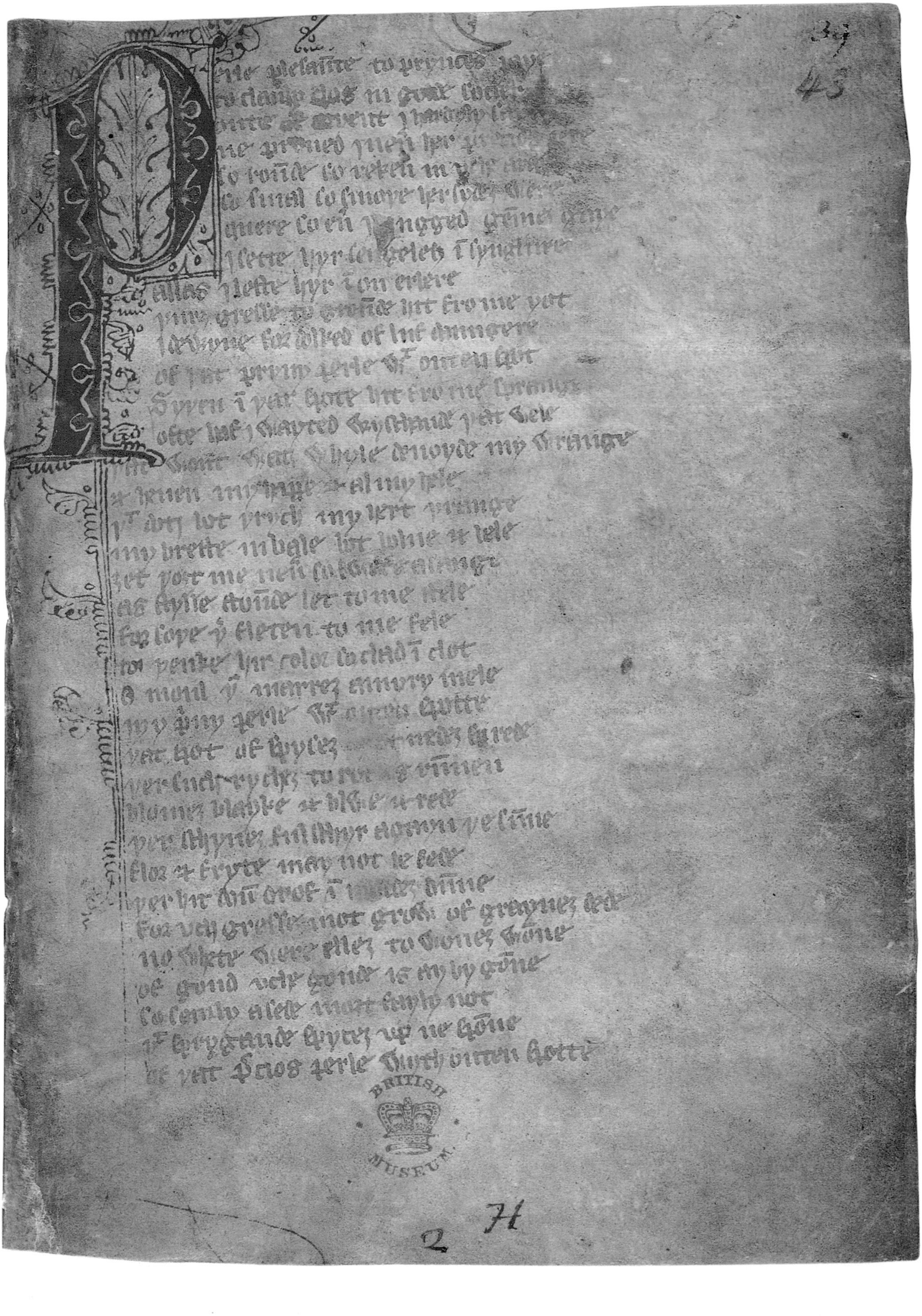

John Gower 1330–1408

ABOVE:

The effigy of John Gower on his tomb in Southwark Cathedral. Representations of three of his most famous works cradle his head.

'Confessio Amantis', John Gower's long poem of about 1390, is one of the most skilled treatments of love in the English language. The poet, of an educated and landed background, refers in his text to both Richard II, who commissioned the work, and, in an early version, at least, to his friend Geoffrey Chaucer, who is encouraged to proceed with his own 'testament of love', 'Troilus and Criseyde'. The narrative, written in Middle-English in deft octosyllabic couplets, relates a dialogue between a priest and his 'confessor', who is encouraged to consider how the seven deadly sins have frustrated his chances of love. In return for his honesty, the priest draws upon a great store of 'goodly' tales, each chosen to teach the man how to overcome sin and find true love. In the beautiful and moving conclusion of the poem, however, the confessor gives up his quest – not only because the priest reminds him of higher truths (symbolised by a gift of black beads) but because he is by now an old man. It is likely that Gower, who possibly practised law, composed his poem in the priory of St Mary Overie, Southwark, where he had lodgings in the latter years of his life. He lies magnificently memorialised in the church there, known today as Southwark Cathedral.

OPPOSITE:

This lavishly decorated manuscript is an early issue (sometimes referred to as a 'publication') of the poem, written out by a professional scribe around the time of the poet's death in 1408. Forty-nine manuscripts of the poem are known. The marginal rubrication (words in red) indicates whether the confessor or the priest speaks and is also used for Latin summaries and notes. Shown here is the beginning of the fourth book (of eight) which features sloth. 'Lachesse', as the confessor reveals, has in the past cunningly prevented him from wooing 'the swete May'. Some of the proverbial phrases in the following passage are still in current use.

Upon the vices to procede
After the cause of mannes dede,
The ferste point of Slouthe I calle
Lachesse, and is the chief of alle,
And hath this propreliche of kinde,
To leven alle thing behinde.
Of that he mihte do now hiere
He tarieth al the longe yere,
And everemore he seith, Tomorwe;
And so he wol his time borwe,
And wissheth after God me sende,
That whan he weneth have an ende,
Thanne is he ferthest to beginne.
Thus bringeth he many a mischief inne
Unwar, til that he be mischieved,
And may nouht thanne ben relieved.
And riht so nouther mor ne lasse
It stant of love and of lachesse:
Som tyme he sloutheth in a day
That he nevere after gete may.
Now, Sone, as of this ilke thing,
If thou have eny knouleching,
That thou to love hast don er this,
Tell on.

My gode fader yis.
As of lachesse I am beknowe
That I may stonde upon his rowe,
As I that am clad of his suite:
For whanne I thoghte my pursuite
To make, and therto sette a day
To speke unto the swete May,
Lachesse bad abide yit,
And bar on hond it was no wit
Ne time forto speke as tho.
Thus with his tales to and fro
My time in tarieng he drouth:
Whan ther was time good ynouh,
He seide, "An other time is bettre;
Thou schalt mowe senden hire a lettre,
And per cas wryte more plein
Than thou be Mouthe derst sein."
Thus have I lete my time slyde
For Slouthe, and kepte nouht my tide,
So that lachesse with his vice
Fulofte hath mad my wit so nyce,
That what I thoghte speke or do
With tarieng he hield me so,
Til whanne I wolde and I might nouht.

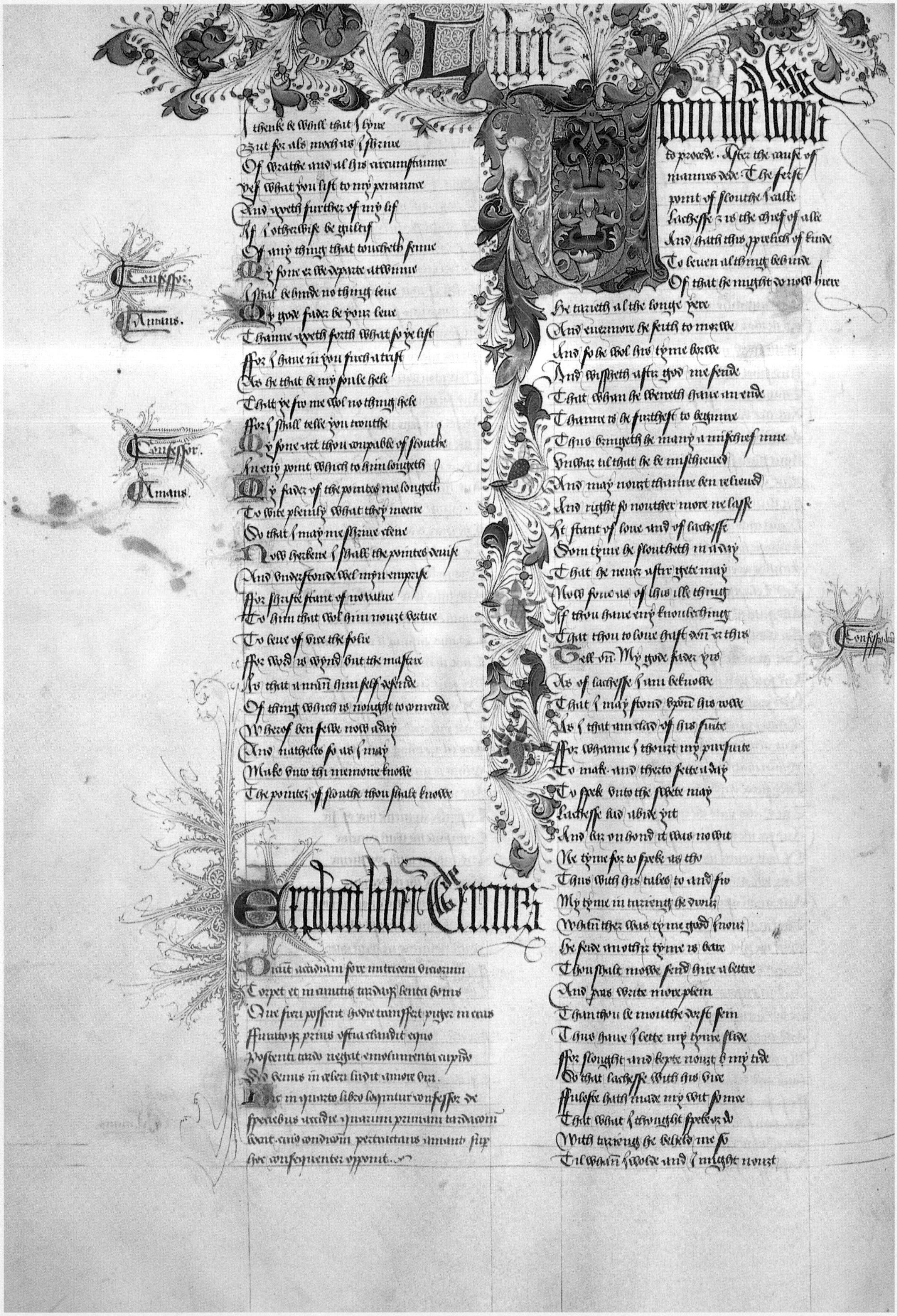

Liber Quartus

I thenke be whil that I lyve
But for als moche as I shrive
Of wrathe and al his circumstance
Yif what you list to my penance
And axeth further of my lif
If I otherwise be giltif
Of eny thing that toucheth sinne
Confessor My sone er we departe atwinne
I shal behinde no thing leve
Amans My gode fader be youre leve
Thanne axeth forth what so ye list
For I have in you such a trist
As ye that be my soule hele
That ye fro me wol no thing hele
For I shall telle you trouthe
Confessor My sone art thou coupable of slouthe
In eny point which to him longeth
Amans My fader of the pointes me longeth
To wite pleinly what they mene
So that I may me shrive clene
Now herkene I shall the pointes devise
And understonde wel myn emprise
For shrifte stant of no value
To him that wol him nouzt vertue
To leve of vice the folie
For word is wynd but the maistrie
Is that a man him self defende
Of thing which is nought to commende
Wherof ben fewe now aday
And natheles so as I may
Make unto thi memorie knowe
The pointes of slouthe thou shalt knowe

Explicit liber Tercius

Dicunt accidiam fore nutricem viciorum
Torpet et in cunctis tardans lenta bonis
Que fieri possent hodie transfert piger in cras
Furatoque prius ostia claudit equo
Poscenti tardo negat emolumenta cupido
Set Venus in celeri ludit amore viri.
Hic in quarto libro loquitur confessor de speciebus accidie quarum primam tardacionem vocant, cuius condicionem pertractans amanti super hoc consequenter opponit.

Upon the lines
to procede After the cause of
mannes dede The ferst
point of slouthe I calle
Lachesse and is the chief of alle
And hath this propreliche of kinde
To leven al thing behinde
Of that he mighte do now here
He tarieth al the longe yere
And evermore he seith to morwe
And so he wol his tyme borwe
And wissheth after God me sende
That whan he weneth have an ende
Thanne is he ferthest to beginne
Thus bringeth he many a mischief inne
Unwar til that he be mischieved
And may nouzt thanne ben relieved
And rizht so nouther more ne lasse
It stant of love and of lachesse
Som tyme he slowtheth in a day
That he never after gete may
Now sone as of this ilke thing
If thou have eny knowleching
That thou to love hast don er this *Confessor*
Tell on. My gode fader yis *Amans*
As of lachesse I am beknowe
That I may stonde upon his rowe
As I that am clad of his suite
For whanne I thouzt my pursuite
To make and therto sette a day
To speke unto the swete may
Lachesse bad abide yit
And bar on hond it was no wit
Ne tyme for to speke as tho
Thus with his tales to and fro
My tyme in tariyng he drouz
Whan ther was tyme good ynouz
He seide another tyme is bette
Thou shalt now sende hire a lettre
And pars write more plein
Than thou be mouthe dorst sein
Thus have I lette my tyme slide
For slowthe and kepte nouzt my tide
So that lachesse with his vice
Fulofte hath mad my wit so nice
That what I thoughte speke or do
With tarieng he helde me so
Til whan I wolde and I mighte nouzt

Geoffrey Chaucer c. 1343–1400

Geoffrey Chaucer was born some time between 1339 and 1346, probably in Thames Street to a 'citizen and vintner of London', and is likely to have studied either at Oxford or Cambridge University. By 1357 he appears to have been a page in the household of Edward III's son, Lionel, Duke of Clarence and in 1359 he 'bore arms' against the French, who captured and successfully ransomed him. His father died in 1366 and shortly afterwards he found himself in the King's service, campaigning again in France. He married, probably by 1366, Philippa, a lady in the Queen's household. This no doubt helped his advancement at court, although it has been suggested, from his literary treatment of matrimony, that the union was not a happy one.

Business took Chaucer to Italy in 1372–1373, where he visited Florence and Genoa and possibly saw the great poets Petrarch and Boccaccio, in whose works he found inspiration. On his return to London, he found continuing favour, being granted a daily pitcher of wine – which later became a 'tun', to be delivered by the King's chief butler, one Thomas Chaucer, probably the poet's son – and taking up a senior position as a customs official.

Living comfortably in Aldgate, in the city of London, Chaucer embarked on occasional secret diplomatic missions abroad, to France, Italy and Flanders. By 1386, however, his professional fortunes had taken a downward turn, with his replacement at court possibly the result of political machinations. It was during this period of hardship, most likely in April 1388, a year after his wife's death, that Chaucer undertook the famous pilgrimage to Canterbury which formed the subject of his late, great and unfinished work, *The Canterbury Tales*.

In 1389 he was appointed Clerk of the King's Works, a worthy post which, nevertheless, failed to compensate for the loss of his earlier positions and was, in any case, short-lived. Further occupation was found for him as a 'forester', with his meagre salary supplemented in 1394 by a pension from King Richard II. Chaucer's financial worries (he appears to have been somewhat profligate) were finally alleviated on the accession of Henry IV, who doubled his previous income and allowed him in 1399 to lease a house in the grounds of the Lady Chapel, Westminster. According to the inscription on his (later) tomb, Chaucer died on 25 October 1400. He is buried in Poet's Corner, in Westminster Abbey.

ABOVE:
Chaucer is one of the earliest English writers to have been accurately represented in portraits. In this illustration of him reading – the pen case around his neck perhaps hints at his trade – the poet's surprisingly sober expression is more than made up for by his jaunty red socks. An account of 1357, from the household of Prince Lionel, where he evidently served as a page, notes that 'an entire suit of clothes, consisting of a paltock or short cloak, a pair of red and black breeches, with shoes, is provided for Geoffrey Chaucer.'

OPPOSITE:
This early copy of *The Canterbury Tales*, dating from the period shortly after the poet's death, shows the prologue. The provenance of the vellum manuscript has been traced back, with a reasonable degree of certainty, to its original owners. By 1800 it had passed into the hands of William Petty, Marquess of Lansdowne, whose collection of manuscripts was acquired by the Library in 1807.

Whan þat Aprill wyth his shoures soote
þe drougth of March haþe perced to þe roote
And baþed every veyne in suche lycoure
Of whiche vertu engendred is þe floure
Whan zephirus eke wyth his swete breye
Inspired haþe in euery holte & heþe
The tendre croppes & þe yonge sonne
Haþe in þe Rame his halfe cours ronne
And smal foules maken melodye
þat slepen alnyght wyth open yhe

So priketh hem nature in her corages
Than longen folke to gone one pilgrimages
And palmeres for to seke straungere strondes
To ferne halowes kowþe in sundre londes
And specialy from euy shyres ende
Of Ingelonde to Canterburi þey wende
The holy blisful martir for to seke
þat hem hay holpen whan þei were seke
It befel þan in þat seson vpon a daie
In Southewerke att þe tabard as I laie
Redi to wende on my pilgremage
To Canterburie wyth ful deuoute corage
At nyghte was come in to þat hostellerie
Wel nyne and twente in a compaynie
Of sundre folke be auenture yfalle
In felauschipe & pilgrimes were þei alle
To warde Canterburi þit wolde ride
The chambres & stables weren wyde
And wele weren esede att þe beste
And shortly whan þe son was to reste
So had I spoken wyth hem euychone
þat I was of her felawschipe anone
And made forward erly for to rise
To take oure waie þere as I yow deuyse
But naþeles while I haue tyme & space
Er þat I ferþer in þis tale pace
Me þenketh it acordaunt to resone
To tell yowe all þe condicione
Of iche of hem so as it semed me
And whiche þei were & of whate degree
And eke in whatte araie þat þei were inne
And att a knyghte þan wol I furst begynne

Chaucer, according to his friend, pupil and fellow poet, Thomas Hoccleve, was 'the first finder of our fair language'. At a time when most important poetry was written in Anglo-Norman or Latin, his use of English played a central role in establishing the literary language we recognise today. Although he composed several major works throughout his life, *The Canterbury Tales* has long been regarded as his comic masterpiece. Probably conceived around 1387 and remaining unfinished at his death, *The Canterbury Tales* introduces readers to a series of memorable characters on the pilgrimage from The Tabard Inn in Southwark, London, to Canterbury. Each provides in their own distinctive voice a rich, often hilarious, and always telling insight into the human condition.

Some eighty-eight manuscript copies of *The Canterbury Tales* survive, attesting to the popularity of the poet's work. None is thought to be in Chaucer's own hand. Indeed, even among the large number of official documents connected with his professional career, it is impossible to establish which, if any, bear his own writing.

ABOVE:
An older Chaucer is represented here in an early fifteenth-century manuscript of 'The Regement of Princes', a long poem by his friend and pupil, Thomas Hoccleve. Chaucer points to a verse in which Hoccleve explains that those who, unlike him, have forgotten the master poet , 'By his peynture may ageyn him fynde'.

OPPOSITE:
This important edition of the works of Chaucer was published in 1896 at William Morris's Kelmscott Press in Hammersmith. The illustrations were designed by Sir Edward Burne-Jones.

HERE BEGINNETH THE TALES OF CANTER-
BURY AND FIRST THE PROLOGUE THEREOF

WHAN

THAT Aprille with his shoures soote
The droghte of March hath perced to the roote,
And bathed every veyne in swich licour,
Of which vertu engendred is the flour;
Whan Zephirus eek with his swete breeth
Inspired hath in every holt and heeth

The tendre croppes, and the yonge sonne
Hath in the Ram his halfe cours yronne,
And smale foweles maken melodye,
That slepen al the nyght with open eye,
So priketh hem nature in hir corages;
Thanne longen folk to goon on pilgrimages,
And palmeres for to seken straunge strondes,
To ferne halwes, kowthe in sondry londes;
And specially, from every shires ende
Of Engelond, to Caunterbury they wende,
The hooly blisful martir for to seke,
That hem hath holpen whan that they were
seke.

BIFIL that in that seson on a day,
In Southwerk at the Tabard as
I lay,
Redy to wenden on my pilgrym-
age
To Caunterbury with ful devout
corage,
At nyght were come into that hostelrye
Wel nyne and twenty in a compaignye,
Of sondry folk, by aventure yfalle
In felaweshipe, and pilgrimes were they alle,
That toward Caunterbury wolden ryde.

The 'Sloane Lyrics' *c. 1400*

ABOVE:

Sir Hans Sloane, who lends his name to the 'Sloane Lyrics', the manuscript of which formed part of his great library.

It has been suggested that this song (illustrated opposite) might refer to an elaborate and much prized piece of jewellery. Although that may be the case on one level, its real jollity lies in its bawdy puns and sly sexual allusions:

> I have a gentil cock – crowyt me day
> he doth me rysyn erly – my matynis for to say
> I have a gentil cock – comyn he is of gret
> his comb is of reed corel – his tayil is of get
> I have gentyl cock – comyn he is of kynde
> his comb is of red scorel – his tayl is of inde
> his leggs ben of asor – so gentil & so smale
> his spors arn of sylver qwyt – in to the wortewale
> his eynyn arn of cristal – lokyn al in aumbyr
> & every nygt he perchit hym – in myn ladyis chambyr

Might this richly suggestive jewel of a lyric have come down to us in a more familiar form? Anyone who has taught, or been taught, one of the jauntiest of Mother Goose's nursery rhymes might well think so:

> Goosey Goosey Gander!
> Whither shall I wander?
> Up stairs, down stairs,
> In my lady's chamber!

The anonymous medieval poet's bright and clear imagery strongly evokes Chaucer's description of the cock Chauntecleer in *The Nun's Priest's Tale*, which also has a red coral comb, azure legs, white spurs, jet black colourings and the quality of 'gentilness'. This fact helps us to date it to about the beginning of the fifteenth century. The manuscript volume in which it appears contains some fifty-seven English carols and seventeen other songs, often referred to collectively as the 'Sloane Lyrics', after Sir Hans Sloane who owned the manuscript. It is thought that the modest book resided, at some earlier stage, on the library shelves of the Benedictine monastery at Bury St Edmunds in East Anglia and that, despite its lack of musical notation, it may originally have belonged to a wandering minstrel.

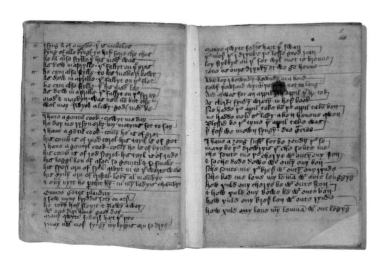

LEFT AND OPPOSITE:

'I have a gentle Cock' appears in an important manuscript volume, sometimes known as the 'Sloane Lyrics', containing fifty-seven English carols (a song with a uniform verse structure and repeating burden) and seventeen other lyrics in English and Latin. The manuscript's hybrid composition reflects the gradual replacement of parchment by paper during the medieval period.

I syng of a mayden · þ is makeles
kyng of alle kynges · to here sone che ches
he cã also stylle · þer his moder was
as dew in aprylle · þt fallyt on þ gras
he cam also stylle · to his moders bowr
as dew in aprille · þt fallyt on þe flour
he cam also stylle · þer his moder lay
as dew in aprille · þt fallyt on þe spray
moder & maydyn · was neuer non but che
wel may swych a lady · godes moder be

I haue a gentil cook · crowyt me day
he doþ me rysyn erly · my matyns for to say
I haue a gentil cook · comly he is of cot
his comb is of red corol · his tayl is of get
I haue a gentyl cook · comly he is of kynde
his comb is of red scorol · his tayl is of inde
his legges ben of asor · so gentil & so smale
his spors arn of sylver qwyt · in to þe worte wale
his eynyn arn of cristal · lokyn al in aumbyr
& euery nyzt he perchit hym · in myn ladyis chaumbyr

Omnes gentes plaudite
I saw myny byrddis setyn on a tre
he tokyn here flyzt & flowyn away
wyt ego dixi haue good day
many whyte federis haþ þe pye
I may non mor syngyn my lyppis arn so drye

Margery Kempe *c. 1373 – c. 1439*

In 1934 the earliest surviving autobiography written in the English language was discovered in wonderfully eccentric circumstances. According to family legend, Colonel W. Butler Bowden, searching in a cupboard at his home near Chesterfield for a ping pong ball, became frustrated at the piles of old books which hampered his efforts, expostulating to a friend: 'I am going to put this whole lot on the bonfire tomorrow and then we may be able to find Ping Pong balls & bats when we want them.' The friend besought him to allow an expert to check the books first. Shortly afterwards, the medieval scholar Emily Hope Allen identified an undistinguished looking manuscript as the 'Book of Margery Kempe', a vivid confessional work dictated in 1436. Before this discovery, all anyone knew of the work were the seven pages of extracts printed by Wynkyn de Worde in 1501.

As she could neither read nor write, Kempe dictated the final version of her book to a priest in her home town of Lynn in Norfolk, with the present manuscript being copied down shortly afterwards by a scribe named Salthows, possibly under her direction. In a work much more intimate and revealing than other writings in the medieval visionary tradition, Kempe relates her severe mental anguish after the birth of the first of her fourteen children, her vision of Christ and spiritual conversion, her three years of sexual temptation, her pilgrimages to Italy and the Holy Land, her vow of chastity in 1413 (evidently accepted by her husband, John, whom she later nursed through six years of illness), her stormy relationship with the church authorities, her meeting with another highly influential woman, the mystic Julian of Norwich, and her later years of prayer and charitable works. There are no records of Margery's death, although we know that her husband and eldest son died around 1431 and that she was still alive in 1439.

ABOVE:

In the absence of any likeness of Margery Kempe we must make do with generic contemporary portrayals of women. Shown here is a woman, with rosary beads, engaged in devotional reading.

BELOW:

A colophon (tailpiece in a manuscript or book) suggesting the scribe's name to have been Salthows.

OPPOSITE:

The provenance of this manuscript is still by no means clear, although an inscription in the volume indicates that it belonged at an early stage to the Carthusian Monastery of Mount Grace, Yorkshire. After a certain amount of prefatory text, Margery's confessional autobiography (written in the third person) begins towards the foot of the page (opposite):

Whan this creatur was twenty yer of age or sumdele mor, sche was maryed to a worschepful burgeys and was wyth chylde wythin schort tyme, as kynde wolde. And aftyr that sche had conceyved, sche was labowrd wyth grett accessys tyl the child was born, and than, what for labowr sche had in chyldyng and for sekenesse goyng beforn, sche dyspered of hyr lyfe, wenyng sche mygth not levyn. And than sche sent for hyr gostly fadyr, for sche had a thyng in conscyens whech sche had nevyr schewyd beforn that tyme in alle hyr lyfe. For sche was evyr lettyd be hyr enmy, the devel, evyrmor seyng to hyr whyl sche was in good heele hir nedyd no confessyon but don penawns be hirself aloone and all schuld be forgovyn, for God is mercyful inow ...

schort tretys of a creature sett in grett pompe &
pride of þe world whech sythen was drawyn to owyr
lord be gret poverte & sekenes schauuo & gret repref
in many dyvers cuntres & places of whech tribulacyons su
schal ben schewed aftyr not in ordyr as it fellyn · but as
þe creatur cowd han mend of hem whan it wer wretyn
for it was xx zer & mor fro tym þis creatur had for
sake þe world and besyly clef on to owyr lord or þis boke
was wretyn · notwythstondyng þis creatur had gret
cownsel for to don wrytyn hir tribulacyons & hir felyng
ys · And a whyte frer proferyd hir to wryte frely yf sche
wold · And sche was warnyd in hyr spyryt þt sche xuld
not wryte so sone · And many zerys aftyr sche was bodyn
in hyr spyryt for to wrytyn · And þan zet it was wretyn
fyrst be a man whech cowd neyþer wel wryten englysch
ne duch · so it was un abyl for to be red but only be
specyal grace · for þer was so mech obloquie & slawndyr
of þis creatur · þt þer wold fewe men beleue þis creatur
And so at þe last a prste was sor mevyd for to wrytyn
þis tretys & he cowd not wel redyn it of a iiij zere
to gedyr & sythen be þe reqst of þis creatur & compel
lyng of hys owyn conscens he asayd a gayn for to
rede it & it was mech mor esy · þan it was a for tyme
And so he gan to wryten in þe zer of o lord a · m ·
cccc · xxxvi · on þe day next aftyr mary maudelyn
aftyr þe informacyon of þis creatur : ~

Cap jo

han þis creatur was xx zer of age or sum dele
mor sche was maryed to a worschepful burgeys of lyn
and was wyth chylde wyth in schort tyme as kynde
wold · And aftyr þat sche had conceyued sche was labowrd
wyth grett accessys tyl þe chyld was born & þan what
for labor sche had in chyldyng & for sekenesse goyng be
forn sche dyspered of hyr lyfe wenyng sche myght not
leuyn · And þan sche sent for hyr gostly fadyr for sche

Charles d'Orléans 1394–1465

Charles d'Orléans was born in Paris into a world of considerable wealth and aristocratic privilege – as might be expected of a nephew of King Charles VI of France. Aged eleven, he married Isabelle, the sixteen-year-old widow of England's King Richard II. In 1407 he endured the first great sorrow of his life, when his father, Louis, was assassinated by Burgundian enemies. Just a year later his mother Valentina died, leaving him both his inheritance and title. Charles married for the second time in the summer of 1410 (his first wife having died in childbirth) and went to battle at Agincourt in 1415. Reputedly pulled from under a mound of corpses, he was held by his English captors for twenty-five years. During his incarceration he would have enjoyed a life of reasonable comfort and privilege, in accordance with his aristocratic status; certainly he moved between various important noble houses, forging strong friendships and putting his considerable intellect and political skill to good use as a mediator in negotiations between England and France.

At some stage, perhaps during his years in England, Charles began a series of lyrics later arranged into a sequence representing the story of the 'lover-prisoner'. The degree to which his narrative is autobiographical has been much debated; although the poems conform to courtly conventions, certain personal details ring true. At some stage between his return to France and his death in 1465 at the old age of seventy, the indefatigable Charles arranged his poems in a manuscript which is known as his 'Livre de Prison'. The original 'Prison Book', which contains both English and French verse, is preserved in the Bibliothèque Nationale in Paris but of the several subsequent manuscripts inspired by the sequence, that featured here is among the most important. Many of the English poems, although not literal translations from the French, clearly derive from the originals and at least one commentator has suggested their author to be none other than Charles himself.

ABOVE:

Another copy of the lyrics, dating from the late fifteenth century, includes a famous picture of the Tower of London, where Charles was held for a period during his long captivity in England. In one of the earliest accurate depictions of London topography (London Bridge and the old St Paul's Cathedral can both be seen), Charles is represented several times. In the centre he can be seen writing a letter seeking money for his release.

OPPOSITE:

The song illustrated here (still awaiting completion by its illuminator) takes the form of a punning confession made to a priest by a lover who has 'stolen a kiss of great sweetness'. Playing upon the religious and linguistic conventions of the time, the lover vows to 'restore' (or revoke) the sin, leaving us – and, presumably, his 'ghostly father' – wondering whether he truly means to repent or has every intention of returning the kiss to his sweetheart.

My Gostly fader y me confesse (My holy father)
First to god and then to yow

That at a wyndow, wot ye how, (you understand how)
I stale a cosse of gret swetnes
Which done was out avisynes (without premeditation)
But hit is doon, not undoon, now

My Gostly father y me confesse
First to god and then to yow

But y restore it shall dowtless (without doubt)
Ageyn if so be that y mow
And that god y make a vow
And elles y axe foryefnes

My Gostly father y me confesse
First to god and then to yow

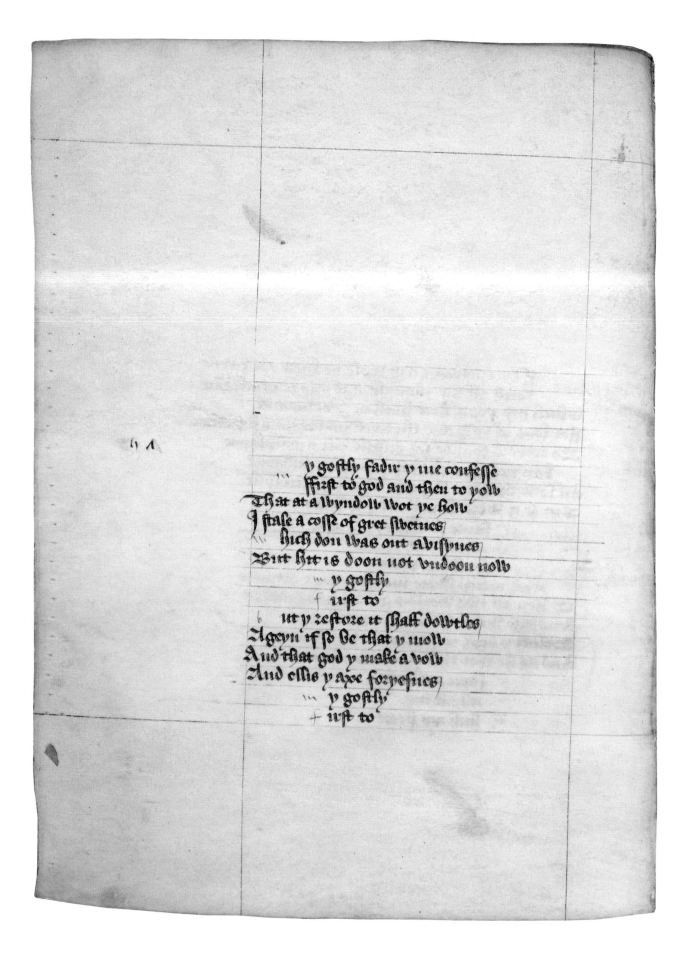

y goftly fadir y me confeffe
ffirst to god and then to yow
That at a wyndow wot ye how
J stale a coffe of gret swetnes
which don was out avisynes
But hit is doon not vndoon now
    y goftly
    first to
But y restore it shall dowtles
Ageyn if so be that y mow
And that god y make a vow
And ellis y axe foryefnes
    y goftly
    first to

Sir Thomas Malory *c. 1416–1471*

The fyrst boke.

¶ Here begynneth the fyrst boke of the moost noble and worthy prince kyng Arthur somtyme kyng of grete Brytayne now called Englande whiche treateth of his noble actes and feates of armes & chyualrye / and of his noble knyghtes of the table roūde and this volume is deuyded in to .xxi. bokes.

¶ How Utherpendragon sente for the duke of Cornewayle and Igrayne his wyfe / and of theyr sodayn departynge agayne.

It befell in the days of þ noble Utherpendragon whā he was kynge of Englande and so regned / there was a mygbty and a noble duke in Cornewayle that helde longe tyme warre agaynst hym. And þ duke was named the duke of Tyntagyll / & so by meanes kynge Uther sente for this duke / chargenge hym to brynge his wyfe w hym for she was called a ryght fayre lady / a passynge wyfe / & Igrayne was her name. So whan the duke & his wyfe were comen to þ kynge / by the meanes of grete lordes they were bothe accorded / & the kyng lyked & loued this lady well / and made her grete chere out of

ABOVE:

Shown here is the beginning of 'The fyrst boke' of Wynkyn de Worde's third edition of *Le Morte D'Arthur*, dating from 1529.

OPPOSITE:

The work of two scribes can be seen here in the unique manuscript of *Le Morte D'Arthur*, with the first eight lines penned in a hand different from that which follows.

Le Morte D'Arthur was composed, at least in part, between 1468 and 1470 while Malory endured one of his many stints in prison. Charged in 1451 and 1452 with attempted murder, extortion, robbery (of Combe Abbey), and rape, the man who was three times a member of Parliament and a knight by 1441, was jailed at least eight times in his life and managed to escape from prison twice. Whether Malory – whose name derives from an ancient Norman word meaning 'unlucky' – was just plain bad or the victim of political intrigue is uncertain. Indeed, until recently virtually nothing was known of him beyond what could be deduced from authorial and editorial references given in his vast prose interpretation of the legend of King Arthur.

It is now accepted that Malory was born at some time between 1414 and 1418 to influential parents and can be identified in the records as the knight of Newbold Revel, Warwickshire. Before his parliamentary representations of Warwickshire, Bedwin in Wiltshire and Waresham in Dorset, it is quite possible that he fought in France; it seems probable, later on, that he became heavily embroiled in the civil strife raging between the Lancastrian and Yorkshire nobility, switching allegiances at least once. Despite his extravagant propensity for trouble, it has been suggested that Malory achieved a degree of prosperity in the latter part of his life, as is witnessed by his burial in the affluent Greyfriars church in the city of London.

In 1485 William Caxton, England's first printer, wrote in the preface to his edition of *Le Morte D'Arthur* (of which only one complete copy survives, in the Pierpont Morgan Library, New York) that he was 'enprised to imprint a book of the noble histories of the said King Arthur and of certain of his knights after a copy unto me delivered, which copy Sir Thomas Malory did take out of certain book of French, and reduced it into English.' The only known manuscript source for the work, written out by two scribes and attributed to 'a knyght presoner sir Thomas Malleorre', was discovered at Winchester College in 1934. Although not necessarily the 'copy' text referred to by Caxton (whose edition contains numerous variants from the manuscript), scholars have demonstrated that it almost certainly passed through his Westminster premises during the period 1480–1483. Crucial to their arguments is the presence, on four of its pages, of offset markings from type used by Caxton.

Spun into a rich and lengthy whole mainly from numerous tales belonging to the French romance tradition, the work was evidently a commercial success from the outset, being twice reprinted by Caxton's one-time assistant, Wynkyn de Worde. Although of undoubted importance and influence – witness its appeal to the gothic imagination of the late nineteenth century and, in turn, the popular interpretations of Hollywood – there is a tradition of critical scepticism which can be traced back hundreds of years. In 1568 Robert Ascham noted that the 'whole pleasure of [the] book standeth in two special points, in open manslaughter and bold bawdry: In which booke those be counted the noblest knights that do kill men without any quarrel, and commit foulest adultery by subtlest shifts.'

IN the begynnyng of Arthure . Afir he was chosyn kynge by aduenture and by grace for the moste pty of the barovns knew nat he was kethir pendragon son But as Merlyon made hit oppynly knowyn . But yet many kyngis and lordis hylde hym grete werre for that cause But well Arthur on com hem aff the moste pty dayes of hys lyff he was ruled by the councell of Merlyon So hit felle on a tyme kyng Arthure seyde vnto Merlyon my lordws wolf let me haue no reste but nedis I muste take a wyff ¶ I wolde none take but by thy councele and aduice ¶ hit ys well done seyde Merlyon that ye take a wyff ffor a man off youre bounte and nobles scholde not be wt onte a wyff . Now is ther ony seyde Merlyon that ye loue more than a nop . ye seyde kyng Arthure I loue Gwenyvere the kyngs doughter of lodegrean of ye londe of Tamelerde the whyche holdyth In his howse the table rounde that ye tolde me he had hit of my fadir Vther And this Damesell is the moste valyaunte and fayryst that I know lyvyng or yet that ever I coude fynde Sertis seyde Merlyon as off her beaute and fayrenesse she is one of the fayrest on lyve . But and ye loved her not so well as ye do I scholde fynde you a Damesell off beaute and of goodnesse that scholde lyke you and please you and youre herte were nat sette But there as mannes herte is sette he woll be loth to retourne . that is trouthe seyde kyng Arthur But Merlyon warned the kyng covertly that Gwenyver was nat holsom for hym to take to wyff . ffor he warned hym that Lancelot scholde loue her and she hym agayne . And so he turned his tale to the aventures of the Sankegreall Thenne Merlyon desyred off the kyng for to haue men wt hym þ scholde enquere of Gwenyver and so the kyng grawnted hym and so Merlyon wente forthe vnto kyng lodegrean of Camylerde and tolde hym of the desire of the kyng þ he wolde haue vnto his wyff Gwenyver his dowter That is to me seyde kyng lodegrean the beste tydyng that I euer herde . that so worthy a kyng off probesse & noblesse wol wedde my dowter And as for my londis I wolde geff hit hym yf I wyste

Robert Henryson *c.* 1439–1506

Robert Henryson is often referred to as a Scottish Chaucerian, a term applied to a group of poets working in late medieval Scotland whose characteristic style echoes the humanism, wit and narrative tone of, as Henryson himself put it, 'the worthie Chaucer'. Although there is some sense in this classification, commentators have increasingly come to view and respect Henryson as an important and original poet in his own right. Retrieving his poetry from Chaucer's far-reaching shadow has, however, proved easier than bringing the man himself into the light. History offers us precious few references to Henryson. Around 1506, the Scottish poet William Dunbar in his elegy 'The Lament for the Makaris', says of death that:

In Dunfermelyne he hes done roune
With Maister Robert Henrisoun.

Another reference can be found in a seventeenth-century manuscript containing a Latin version of Henryson's poem 'The Testament of Cresseid' (a sequel to Chaucer's 'Troilus and Criseyde') which notes that it was 'made & written by one Mr Robert Henderson sometimes cheife schoole master in Dunfermling'. Otherwise, no convincing record can be found of Henryson's attendance at the Scottish universities of the time, Glasgow and St Andrews, and it has been suggested that he may have graduated abroad before taking up a teaching position at the school associated with Dunfermline Abbey.

In addition to his 'Testament of Cresseid', a number of poems can be ascribed to Henryson, among them 'The Tale of Orpheus and Erudices his Quene.' Although his 'Morall Fabillis of Esope' also take a famous source from antiquity as their starting point, their style is unmistakably rooted in the poet's Scottish background.

ABOVE:
The second, third and fourth verses of Henryson's 'Tail of the Cok and the Jasp'.

LEFT:
This representation of a cockerel and his jewel is from a manuscript copy of Aesop's fables dating from around 1477.

OPPOSITE:
This charming manuscript of Henryson's 'Fables', written out in an anonymous hand, was produced one year after the first printed edition of 1570. The first verse of his 'Tail of the Cok and the Jasp' describes how the brisk, bold, and self-satisfied Cock discovers a jewel accidentally swept out of a house:

Ane Cok, sum tyme, with feddram fresch and gay,
Richt cant and crous, albeit he was bot pure,
Fleu furth upon ane dung hill sone be day:
To get his dennar set was al his cure.
Scraipand amang the as, be aventure
He fand ane Jolie Jasp, richt precious,
Wes castin furth be sweping of the hous

The taill of the Cok and the Iasp

Ane cok sum tyme with feddrin fresch & gay
Richt cant and crous albeit he was bot pure
Fleis furth vpoun ane dung hill sone be day
To get his denner set was all his cure
Scraipand amang the ass be auenture
He fand ane Iolie Iasp richt preciuss
Was casten furth be sweping of the hous
Te

The arrival of the printing press in Britain at the end of the fifteenth century far from spelt the end of the manuscript as a means of distributing literary texts. As late as the 1660s Katherine Philips seems to have positively mistrusted print (in a turbulent political age where discretion was all), while John Donne saw no collection set in type during his life and was known to his admiring contemporaries almost exclusively through circulated manuscripts. George Peele's 'Anglorum Feriae' of 1595 – written for no less a personage than Queen Elizabeth I herself – evidently had to wait until 1830 before it was published.

Given the proliferation of Donne's verse in manuscript anthologies, it seems surprising that only three poems appear to have survived in his own hand. Yet as for the preceding generations of writers, rarely was any importance attached to an author's own manuscript *per se*. It is entirely possible that handwritten texts by Shakespeare (of which only one highly disputed example exists) and Marlowe (in whose hand we have nothing at all), once no longer required, ended up lining pie dishes or were put to even less dignified use in the Elizabethan 'jacques', as the 'saucy poet' John Harington might have put it. The fact that all the examples here are, indeed, written at least partly in the hand of their authors makes them, therefore, extremely rare among the considerable number of sixteenth- and seventeenth-century manuscripts which have descended to us.

In many cases the existence of autograph manuscripts can be owed to sheer good fortune, such as Thomas Traherne's 'Commentaries of Heaven' which, flitting in and out of London sale-rooms in 1844 and in 1854 (unidentified) was eventually rescued from a Lancashire rubbish-tip in 1967. 'Believe as you List', a play written in Philip Massinger's own hand and marked up as a prompt copy, was rediscovered 'among a mass of rubbish' in 1844. Harington's poetical manuscript, covered in ink smudges and compositors' instructions, is the only known Elizabethan example to have somehow escaped from the printer's workshop once set in type. The album of verse, kept close by Thomas Wyatt through the thick and thin of missions abroad, imprisonment and the fever to which he eventually succumbed,

seems to have narrowly avoided destruction at the hands of its subsequent owners, who casually treated it as scrap paper for their doodlings, sums and commonplace musings. We should rather celebrate the rare survival of one half of the 'loose Papers' bequeathed by Samuel Butler to his friend William Longueville than mourn the loss of the other.

Occasionally, enough importance was attached to an author's manuscript at the time of its creation to secure its preservation. 'The Masque of Queens' was composed for the New Year festivities at Whitehall Palace in 1609 and written out by Ben Jonson, in his elegant secretary hand, for presentation to Henry Prince of Wales, thus entering the royal library. In other cases posterity has later collectors to thank. Sir Thomas Browne's notebooks caught the eye of Sir Hans Sloane, another physician with literary tastes, and were it not for William Petty, 1st Marquess of Lansdowne, whose collection was acquired for the nation in 1807, by far the most significant autograph manuscript by John Dryden would be lost to us.

The fact that Dryden's poem remained unidentified until 1966 raises the exciting prospect of other important autographs quietly waiting to be discovered, possibly beneath our very noses. Just one sonnet in draft by Shakespeare would cause an academic hysteria well worth seeing. But perhaps, after all, this increasingly secular age was the least suited for the long-term preservation of literary manuscripts. Gone were the didactic texts inscribed on vellum, bound between boards of oak and designed to last. With playwrights competing against one another to satisfy the rapacious appetite for popular entertainment, poets chasing wildly unpredictable preferment and patronage at Elizabeth's court, and everyone subject to the continual vicissitudes of strife at home or abroad, who – apart, of course, from Sir Thomas Browne – would spare a thought for posterity?

Sir Thomas Wyatt 1503–1542

ABOVE:

A portrait of Sir Thomas Wyatt after Hans Holbein.

BELOW:

Wyatt's short autograph poem, which finds a neat conceit for the irrepressible course of love, is surrounded on the page by a variety of later writings and mathematical workings by various members of the Harington family, into whose possession the manuscript fell.

Sir Thomas Wyatt was born at Allington Castle, Kent, in 1503. Educated at Cambridge University, he was twice imprisoned by Henry VIII: first in 1536 for his close association with Anne Boleyn and secondly (and more seriously), in 1541, for his support of Thomas Cromwell, whom the King executed in 1540. Egerton Manuscript 2711 was acquired by the British Museum Library in 1889. Its 136 surviving leaves contain 107 of Wyatt's poems, his penitential psalms, two letters and three other poems, one by Henry Howard, the Earl of Surrey.

During this period one would expect such a collection, even if compiled during the author's lifetime, to comprise copies rather than original autographs. But in this case, several of the poems are indeed written in Wyatt's own hand with many of the remaining scribal copies bearing his own corrections and revisions. The album, which establishes the Wyatt canon, was kept from 1537 until his death in 1542 of a fever, contracted at Sherborne, Dorset (where he lies buried), after an exhausting ride towards Falmouth on a diplomatic mission. As such, it probably accompanied him abroad before his second spell in prison, while he served his king as Ambassador to Charles V. Certainly his departure from Spain in June 1539 is recorded in his handwritten epigram 'Tagus farewell'. The volume later came into the possession of the Harington family, whose various members carelessly employed it for doodlings, mathematical equations, miscellaneous prose musings and scribbles.

Transcription of the poem illustrated opposite:

What rage is this? What furour of what kynd?
What powre, what plage doth wery thus my mynd?
With in my bons to rancle is assind
        What poyson, plesant swet?

Lo se myn iyes swell with contynuall terys
The body still away sleples it weris:
My fode [n]othing my faintyng strength reperis,
        Nor doth my lyms sustayne.

In diepe wid wound the dedly stroke doth torne
To curid skarre yt neu shalle retorne.
Go to, tryvmph, reioyse thy goodly torne,
        Thi frend thow dost opresse.

Opresse thou dost and hast off hym no cure
Nor yett my plaint no pitie can procure
Fiers tygre fell, hard rok with owt recure
        Cruell rebell to love!

Ons may thou love neu belovffd agayne
So love thou still & not thi love obttayne
So wrathfull love, with spite of lust disdayne
        May thret thy cruellty hert.

ABOVE:
The complexity of Wyatt's working
methods are much in evidence in this
autograph draft of a poem preoccupied
with the torments of 'wrathfull love'.

Launcelot Andrewes 1555–1626

ABOVE:

The sumptuous gilded figure of
Bishop Launcelot Andrewes,
added in *c.* 1910 to the sixteenth-
century reredos in Southwark
Cathedral. His tomb stands
nearby.

The 1611 revision of the Bible, made for King James I and known as the 'Authorized Version', is one of the great glories of English prose. Regrettably the manuscript of it is lost. It was last heard of as having been sold, together with the copyright, to the King's Printer, Robert Barker, who died in 1645. The work of revision was entrusted to about fifty distinguished scholars who took the Bishops' Bible of 1568 as a basis but nevertheless had the Hebrew and Greek texts before them as they proceeded. Work began in 1607.

First on the list of divines appointed to the task was Launcelot Andrewes, then Bishop of Chichester. He was born in Barking, Essex, and educated at Pembroke Hall, Cambridge. In the early stages of his career he was chaplain to Queen Elizabeth I and Dean of Westminster. In 1609 he became Bishop of Ely and in 1618 Bishop of Winchester.

Andrewes's reputation for great scholarship – he is said to have mastered six ancient languages – ensured his work on the Book of Joshua and the books following it as far as Chronicles, as well as on the five Books of Moses. He was an immensely respected church leader whose very presence awed the often lewd King James into decency. T. S. Eliot considered Andrewes's sermons among the finest written but of even greater beauty are his prayers, *Preces Privatae*, published in 1648. The saintliness of his nature is touched on in the exhortation to be found near his tomb in Southwark Cathedral: '…stay, it will be worth thy tarrying to know how great a man is here…'.

RIGHT:

The opening of the Book of
Genesis in the 1611 Authorized
Version of the Bible, one of the
great glories of English prose.
Launcelot Andrewes was one of
about fifty distinguished scholars
appointed to the task of its
production.

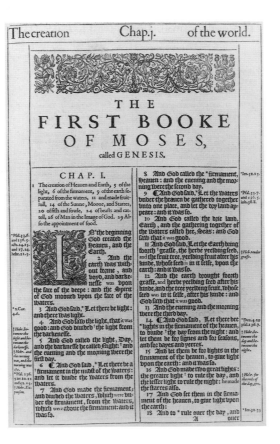

OPPOSITE:

This letter was written, early in
Andrewes's career, on 24 May 1589,
to Sir Francis Walsingham, one of
Queen Elizabeth's privy council-
lors. Walsingham was instru-
mental in Andrewes's obtaining
the living of St Giles, Cripplegate,
and in his becoming a prebend of
St Paul's Cathedral. The hand is
beautifully measured and fluent.

I doe, in humble manner, crave pardon of yo[u]r Honor, in y[a]t J
have not my self attended, in y[e] redeliverie of th'enclosed;
to render to y[i]s H. my bounden dutie of thanks, for the
cotents thereof.   Being, besides myn exercise to Morrow,
on Monday morning bid y[e] Feast of my Fathers Company
to p[re]ach at Deptford: J promised my self fro[m] yo[u]r Honor,
a favorable dispensation, for y[e] forbearing of my presence till then.
What tyme, J shall awaite on yo[u]r Honor, to present unto
yo[u]r same, my professed humble thanks, and not my thanks
only, but my service and my self to, to be ordered and employed
by y[i]s H. every way.   The same of verie right and dutie
belonging to y[i]s H: as well, in regard, of yo[u]r Honors great
bountie to me these yeares past: (w[hi]ch while J live J am
bound to acknowledg:) as now, for y[e] instant procurement
of these 2 prebends, the one of them no sooner ended,
but y[e] other streight begoon.   They are to me both,
sufficient witnesses of yo[u]r Honors care for my well doyng,
and mindfulnes of me upon any occasion: my prayer to God
is, y[a]t J may not live, unworthy these so honorable dealings
but y[a]t in some sort, (as his holy wisdome shall appoint
J may prove serviceable to yo[u]r Honor, and to, yo[u]r Honors
cheef care, his Church of o[u]rs.   what y[i]s H
hath, or shall, further vouchsafe to promise, in my name, in
this, or ought else by me to be done: shalbe J trust so
satisfied, as shall stand to yo[u]r Honors lyking, every way.
So recommending, to y[i]s H. y[e] perfeting of yo[u]r Honors owne
benefite,   w[i]th my verie humble dutie, J end.
The L. Jesus, of his great goodnes, graunt unto this Realme
long to enjoy yo[u]r Honor.   Amen.   May 24.

Yo[u]r Honors in all humble dutie
and service so most bound.

L. Andrewes

Sir John Harington c. 1561–1612

ABOVE:
The elaborate title page of this first printing of *Orlando Furioso* includes a portrait of the handsome author and his distinguished looking dog, Bungy.

'When thou doste feel creeping tyme at thye gate, these fooleries will please thee less.' One piece of foolery may have been on her mind more than most when Queen Elizabeth I uttered these sobering words in 1603 in the closing weeks of her life to her godson, the 'saucy poet' Sir John Harington. Some seven years earlier, in 1596, he had published *A New Discourse of a Stale Subject, called the Metamorphosis of Ajax*, a work whose title teasingly hints at its surprising contents. A 'jacques', or what is still sometimes called a 'john', was Elizabethan slang for a privy or toilet. Harington's carefully illustrated satire, which perhaps predictably failed to secure him the royal praise for which he hoped, proposed a detailed prototype of what is instantly recognisable today as a flushing lavatory – a convenience which, as it turned out, failed to find ready employment until the nineteenth century.

A more serious but less celebrated work is Harington's translation of *Orlando Furioso*, originally written by the Italian Ludovico Ariosto and published in 1532. Harington was reputedly banished from court by Elizabeth for corrupting her ladies with translations plucked from the 'less seemly' parts of the text and charged not to return until he had completed a full English version. He took up his task with gusto and it appeared in 1591. After a spell in Ireland with the ill-fated Earl of Essex and many subsequent years negotiating the vagaries of the royal court (upon which he commented with great flair in the letters and miscellaneous writings published in 1769 under the title *Nugae Antiquae*), Harington died at his home of Kelston, near Bath, on 20 November 1612. His entry in the British *Dictionary of National Biography* describes him as a man 'entirely destitute of restraint'.

RIGHT:
Shown here is the page of *Orlando Furioso* set from the manuscript.

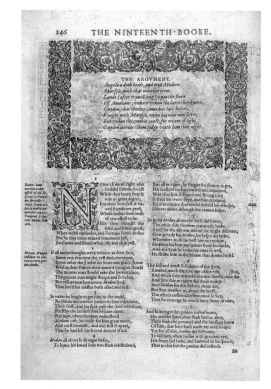

OPPOSITE:
This manuscript, written out at least in part by Harington himself, is thought to be the only surviving Elizabethan poetical manuscript known to have been the copy text for a contemporary printer. Although the manuscript, which comprises only part of Harington's translation of *Orlando Furioso*, is essentially a fair copy, it does contain last minute revisions and additions. Thus in the second stanza shown here, the word 'prices' is replaced by 'soverayns'. The manuscript bears smudges of ink from the workshop and various instructions for setting the type. The author uses different hands for his marginal annotations and the introductory 'arguments' which preface each of the poem's books.

N. 3
—————
145

N. 4
—————
146

The Argument of the 19. booke.

Angellyca doth heale, and wed Medore :
Meonfesta, with that other worthy crew,
Landes (after travell long) vppon the shore
Of Amazons; where when the law they knew,
Gwydon, that thither came but late before,
Foreght with Meonfesta, who hir nynt men slew;
but when the combat ceast, for want of lyght,
Gwydon intreated them lodg with him that nyght.

1
None can deem ryght who faythfull frends do rest,
whyle they bear sway, and rule in great degree,
for then both fast and fayned frends are prest,
whose fayths seem both of on effect to bee :
but then reuolte the faynt and fayned guest,
when welth convoynd, and fortune seems to flee.
but hee that loud indeed remayneth fast,
and loud and serud when lyfe and all ys past.

2
Of all mens thoughts vpon wrytten in theyr fate,
some one that now the rest doth overthrow,
some other tale that mounts hir grace,
when at theyr prime theyr inward thoughts shewd know,
the meaner man should take the better place,
the greater man myght stoop, and sit below,
but tell wee now how poor Medoro sped,
that loud his master both alyve and ded.

3
In vayn he sowght to get him to the wood,
by blynde and narrow pathes to him vnknown,
theyr swyft, and his slow pase the same withstood,
forst by the burden that he bare alone:
but now, when Clorydano vnderstood
Medoros pase he made for him great mone,
and curst him selfe, and was full yll apayd
that he had left his frend devoyd of ayd.

Medoro all about

19

Divers haue written to this
effect of the fickilnes of frends
but specially, Ovid.
Donec eris fœlix multos
numerabis amicos
Tempora si fuerint nubila
solus eris.

Horace. vulgus infidum
vt meretrix retro per-
iura cedit.

George Peele 1558–1597

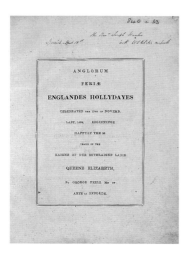

ABOVE:

The first known printing of Peele's 'Anglorum Feriae' was issued privately in 1830 by the owner of the manuscript, W. Stevenson Fitch, postmaster of Ipswich. The title page is shown here and reveals that the publication, in effect a slight pamphlet, was presented by Fitch to a Reverend Joseph Hunter.

George Peele, born a Londoner, undertook his schooling as free scholar at Christ's Hospital, of which his father was clerk, and subsequently at Oxford University, where he gained a reputation as a skilled poet and translator. He was a student first at Broadgates Hall (now Pembroke College), and later at Christ Church, graduating as a 'Master of arte' in 1579. Peele's adult life in London was characterised by literary effort and dissipation in equal measure. No sooner had he left Oxford than the governors of Christ's Hospital, who had helped to fund his studies, commanded his father to 'discharge his house' of him. By 1585, Peele had married into a certain amount of wealth, which he set about squandering. He had also helped to produce two plays in Oxford, seen his first work, *The Arraignment of Paris*, acted on the stage, and had created his first pageant. There is evidence to suggest that he was in all likelihood an actor as well as a playwright, an occupation which doubtless enhanced his opportunity for exuberant behaviour. One friend described him as 'the chief supporter of pleasance now living'. He died in about 1597 of (according to one source) 'a loathsome disease'.

November 17 marked a special occasion for the Elizabethans, this being the day, in 1558, that the young Queen ascended to the throne. By 1595 the annual celebrations had grown into perhaps the most important and lavish festival in the English calendar. One spectator evidently impressed by the pageantry that year was George Peele. His last known work 'Anglorum Feriae' (shown opposite), a poem written in the blank verse for which he is celebrated, gives a lively account of the day's jousting. Whether it was printed at the time is not known, but Peele, once commissioned by Lord Burghley to compose verses to the Queen, no doubt hoped to win high favour with his patriotic piece.

RIGHT:

This dramatic fifteenth-century illumination in a French Romance shows a joust before royalty. An Elizabethan audience such as that to which Peele belonged would have enjoyed a similar spectacle, as described in his 'Anglorum Feriae'.

ABOVE:

Peele's autograph poem 'Anglorum Feriae' of 1595 has descended to us in this
manuscript alone, an important survival from the Elizabethan age – albeit one
badly damaged by unknown corrosive substances in the nineteenth century.

William Shakespeare 1564–1616

'He was not of an age, but for all time'. Ben Jonson's verse tribute in the first collected edition of Shakespeare's plays (the posthumously published 'First Folio' of 1623, prepared by his fellow actors) is perhaps English literature's most prescient. The young love of Romeo and Juliet, the mature love of Antony and Cleopatra, the jealousy of Othello, the ambition of Lady Macbeth, the anguish of Hamlet and the foolishness of Falstaff strike us with the enduring force of truth.

ABOVE:
Shakespeare's celebrated portrait from the title page of the *First Folio*, of 1623. The work of Martin Droeshout, it was confirmed as a likeness by the playwright's friend and colleague, Ben Jonson. Done posthumously, it was probably based on a painting which has not survived.

William Shakespeare was born to a prosperous, middle-class merchant in Stratford-upon-Avon, where he attended school and met the older Anne Hathaway, whom he married in 1582 and with whom he had three children. By 1589, possibly after working as a humble provincial schoolmaster, he had established himself as a dramatist in London and he soon became a leading member of the Lord Chamberlain's Men. His long and evidently very profitable association with this theatrical company as both actor (he played the ghost, for example, in *Hamlet*) and playwright, saw him working at the Globe Theatre, in which he held a share, from 1599, and the Blackfriars Theatre, of which he was a leaseholder, from 1608.

Among Shakespeare's earliest work may be counted two long poems (perhaps written when London's theatres closed due to plague in the early 1590s), his mysterious, musical, richly dark sonnet sequence and the violent play *Titus Andronicus*. Over the next two decades he would bring a steady stream of plays to the stage, including histories, comedies, tragedies, tragicomedies and the so-called 'problem plays' which defy traditional classification. Shakespeare's most haunting work, *The Tempest*, was performed for King James I in 1611 before his retirement to Stratford-upon-Avon and is often seen as his swansong. He died on 23 April 1616 and lies buried in Holy Trinity Church, Stratford-upon-Avon.

The extreme rarity of manuscript sources by or relating to Shakespeare has long served to heighten the intense speculation surrounding his identity. Indeed, some have gone so far as to argue that no such person existed, being but a convenient front for other writers. However, this lacuna in the record is perhaps not as surprising as it seems. After all, little else has come down to us from his numerous contemporaries, many of whom were at the time equally well regarded and successful. Indeed, scripts of only 18 of his 37 plays appeared in print in his life-time. Of these, the 'good quartos' probably derived from original manuscript

OPPOSITE:
Shakespeare's three-page contribution to 'The Book of Sir Thomas More' comprises a new beginning for the sixth scene in the play, in which More, with his formidable powers of speech, quells a riot against the Lombard and French aliens in London. The hand is a typical secretary type of the time, but does bear certain idiosyncratic characteristics which have helped scholars to attribute it to Shakespeare – most notably a recurrent 'spur' on the character 'a'.

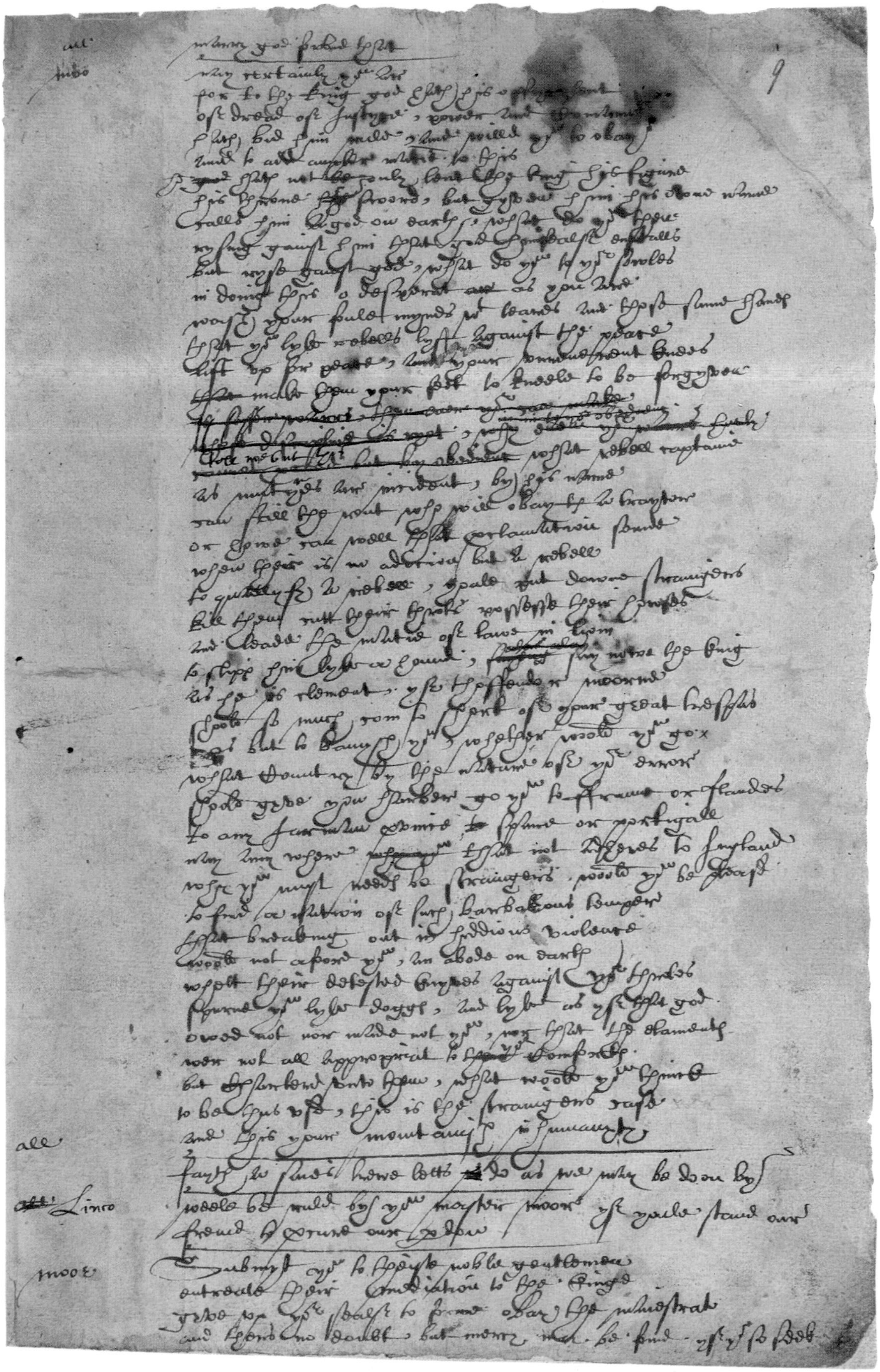

all. marry god forbid that
moo. nay certainly you ar
for to the king god hath his offyc lent
of dread of Iustyce, power and Comaund
hath bid him rule, and willd you to obay
and to add ampler maiestie to this
he hath not only lent the king his figure
his throne and sword, but gyven him his owne name
calls him a god on earth, what do you then
rysing gainst him that god himsealf enstalls
but ryse gainst god, what do you to your sowles
in doing this o desperat as you are.
wash your foule mynds wth teares and those same hands
that you lyke rebells lyft against the peace
lift vp for peace, and your vnreuerent knees
make them your feet to kneele to be forgyven
~~is safer warrs, then ever you can make~~
~~whose discipline is ryot;~~ in in to yor obedienc. why even yor hurly
cannot proceed but by obedienc what rebell captaine
as mutyes ar incident, by his name
can still the rout who will obay a traytor
or howe can well that proclamation sounde
when ther is no adicion but a rebell
to quallyfy a rebell, youle put downe straingers
kill them cutt their throts possesse their howses
and leade the maiestie of lawe in liom
to slipp him lyke a hound; say nowe the king
as he is clement, yf thoffendor moorne
shoold so much com to short of your great trespas
as but to banysh you, whether woold you go.
what Country by the nature of yor error
shoold gyve you harber go you to ffraunc or flanders
to any Iarman province, spane or portigall
nay any where why you that not adheres to Ingland
why you must needs be straingers, woold you be pleasd
to find a nation of such barbarous temper
that breaking out in hiddious violence
woold not afoord you, an abode on earth
whett their detested knyves against yor throtes
spurne you lyke doggs, and lyke as yf that god
owed not nor made not you, nor that the elaments
wer not all appropriat to yor Comforts.
but Charterd vnto them, what woold you thinck
to be thus vsd, this is the straingers case
and this your mountanish inhumanyty

all. fayth a saies trewe letts us do as we may be doon by
Linco. weele be ruld by you master moor yf youle stand our
freind to procure our pardon

moor. Submyt you to theis noble gentlemen
entreate their mediation to the kinge
gyve vp yor sealf to forme obay the maiestrat
and thers no doubt, but mercy may be found yf you so seek

RIGHT:
The house secured by Shakespeare's signature on the first tag of this deed lay beside and partly over what had once been the lodging of the Prior of Blackfriars. It appears to have been associated with Catholic intrigue (particularly the hiding of priests and papists). One description from about 1586 notes that 'it hath sundry back-dores and bye-wayes, and many secret vaults and corners', while another commented on its 'many places of secret conveyance' communicating with 'secret passages' leading to the Thames.

sources or official playhouse copies, while the 'bad quartos' comprised unofficial texts remembered, or partially remembered, by audiences or actors ('quarto' meaning a book made from sheets of paper folded four times, as opposed to 'folio' in which the paper is folded once). Comparison between often widely differing quarto and posthumous folio texts has kept scholars engaged for generations in trying to establish Shakespeare's original words – words which may well have met an ignoble fate lining pie dishes or, worse still, serving as the Elizabethan equivalent of lavatory paper.

Six signatures of Shakespeare survive, although doubts have been raised as to whether some or all of these were actually signed by him, or by legal functionaries. Three are on his will, one on a legal document in the Public Record Office and two on documents relating to the purchase of a property (one in the Guildhall Library, London, and the other, shown here, in The British Library). The mortgage deed, discovered in 1768 and once belonging to the celebrated Shakespearean actor David Garrick, bears the abbreviated signature 'Wm. Shakspe'. It is dated 11 March 1613 and evidently completes the purchase by him, with the help of three trustees, of a gate-house in the precinct of 'the late black ffryers, London'.

There is only one literary manuscript which would appear to bear proof of Shakespeare's pen. The collaborative play 'The Book of Sir Thomas More' is mostly in the hand of Anthony Munday, but three pages (one illustrated on the previous page), with extensive corrections, are generally attributed to Shakespeare himself. The imagery, style and spelling have led commentators to this

LEFT:

This seventeenth-century view of London clearly shows the Globe Theatre. Finally demolished in 1644, it had been entirely rebuilt after a fire in 1613 caused by gunpowder special effects used in *Henry VIII*. The view also shows Blackfriars on the opposite side of the river.

BELOW:

This panoramic view by William Smith dating from 1588 shows London as it was during Shakespeare's first year of residence there. The Rose Theatre, in which he performed, would open on the South Bank in 1592, to be followed, in 1599, by the Globe Theatre. They lay close to the two circular bull and bear baiting enclosures, clearly visible here, and would be reached by playgoers from Westminster and the City by ferry or London Bridge.

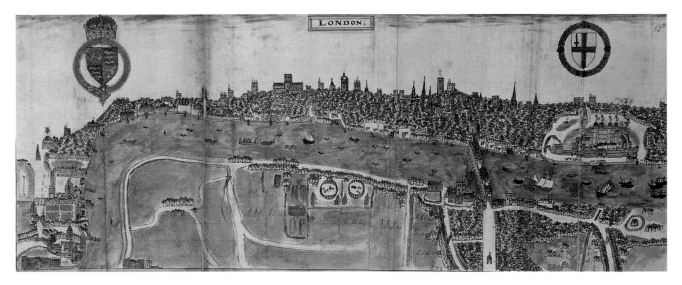

conclusion, together with a comparison with the six surviving signatures. The play, which involved the efforts of some five dramatists around the mid-1590s, was probably never performed, although Thomas Goodal, whose name later appears in the margin of the manuscript, was an actor with the company known in 1592 as Lord Strange's Men, for whom Shakespeare was then writing.

Sir Walter Ralegh *c.* 1552–1618

ABOVE:

An engraved portrait of Sir Walter Ralegh from a 1652 edition of his *The History of the World*.

BELOW:

This is one of a number of maps of ancient Biblical lands drawn, watercoloured and annotated by Ralegh as part of his research for his *History of the World*.

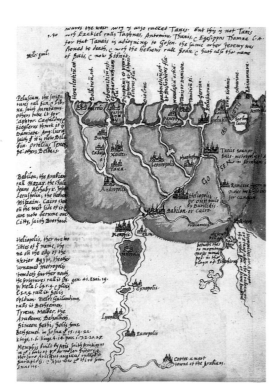

From 1603 to 1616, Sir Walter Ralegh, courtier, coloniser, historian, soldier, poet and first importer to England of tobacco and potatoes – one might say the very model of the Renaissance man – was imprisoned in the Tower of London. He had, in fact, been there before, in 1593, when he infuriated his doting Queen by planning to marry a maid of honour. On that occasion he was quickly released and back in royal favour by 1597, having searched for gold in South America to swell Elizabeth's coffers and sacked Cadiz. Elizabeth's successor, however, was not so easily impressed. Almost as soon as he acceded to the throne, James I accused the flamboyant Ralegh of conspiracy to treason and locked him away.

It was during this long incarceration that Ralegh embarked upon his *History of the World*, dedicated to 'Her, whom I must still honor in the dust.' A notebook kept by Ralegh while in the Tower (illustrated left and opposite) reveals that his time there was hardly that of the desperate prisoner; extensive lists record the contents of his excellent library, while the presence of other hands in the volume points to his use of assistants as he conducted his research. The carefully drawn, annotated and coloured maps charting ancient Biblical lands were, however, all his own work, as was the fairly copied poem on its final page which forms part of (perhaps the conclusion to) a series of poems inspired by his fluctuating relationship with Elizabeth, or 'Cynthia'.

Ralegh's *History,* which started with the Creation but only reached 130BC, appeared in an impressive folio volume in 1614 and, despite a sour reception by the King, was widely admired. Two years later, longing for freedom and adventure, he secured his release from the Tower by volunteering to hunt for gold in South America. The mission was a tragic failure; his son was murdered and on his empty-handed return suspicion mounted that he had invented his story of a gold mine promising untold riches (his 1596 *Discoverie of Guiana* included a description of 'Eldorado'). The old charge of treason was revisited upon his head, which he lost to the executioner on 29 October 1618. He was said to have faced his death bravely, responding to one in the crowd who objected to his head not facing east: 'what matter how the head lie, so the heart be right?'. His body was buried in the chancel of St Margaret's church, Westminster; his head was embalmed by his wife, Elizabeth Throgmorton, the very maid who had inspired Elizabeth's jealousy. If the story is to be believed, she carried it with her at all times for the rest of her life in a red leather bag.

OPPOSITE:

It is thought that Ralegh composed these verses possibly between 1597 and 1601, perhaps to be read at a specific occasion before the Queen herself. Why he should have so carefully copied the verses into a notebook largely devoted to his *History*, quite some time after Elizabeth's death, remains unclear. Two suggestions are that he may have been intending to dedicate the *History* to Elizabeth or that he actually started to keep the notebook from an earlier date than that commonly supposed.

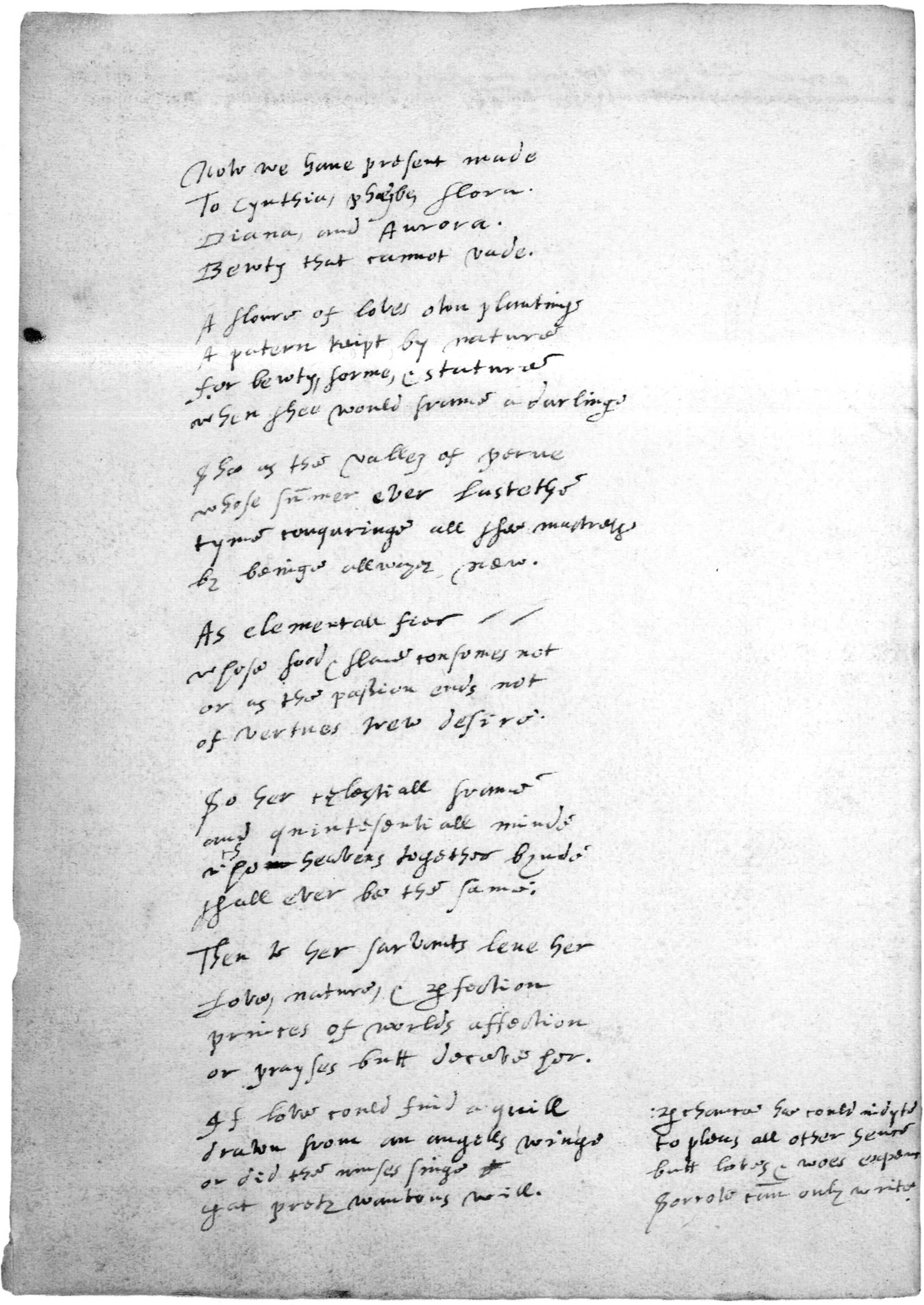

Now we have present made
To Cynthia, Phœbe, Flora
Diana, and Aurora.
Bewty that cannot vade.

A flower of loves own planting
A patern kept by nature
For bewty, forme, & stature
When shee would frame a darling.

Shee is the valley of Joyne
Whose sūmer ever lasteth
Tyme conqueringe all shee masketh
By beinge allwayes new.

As elementall fier //
Whose food & flame consumes not
Or as the passion ends not
Of vertues new desire.

So her celestiall frame
And quintessentiall minde
These seasons togethor bynde
Shall ever be the same.

Then to her servants leave her

Loves, natures, & affection
Princes of worlds affection
Or prayses butt deceive her.

If love could find a quill
drawn from an angells winge
or did the muses singe
yat prety wanton will.

Yf Saturne her could indyte
To please all other sence
butt loves & woes expence
Herself can only write.

Ben Jonson 1572/73–1637

ABOVE:

This imposing portrait of Jonson is taken from a set of his *Works* published in 1640. Before him in the lower corners of the frame are finely bound books with clasps.

'O rare Ben Jonson' reads the memorial slab on his grave in Westminster Abbey and his standing today is such that, in any other language, he would be honoured by many as the national playwright. Jonson, an imposing and powerful man, the son of a clergyman of Borders descent, was educated at Westminster School and became in turns a bricklayer, a soldier in the Netherlands, an actor and finally a playwright. He was imprisoned in 1597, following an appearance in Thomas Nashe's 'The Isle of Dogs' which gravely offended the authorities, and a year later he killed a fellow actor, Gabriel Spencer, in a duel, narrowly escaping execution. Jonson became a devoted friend, admirer and theatrical colleague of Shakespeare, tutored Sir Walter Ralegh's son, travelled through Europe, held court at the Mermaid and Devil taverns before John Donne, George Chapman, Francis Beaumont and John Fletcher, and was lauded by James I, who made him in effect Poet Laureate.

Jonson's major plays, written for the London stage, belong to the period before 1616 when he published a folio collection of his *Works* – the first attempt to elevate the art of the stage play. From 1605, however, he increasingly turned to the composition of masques for the court, prompted by the wishes of James's consort, Anne of Denmark. The court masque, an entertainment combining drama, poetry, music and dance in lavish settings, enjoyed an enormous vogue with English monarchs from Elizabeth I to Charles I. The one illustrated here, 'The Masque of Queens', was composed for the New Year festivities at Whitehall Palace in 1609, though in the event it was not performed until Candelmas (2 February). The parts were taken by noble ladies of the court, and the sets and costumes were designed by Inigo Jones. The sketches for these still survive in the collection of the Duke of Devonshire.

'The Masque of Queens' came to the Library, by the authority of George II, in 1757 among the collection of Royal Manuscripts formed by successive sovereigns of England. That collection of nearly 2000 volumes had been stored in an old dormitory in Westminster School. The manuscript's having gone into the Royal collection spared it the fate of many of Jonson's papers which were sadly destroyed with the rest of his library in a fire in his lodgings in 1623.

LEFT:

A portrait of Henry, Prince of Wales, published in 1612.

OPPOSITE:

The autograph manuscript of 'The Masque of Queens' comprises twenty folios of Jonson's late-English mixed hand (showing both italic and secretary characteristics). It was written out for presentation to Henry, Prince of Wales, who was to die prematurely in 1612. Here we have the preliminary address to the prince. The underlined words are given extra stress by being written in a pronounced Italic hand.

Humanitye, is not the least honor of ye Wreath. For,
if once the worthy Professors of these learnings shall
come (as heretofore they were) to be the care of
Princes, the Crownes theyr Soueraignes weare will
not more adorne theyr temples; nor theyr stampes
liue longer in theyr Medalls, than in such Subiects
labors. Poetry, my Lord, is not borne wth euery man;
Nor euery day: And, in her generall right, it is now
my minute to thanke yor Highnesse, who not only
do honor her wth yor care, but are curious to exa=
mine her wth yor eye, & inquire into her beauties,
and strengthes. Where, though it hath prou'd a worke
of some difficulty to mee to retriue the particular
authorities (according to yor gracious command, and a
desire borne out of iudgment) to those things, wh.
I writt obt of fulnesse, and memory of my former
readings; Yet, now I haue ouercome it, the reward
that meetes mee is double to one act: wh is, that
thereby, yor excellent vnderstanding will not only iusti=
fier mee to yor owne knowledge, but decline the
stiffnesse of others originall Ignorance, allready
armd to censure. For wh singular bounty, if my
Fate (most excellent Prince, and only Delicacy of
mankind) shall reserue mee to the Age of yor Actions,
whether in the Campe, or the Councell Chamber, ÿ
I may write, at nights, the deedes of yor dayes; I
will then labor to bring forth some worke as wor=
thy of yor fame, as my ambition therin is of yor
pardon.

   By the most trew admirer of yor Highnesse Vertues,

     And most hearty Celebrater of them.

MVSEVM
BRITAN
NICVM

      Ben: Jonson.

        The

Sir Fulke Greville 1554–1628

ABOVE:

An engraved portrait of Sir Fulke
Greville from Edward Lodge's
four-volume work *Portraits of
illustrious personages of Great
Britain, engraved from authentic
pictures in the Galleries of the
Nobility, and the public collections of the country, with biographical and historical memoirs of
their lives and actions* (1821–34).

Born in 1554 into a noble Warwickshire family, Fulke Greville attended Shrewsbury School where he met Sir Philip Sidney, establishing a close friendship which would endure through their adventures in the literary world of the Elizabethan court. Greville, who helped to bear Sidney's coffin at St Paul's in 1586, played an important part in preserving and publishing the works of his friend. *The Life of Sir Philip Sidney*, which he started around 1610, helped to establish a literary reputation which has long since eclipsed his own, when it finally appeared in 1652.

In 1621 Greville became first Baron Brooke after a successful career as a much favoured, if occasionally chastised, subject of Elizabeth I (a figure above all others revered and mythologised by poets and playwrights of the age), and subsequently James I, who granted him the magnificent gifts of Warwick Castle and Knowle Park. His distinguished and colourful life came to a violent end in 1628 at his London house in Holborn at the hands of Ralph Haywood, an old servant who felt slighted after discovering his exclusion from his master's will. Haywood killed himself immediately after stabbing Greville who struggled on in agony for a month. The man who met his death through perceived parsimony used his final strength to bequeath large sums of money to the surgeons and attendants who ministered to him. Described by C. S. Lewis as a writer of 'genuinely didactic verse…utterly unadorned and dependent for interest almost exclusively on its intellectual content', the inscription of his own devising, which can still be seen on his tomb in St Mary's Church, Warwick, reads simply, 'servant to Queen Elizabeth, councillor to King James, and friend to Sir Philip Sidney'.

In 1968 The British Library acquired six vellum-bound manuscripts containing the poems, plays and one prose piece by Greville. Sometimes known as the Warwick manuscripts, after their former home, they comprise the work of a known scribe charged with the task of compiling fair copies of Greville's works. The great importance of these copies lies not only in the fact that they were compiled under the direction of their author, but that they include extensive revisions in his own hand, a fact leading one scholar to note that they represent 'the most substantial, authorized manuscript text that has come down to us of any distinguished Elizabethan or Jacobean poet'.

LEFT:

Sonnet 77 from a rare copy of the 1633 edition of *Certain Learned and Elegant Workes,* printed on oversized paper. Despite the care Greville evidently took to preserve his work, he published nothing during his own lifetime. That task was left to his friend and co-executor Sir John Coke, who saw *Certain Learned and Elegant Workes* through the press in 1633, an edition which does not appear to have used the Warwick manuscripts as copy texts but some later source.

OPPOSITE:

Shown here is the opening of Sonnet 76 from the sequence *Cælica,* probably written out in the year 1619. The neat scribal copy contrasts vividly with Greville's revisions.

The heathen Gods, first in powre, witt, birth,

yet worship'd for their worth, and loue to men,

At first kept stations between heauen and earth,

A like iust to the Castle and the Denn.

Ocasion, Meritt, nature dulie weigh'd,

And yet in showe, no rule, but will obey'd.

Till tyme and selfenesse wch turnd worth, to artt,

Loue into complements, and thyngs to thought,

formd new pictures to enthrall mens hartt,

By lawes, wthin while tyrones seemd ouer-wrought.

Powre sweetly surpriz'd this faith, off man,

And tak't his freedome at more then hee can.

for to the Scepters while powre doth reserue,

As well the prastique, as expounding sence

thes lawes, from wth not fleshe can paynetlesse swerue,

They being Engmes off omnipotence.

With equall powre, is not vnequall man,

Then swetly, tak't at wth, more then hee can?

Robert Herrick 1591–1674

ABOVE:

A portrait bust of Herrick, set in an elaborately mythic landscape, from his *Hesperides* (1648).

ABOVE:

A picture of Dean Prior Church, from an 1882 edition of the poet's works. Herrick ministered at the church from 1629 and was buried there in 1674.

Robert Herrick was little over a year old when his father, a goldsmith, fell to his death from the window of his London house. The strong suspicion of suicide may have played its part in his son's failure to visit his place of burial, at St Vedast's Church (which still stands, albeit rebuilt, in the shadow of St Paul's Cathedral) for thirty-five years. In his poem 'To the Reverend shade of his religious Father', he asks forgiveness:

> That for seven lusters I did never come
> To do the rites to thy religious tomb;
> That neither hair was cut, or true tears shed
> By me, o'er thee, as justments to the dead,
> Forgive, forgive me; since I did not know
> Whether thy bones had here their rest or no.

Along with his six siblings, Herrick came under the guardianship of his wealthy uncle, to whom he was apprenticed as a goldsmith. He gave up his craft, however, when he decided to enter St John's College, Cambridge in 1613, as a 'fellow-commoner'. He moved to Trinity Hall in 1616 to pursue legal studies and graduated in 1620, by which time he had begun to establish himself as an accomplished poet. Subsequent lively years spent in London among a group of poets devoted to the charismatic Ben Jonson – at, as he recalled, 'the Sun, the Dog, the Triple Tun' – helped to consolidate his literary credentials (and, perhaps, nurture what became a lifelong aversion to the idea of marriage). The direction of his professional life was affirmed with his ordination, in 1623, as an episcopal minister.

Six years later, Herrick entered into an ambiguous period of existence. Appointed in 1629 as vicar of Dean Prior, Devonshire, his rural life, shared with a devoted servant 'Prew', whom he immortalised in verse, a spaniel called Tracie ('no eye shall ever see/For shape and service, Spaniell like to thee'), possibly a tame pig with a taste for beer, and numerous other animals, provided ample opportunity to compose, by his own admission, some of his finest work. It also, however, brought him into contact with locals whom he at times regarded 'rude almost as rudest savages' and inspired in him a frustrated longing for the sophisticated and exciting city life which he had left behind.

It was Herrick's political convictions which finally saw him back in his beloved London. A staunch Royalist, he was ejected from his living by the forces of the Commonwealth in 1646. Whatever he may have thought of the style of his dismissal, Herrick was delighted to be leaving his 'long and dreary banishment', vowing never to return until 'rocks turn to rivers, rivers turn to men'. He settled in Westminster where, although having little of his own money, he was able to rely upon his wide and wealthy circle of friends and family. His return to the centre of literary life (at the expense, it would seem, of his devotional obliga-tions) must have played its part in inspiring him to bring to press his first and only collection of verse, *Hesperides*, in 1648. Herrick was eventually restored to his rural living in 1662 and, despite his earlier protests about village life, there he appears to have remained for the rest of his days. An entry in the church register records that 'Robert Herrick, vicker, was buried ye 15th day of October 1674'.

Chorus

Is, is there nothing cann withstand
The hand
Of Time: but that it must
Be shaken into dust?
Then poore, poore Israelites are wee
now fre
But cannot shun the Graues captivitie.

Alas Good Browne! that Nature hath
No bath
Or vichuous herbes to stray me.
To boyle thee yong againe
yet could she (Kind) but back command
Thy breath
Hir self would else ere thou shuldst be Inmand.

But (ah) the golden Ewer by stroke
Is broke.
And now the Almond Tree
With teares, with teares we see
Doth howle bye and with ill fall
Do all
The daughters dye, that once were musicall.

Thus yf weake builded man cam saye
A day
He liues tis all, for why
He's sure at night to dye.
For fading man in fleshly home
Doth rome
Till he his graue find, His eternall home.

Then farewell, farewell man of nee
Till when
For as the mourners meet
Pale visagd in the street
To speake of this our britle birth
In earth)
We meet with thee triumphant in our mirth.

Trinitall Halls
Exeqiues.

RIGHT:
Although there survives a series of important letters written by Herrick while at Cambridge to his uncle (mainly asking for money), and copies of his verses were widely circulated, this elegy written in a fine italic hand is the only known literary autograph which has been attributed to Herrick beyond doubt. It was while a student in his last year at Trinity Hall, Cambridge, that he was evidently invited to compose a formal piece on behalf of his college to mark the death of John Browne, a fellow of neighbouring Caius College.

Philip Massinger   1583–1639

'March 10, 1639, buried Philip Massinger, a stranger'. These words, written in the parish register of St Saviour's Church in London (now Southwark Cathedral) record the passing of a man who has been described as one of the most serious professional dramatists of the post-Shakespearian period. Although 'stranger' here simply means that Massinger was not of that particular parish, its use seems ironic given his long and close association with one of its most significant landmarks, the Globe Theatre.

Massinger was born in Salisbury, the son of a gentleman employed at Wilton House by the Herbert family, the Earls of Pembroke. He attended Oxford University, sponsored by the Earl, but left without a degree, having 'applied his mind more to poetry and romances for about four years or more than to logic and philosophy'. He arrived in London in 1606 and soon established a reputation as a playwright, albeit one in a state of constant impoverishment. As was typical of the age, Massinger collaborated on many plays, his associates including Thomas Middleton, William Rowley and Thomas Dekker. His greatest collaborator and friend, John Fletcher, died in 1625, from which point Massinger wrote almost exclusively for the King's Men which only a few years previously had employed Shakespeare as its leading dramatist.

Of the fifty-five plays in which Massinger was known to be involved, twenty-two are lost. Among those that survive, fifteen are thought to be his work alone. One of the most important of these is *Believe as you List*, a tragedy which he had been forced to rewrite after it was rejected a licence on 11 January 1630 by the Master of the Revels, on the grounds that 'it did contain dangerous matter, as the deposing of Sebastian, King of Portugal, by Philip II, and there being a peace sworn betwixt the kings of England and Spain'. The play survives in a manuscript copy, shown here, written out by Massinger himself. Adding to its rarity and interest is the fact that the document is marked up as a prompt copy and includes the names of the King's Men who performed the play on 7 May 1631, together with an endorsement by the Master of the Revels permitting its performance.

RIGHT:
An engraved portrait of Philip Massinger, from an eighteenth-century edition of his works.

BELOW:
The final page of the play bears an endorsement written out and signed by the Master of the Revels, Sir Henry Herbert. It reads: 'This Play, called Believe as you List may be acted this 6 of May 1631'.

OPPOSITE:
The autograph manuscript of Massinger's *Believe as you List* was rediscovered 'among a mass of rubbish' in 1844. After it was edited and published in 1849 the manuscript passed through the hands of a number of collectors before being purchased for the nation at auction in 1900. Shown in the margins are various notes written for the benefit of the prompt.

on this or this. in death I must conclude
the Roman conquest. how: am I griev'd
for escape, and dilde in their opinion that
I am beside my expectacions?

Harry:
wilson: &
Boy ready for
the song at ye
Arras

will not the losse of my life quitt the cost?
o rare frugalitie! will they force mee to
bee mine owne hangman? & beare still that guilti
of crimes not to bee nam'de? remaine such favor
by the iudges donne, and is my innocence
(to oppresse innocence of a starr cross'd kinge
holds more contemptible. my better angell
though wantinge power to alter fate discovers
their fellies purpose'd. yes, yes, 'tis soe.
my sodiste death will not suffice. they ainde at
my soules perdicion, and that too him
a fewe howers more of miserie betray how?
noe stile is free still. I shall soe returne
from whence it came, & in soe purenes'se triumph
o're tyrannie, ofrainde, and fetterd.

flaminius: O the divell!
Thou art weake. this will not doe.

Metellus: marke how steele stand

Ent: Taylor
(with ... to water)
Sempronio: the honor is intend ~ friends
for the quittinge ~ brought my life out.

Taylor: Heere's ~ take this though course it will kill hunger
it is your dayly pittance, yet when you please
your comons may bee minded.

Antiochus
Taylor: showe mee the way
Confesse your selfe to bee a cuninge knaue
the matter's traind. out if you will bee
still kinge of the creations feede on this, & line
you shall not say wee staruie you.   Exit Taylor.

Antiochus: stay I'll feed those.
and take this cruell pittie backe againe.
to him that sent it. this is a tyrannie
that doth transcende all presidents! my soule
but even now this lumpe of clay her prison
of it selfe in the want or nourish ment springe,
had shooke of her like feathers, and prepar'd
her selfe to make a nobl flight as set
at libertie, and now this separation
againe mint'd. you for whose curious pallat
the elements are ransack'd looke vpon
this bill of fare by my penurious steward
vicetied, send to a famishd kinge.
and warnde by my example, when your tables
cracke not with the weight of dishes, and the fetcht daintied
dispute not with their bounties. what shall I doe?
yf I refuse to touch, & taste these course,
& homely Cates, I fasten my owne fate,
& soe with willingnesse embrace a sinne
I shoulde have fird from. noe the eate,
& yf at this poore rate life can continue
I will not throwe it of.

flaminius: I pine with envie
to see this constance.
· intell bid your prospectie enter

~ Enter aboue flaminius
metellus. Sempronio ~ *(struck through)*

~ Enter Taylor with
browne bread & a
wooden dishe of
water.

The Lute strikes
& then the songe.   ~ & for subtlest magicke! ~ Sempro: ~ ...

John Milton 1608–1674

ABOVE:
An engraved portrait of Milton.

BELOW:
This pencil drawing of 1817, by John Buckler, shows Milton's house at Chalfont St Giles, Buckinghamshire. Here he completed *Paradise Lost* (1667).

'The main benefits of conjugal society', said Milton, 'are solace and peace', and these sentiments derived from personal experience. Classically educated, highly cultured, and travelled (he went to see Galileo in prison in Florence), Milton married the sixteen-year old Mary Powell in 1642. They were together for six weeks before she left him. She abandoned their home in St Bride's Churchyard, off Fleet Street, according to John Aubrey, because 'she found it very solitary; no company came'. It may, therefore, not be surprising to find in part of the *Commonplace Book* illustrated here a preoccupation with matrimony and divorce. Passionate in his defence of the individual in society, Milton produced a flurry of pamphlets on the subject of divorce between 1643 and 1645, *The Doctrine and Discipline of Divorce* having, in its second edition of 1644, an address to Parliament itself. Of course, the time was ripe: the abolition in the 1640s of the episcopacy and the ecclesiastical courts with their fierce control was the biggest disturbance to the marriage laws England had witnessed since the twelfth century. This was to be short-lived, however, for 1660 saw the return to the old order. It was not until 1969, incredibly, that Milton's plea – that full divorce may be allowed in England on the grounds of incompatibility and mutual hatred – became at last enshrined in law. Leo Abse revived Milton's spirit to get the Divorce Reform Bill through Parliament in that year.

In the event, Milton's wife returned to him in 1645. She died in 1652 and he married twice more, wives and children satisfying his scribal needs through the great poems of his later years, including the epic *Paradise Lost*, whose publication in August 1667 had been delayed by both the Great Plague and the Great Fire of 1666. One of the great independent spirits of English literature, fiercely protestant, anti-episcopalian and anti-Royalist (in 1649 he was appointed as Latin secretary to the Council of State), Milton was buried nevertheless next to his father among the Anglican fold in St Giles without Cripplegate in London's Barbican, the spot now marked by an easily-missed inscription at the foot of the pulpit steps. This manuscript was bought by the British Museum Library in 1900.

OPPOSITE:
Milton's *Commonplace Book*, written in Latin and containing references to books on ethical, economic and political matters, was compiled *c.* 1630–1650. The folio relating to divorce, shown here, is from the period 1643–1646. It is in Milton's own strong, purposeful hand, though we have elsewhere the hands of amanuenses upon whom he became increasingly dependent as his sight failed.

in judicia translatâ esse divortii causâ videtr ex quo Canonici lucrû inde reportare
authoritatemqᵤ uberrimam posse didicerunt Hist. Concil. Trident. 67. p.

Quæstiones innumeræ de divortiis incertâ solutione tractantr Concil. Trident. l. 8. p. 729 ⓔ et
737 ⓔ.

ritus publicè celebrandi matrimonii multis post apostolos seculis introducti sunt Concil. Trid.
l. 8. 772.

vide de bonis | Causæ matrimoniales ad civilê magistratû ptinebant priusquã ecclesiastici p socordiam
Ecclesiasticis. | principû eas earum judicia invasere. Concil. Trident. l. 8. 772.

Carolus magnus uxorem Theodorani repudiat, non redditâ ejus rei aliquam ratione
Girard. Hist. Franc. l. 3. p. 146. et Hildegardam duxit.

Post quinquennalem mariti absentiam, si incertum fuerit ubi sit, uxori conceditr cum
alio nuptias facere. Manuelis patriarchæ constantinop: sententia. Jus Græco-
Roman. p. 239. bixt autem hic patriarcha circa an. 1216.

Religionis causâ divortium fieri posse statuit Matthæus Monachus, sive orthodoxus ita
vult, non tantum si ab altero deseratr, in illo enim negotio non simplex
ευδοκια, infidelis ad cohabitationem requiritr, sed utriusqᵤ συνευδοκια
secundû Pauli sententiam; ait etiam ab Theodoto patriarcha ita statutû
vide lib. matrimonial. apud Jus Græco Roman. p. 507.
Guntarius archiepiscopus Colomiensis, et Tergaudus Trevirensis Lotharium Lotharingiæ ducem
repudiatâ Tibergâ p astradam inducentem approbaverunt. Thuan. l. 78. b. 555.

Pro divortio vide Bodin. repub. l. 1. c. 3.

                         Renatus Lotaringiæ dux repudiatâ ob deformitatem, et sterilitatem uxorem
                         Margaretâ et vivente et philippam superinduxit, nec tamen ejus ex
✶ Belgiæ et protestan- | Philippâ filius hæreditate dejectus. Thuan. hist. l. 24. p. 734.
tium defensor ——————— | Wilhelmus Arausionensis abdicatâ a se ob mores uxore Annâ
                         Mauritii Saxonis p viri filiâ Carlotam Borboniam Monpenserii
                         filiam duxit. Thuan. hist. l. 60. p. 72.

ˣ non regi solum, sed civibis | Joannes Basilii filius Moschorum dux, uxore repudiatâ, quod, quoties
Baro ab Herber. de Mesch: | vult, illi moribus patriis licet, novam ducit. Thuan. hist. l. 72. p. 471.
Propter impedimentum naturale Vincentius Mantuæ princeps Alexandri Farnesii
filiam repudiat aliâ superinductâ. Thuan. l. 80. p. 783.
Henricus 4ᵗᵘˢ Galliæ rex Margaritam uxorem ob mores quamvis
cognationis obtentu repudiavit, multisqᵤ exemplis id sibi quoqᵤ
licere demonstrat, quod alii ante se reges varias ob causas fecissent
Thuan. hist. l. 123. p. 885.

Sir Thomas Browne 1605–1682

'Were the happiness of the next world as closely apprehended as the felicities of this, it were a martyrdom to live.' Thomas Browne's words, from his short treatise *Urne-Buriall*, epitomise his fascination with what lies beyond the observable world. Born in London, Browne travelled widely in Europe before settling permanently in Norwich in 1637 to practise medicine, in which discipline he was widely celebrated: when he received his M.D. from Oxford University in 1637, he had already practised for a period in Oxfordshire, had spent time in the great medical centres of Montpellier and Padua, and had received a doctor's degree from Leyden University.

Browne married Dorothy Mileham in 1641 and the couple had twelve children. His life, from this point, seems (in the absence of a great deal of biographical information), to have been dedicated to the calm execution of his professional and domestic duties, and to his remarkable prose reflections. His first great work, in which he reveals his life to have reached 'a miracle of thirty years', was *Religio Medici* (published in an unauthorised edition in 1642), a wide-ranging exploration of personal faith. *Urne-Buriall*, published in 1658, is a short work and perhaps Browne's best regarded. Written in a style celebrated for its subtle beauty and power, it takes as its starting point 'the Sepulchrall Urnes lately found in Norfolk' before considering, in an impressively grand historical and geographical sweep, the profound and insistent question of what becomes of us after death. Browne published nothing after this, but corresponded widely with learned men, among them the diarist John Evelyn. A confirmed Royalist throughout the civil war, he was knighted in 1671 by Charles II and died on his birthday on 19 October 1682. He lies buried in the church of St Peter Mancroft in Norwich.

RIGHT:

An engraved portrait of Sir Thomas Browne.

BELOW:

Frontispiece of *Urne-Buriall* from the first edition, published in 1658. The legend reads: 'See, I am now what can be lifted with five fingers'.

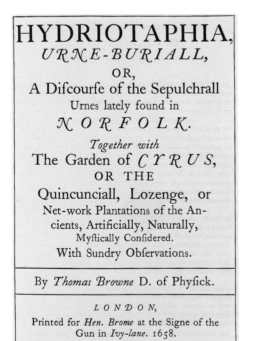

OPPOSITE:

This manuscript volume contains a number of drafts of writings by Browne, among them passages incorporated with various alterations in the published version of *Urne-Buriall*. It was one of a number of manuscripts of Browne and of his son and grandson, Dr Edward and Dr Thomas Browne, bought by the collector Sir Hans Sloane after the grandson's death. The first sentence of the passage, written in Browne's difficult hand, reads: 'Could we truly apprehend heaven or were the happinesse of the next world as sensible as that of this it were a martyrdome to live, & to those who conceive not life after death it is an Hell to dye'.

Could wee truly apprehend honour onely by happinesse
of the next worke as sensible as that of this it were
a martyrdome to live; & to those wee concern not
life after death this — an Egg to dye. twe onsters
more wonder but its spirit of many of the heathens
that durst despise death; & loved not in sure of
a small dissolution — since by us durst continue
death when they honour nor life hereafter could
have respond to live — God by knowing in
experia by God the admiralty of no better nature
on our selves wee dye in consume while
better they durst see nothing — and not to
returnd into their . . .

. . . not . . . valour and . . . sometimes . . .
. . . will but strongly not les men cowards but
by prowesse of humility contempt of . . .
the world . . . but above before that of
men in some principles . . . . Reward . . .
. . . . . . to . . .
ways of . . . & . . . .
. . . .
. . . .
valorous.

John Dryden 1631–1700

Dryden was born into a landed Northamptonshire family whose sympathies during the Civil War were firmly against the King. Indeed, his uncle, Sir Gilbert Pickering, became chamberlain to Cromwell himself during the Protectorate and the elegy illustrated here, 'Heroique Stanza's, Consecrated to the glorious memorie of his most Serene and Renowned Highness Oliver Late Lord Protector of this Common-Wealth etc. Written after the Celebration of his Funeralls', bears witness to Dryden's loyalties at that time.

Cromwell died on 3 September 1658, succeeded to the Protectorate by his son, Richard. His body was embalmed and the funeral in Westminster Abbey was fixed for 9 November but because of the elaborate nature of the preparations, costing an amazing £60,000, it was put off until 23 November. Dryden's opening stanza speaks of the premature effusions of fellow writers who had not anticipated such a delay. He himself was not beyond criticism, however, earning a reputation as something of a politically self-serving creature (and one castigated, while a scholar at Trinity College Cambridge for 'disobediency' and 'contumacy'.) Just one year after his tribute to Cromwell, he was enthusiastically versifying upon 'the Happy Restoration and Return of His Sacred Majesty'. Under the new régime of Charles II, Dryden flourished as a playwright, became Poet Laureate in 1670 and produced a new panegyric in the form of his opera *Albion and Albianus* in 1685, again eulogising the monarch.

Having become a Roman Catholic in about 1686, he lost the laureateship to Thomas Shadwell on the accession of William and Mary, but in these later years he had become a grand old man of letters and was accorded a final resting place, surprisingly, given his faith, in Poet's Corner, Westminster Abbey. Cromwell had been removed from the Abbey in 1661 and we can perhaps look to this manuscript for a lasting contemporary memorial to the Protector.

RIGHT:
An engraved portrait of the author from *The Dramatick works of John Dryden* (1717).

BELOW:
A rare example, preserved at The British Library, of the Great Seal of Oliver Cromwell, Protector, dating from around 1657.

OPPOSITE:
'Heroic Stanzas', published in 1659, was Dryden's first major work and this manuscript is by far the most important in his hand to have survived; very little else is extant and even this manuscript, thirty-seven stanzas in all, covering four sides, lay unidentified until quite recently. It was among some miscellaneous papers gathered by William Petty, 1st Marquess of Lansdowne, who died in 1805. Petty's collection was acquired for the national collection in 1807 and the Library catalogue published in 1819 failed to identify the manuscript as autograph. It was an Italian academic, Anna-Maria Crinò, who made this important discovery in 1966.

Heroique Stanza's,
Consecrated to the glorious ~~memory~~ memorie
Of his most Serene & Renowned Highness
OLIVER
Late Lord Protector of this Common=wealth. &c
Written after the Celebration of his funeralls.

And now 'tis time; for theire officious hast
Who would before haue borne him to the Sky
Like Eager Romans, ere all rites were past
Did let too soone the sacred Eagle fly.

2

Though our best notes are treason to his fame
Joynd with the loud applause of publique voice,
Since Heav'n what praise wee offer to his name
Hath renderd too authentiq by its choise:

3

Though in his praise no Arts can liberall bee,
And they whose Musds haue the highdst flowne
Add not to his immortall memorie;
But do an Act of friendship to theire own:

4

Yet tis our duty and our intrest too
Such Monuments as wee can build to raise;
Lest all the world prevent what wee should do
And claime a title in him by theire praise.

5

How shall I then begin or where conclude
To draw a fame so truly Circular?
For in a round what order can bee shewd,
where all the parts so equall perfect are?

6

His grandeur hee deriv'd from Heav'n alone;
For hee was great e'r Fortune made him so.
And warrs, like mists that rise against the Sunne,
Made him but greater seeme, not greater grow.

Katherine Philips 1631–1664

ABOVE:

A bust portrait of the 'matchless Orinda', as Katherine Philips was known, from the 1667 edition of her poems.

Katherine Philips has only recently emerged as one of the most intriguing literary figures of the mid seventeenth century. She was born Katherine Fowler to a prosperous London cloth merchant and sent to board at a fashionable Presbyterian school in the nearby town of Hackney. It was here that she began to develop the talent for cultivating friendships – especially with women – which would later see her presiding as the 'matchless Orinda' over a select society of erudite and fancifully named friends.

At the age of seventeen, Katherine married the Welshman James Philips, the eldest son of her stepfather. The match seemed an improbable one. While James ('Antenor' in her verse), who was three times her age, successfully pursued high office under Oliver Cromwell, she staunchly defended her independence, aligning herself in print from 1651 onwards with poets espousing Royalist sympathies. However, although political opponents sought to exploit such differences the union proved strong, witnessing the birth of a daughter and a son (who survived only forty days).

With their political fortunes reversed during the Restoration, Katherine put her court and social connections to good use protecting her husband. It was while travelling to Ireland in 1662, to press a claim to lands on his behalf, that she completed a translation of the play *Pompée* by her French contemporary Pierre Corneille. Performed in February 1663, it was the first play brought to the British or Irish stage by a woman. Its great success, swiftly giving rise to editions in Dublin and London, set the seal on her reputation. It also, however, encouraged the appearance in 1664 of a supposedly unauthorized collection of her poems which she insisted was withdrawn, evidently fearing that it might compromise her usual discretion. The first legitimate collection of Philips's verse appeared posthumously in 1667, prepared by Sir Charles Cotterel ('Poliarchus'), a close friend to whom she addressed a series of letters published in 1705. During her lifetime, the majority of her verse was circulated and read in manuscript by an exclusive and carefully chosen audience.

Philips succumbed to smallpox in 1664, which she had only just described, in a poetic elegy to the Earl of Warwick's only son, as 'That fierce Disease, which knows not how to spare/The Young, the Great, the Knowing, or the Fair'. She died in Fleet Street on 22 June and was buried in the church of St Benet Sherehog, barely two years before it was destroyed in the great Fire of London.

POEMS.

122

When you muſt Heav'n delay, or Him forſake?
Yet ſince thoſe joys you made ſuch haſte to find
Had ſcarce been full if he were left behind,
How well did Fate decide your inward ſtrife,
By making him a Preſent of your Life?
Which reſcu'd Bleſſing he muſt long enjoy,
Since our Offences could it not deſtroy.
For none but Death durſt rival him in you;
And Death himſelf was baffled in it too.

Upon Mr. Abraham Cowley's Retirement.

ODE.

1.

NO, no, unfaithful World, thou haſt
  Too long my eaſie Heart betray'd,
And me too long thy Foot-ball made:
But I am wiſer grown at laſt,
And will improve by all that I have paſt.
I know 'twas juſt I ſhould be practis'd on;
  For I was told before,
And told in ſober and inſtructive lore,
How little all that truſted thee have won:
And yet I would make haſte to be undone.
Now by my ſuff'ring I am better taught,
And ſhall no more commit that ſtupid fault.
    Go, get ſome other Fool,
    Whom thou mayſt next cajole:
On me thy frowns thou doſt in vain beſtow;
      For I know how
To be as coy and as reſerv'd as thou.

2.

In my remote and humble ſeat
Now I'm again poſſeſt

Of

LEFT:

The printed text of the first stanza of Philips's Ode 'Upon Mr Abraham Cowley's Retirement' from the 1667 edition, reveals in the third line an intriguing variant from the manuscript text.

OPPOSITE:

This autograph undated fair copy of Philips's Ode 'Upon Mr Abraham Cowley's Retirement' was recently discovered among the papers of the diarist John Evelyn, who may have had it from his father-in-law, Sir Richard Browne.

No, No, unfaithfull world thou hast
Too long my easy heart betray'd
And me too long thy captive made
But I am wiser grown at last
And will improve by all that I have past.
I know 'twas Just I should be practisd on
           For I was told before
And told in sober, & instructive love,
How little all yt trusted thee have won,
And yet I would make hast to be undone
But by my sufferings I am better taught
And will no more comit yt stupid fault
           Go get some other foole
           Whom thou mayst next cajole
On me thy frowns thou wilt in vain bestow
           For I know how
To be as coy, & as reserv'd as thou

2.

In my remote & humble seat
      Now I'm again possess'd
      Of that late fugitive my Brest
From all thy tumults, & from all thy heat
I'le find a quiet, & a coole retreat
      And on the fetters I have worne
Look with experienc'd & revengefull scorne
     In this my soveraign=Privacy
    'Tis true, I cannot govern thee

Thomas Traherne 1637–1674

ABOVE:
The little church of St Mary's, a stone's throw from the Thames, in Teddington, Middlesex, as it is today. Both Traherne and his patron, Sir Orlando Bridgeman, are buried within.

'An unknown seventeenth-century poet' was revealed to the world for the first time in *The Athenaeum* in 1900. Two manuscript volumes had been discovered quite by chance a few years earlier on London bookstalls, one containing poems, the other a prose work, the 'Centuries of Meditation'. At first thought to be from the hand of Henry Vaughan, they were subsequently discovered to be by Thomas Traherne, son of a Hereford shoe-maker and Rector of Credenhill.

So began the quite romantic emergence of this writer, and the manuscript illustrated here, 'Commentaries of Heaven', continues the tale. It is known to have passed unidentified through London sale-rooms in 1844 and in 1854 (when it sold for two shillings), but in 1967 it was found, amazingly, on a Lancashire rubbish-tip. When the finder emigrated to Canada, it went with him and there, in the University of Toronto, its author was recognised. It was purchased by The British Library in 1984.

Traherne's manuscript, compiled *c.*1673–74, is an encyclopaedia of religious and moral subjects, all seeds for meditation, evidently curtailed abruptly by his death. Its ninety-four entries proceed alphabetically from 'Abhorrence' ending with 'Bastard'. Indeed, the 'Commentaries' could have opened like the 'Centuries' with the preamble 'An empty book is like an infant's soul…I have a mind to fill it with profitable wonders', for the manuscript is invested with a sacred quality as if it is an end in itself.

Traherne did well for himself. In 1669 he became domestic chaplain to Sir Orlando Bridgeman, Lord Keeper of the Great Seal and Lord Chief Baron at the trial of the regicides in 1660. He and Traherne died within months of each other and both are buried in the little church of St Mary's in Teddington, to which they had retired together, by the river Thames. No portrait of Traherne is known to exist and a tiny contemporary verbal picture of him as 'a man of cheerful and sprightly temper' has to fill the gap.

LEFT:
Traherne's elaborate title page – an unusual thing in a manuscript – is drafted out in imitation of a printed work and acts as a clarion call to meditation.

OPPOSITE:
The folio shown here from Traherne's 'Commentaries of Heaven', *c.* 1673–74, dealing with the 'Atom' (a 'great Miracle in a little room'), is a typical product of the growing scientific rationalism of the Restoration as, indeed, is the manuscript's projected journey through boundless knowledge. The manuscript is written in a beautifully clear and elegant hand, its author's corrections nevertheless revealing it to be, to some extent, a working document.

Atom.

The Designe.

An Atom is a marvellous Effect of Almighty power, or a great Miracle in a litle Room: perhaps I may say, it is an infinit Miracle in no Room; for it is so small, y̌ it taketh up no place at all, but fill oth an indivisible Point of Space. yʒt is there an unsearchable Abyss of Wonders contained in it; innumerable Difficulties, uses, Excellencies & pleasures concentering in its Womb, for our Instruction & Happiness; y̌ Clear Knowledg of w͏ᵉ will make us expert in y̌ Chiefest Mysteries of GOD & Nature. We may treat of it either Physicaly, or Metaphysicaly: y̌ Metaphysical notion of it, helpeth much in y̌ Mysteries of Felicitie, y̌ Physical in y̌ Secrets of Nature. In y̌ Metaphysical Treatise we designe y̌ Confusion of Atheists, but chiefly y̌ Accomplishmͭ of y̌ Soul, in Comunion wͭh GOD: in y̌ Physical Consideration of it, an Hypothesis, (so much desired by learned men) wherby to Explicate y̌ Phænomena of Nature, as they are observable in y̌ Univers, for y̌ Compleating of y̌ Body of Natural Philosophie, so far as we are able to contribute therunto. for y̌ least things being y̌ Basis of y̌ Great, & y̌ Seed of all, these Atoms are of important Consideration, bec. y̌ clear Sight of yͫ is like y̌ Knowledge of first Principles, aiding us in y̌ Discovery of all Causes & Effects whatsoever. In y̌ Delineation of wͨͪ wͭʰ out taking notice of other mens Errors, we shall draw a ~~straight & Cleare~~ clear & even Rule, wͨ will measure it self, & others Deviations.

Its Etymologie.

Atom is a greek Word derived from ἀ priv: & τεμνω, Scindo, signifying a Part of Matter y̌ cannot be cut or divided aʒunder

Its Nature

An Atom, according to y̌ true & full Importance of y̌ Word, is a Material particle absolutly incapable of being Divided And in this Sence y̌ Word is taken by Philosophers. Its Nature is made up of its Essence & Affections.

Its Essence

Concerning y̌ Essence of an Atom litle can be said, but y̌ it is a Material Existence, invisible & Indivisible, having neither Bulk nor figure, but apt to assist as a Part towards both. Of its Affections more may be Spoken.

Its Obscuritie

An Atom ~~therefore~~ certain kind of is like y̌ Heavens, a retired Quintessence, far removed from all Elementary Qualities. The Affections wͨͪ are generaly observed in other things appear not in yͭ: for want of w͏ᵉ it is inter non Entia, to a vulgar Soul. Common People cannot so much as Shape y̌ Maner of its Existence. It is difficult wͭʰ yͫ to believ y̌ Realitie of such a Creature: much more to apprehend its Inclinations & Properties, Matter, Forme, Qualitie & Appearance. Tho by Nature y̌ Soul was made Capable of Managing any Argumͭ, from a Theme infinitly great, to an Object infinitly Small; nothing by Vastness exceeding its Capacitie, or by litleness evading its Acuteness. An Atom poseth y̌ Wits of y̌ most curious among men, & feedeth y̌ Intelligence of y̌ Sublimest Angel.

Its Claritie

To men, restored to y̌ Claritie of their Knowledg, an Atom is an Object as Apparent as y̌ Sun; every Qualitie in it being as obvious, as y̌ figure & Color of a more Solid Bodie. The vail, or Miste being removed in y̌ Purity of infinit & Eternal Light, y̌ Soul apprehendeth it as effectualy as y̌ Ey, or Hand, doth things fitly proportioned to yͫ. for notwithstanding its Na[ked]kedness, in being divested of all those Accidents, wͭʰ wͨʰ we commonly converse, it hath a fulness of Attributes by wͨ it may be Known. Its Original, Order, Existence, use & End, Operations & Circumstances (perhaps innumerable) may be

Samuel Butler 1612–1680

'And having thus lived to a good old age, admired by all, though personally known to few, he departed this life in the year 1680, and was buried at the charge of his good friend Mr. Longueville, of the Temple, in the yard belonging to the church of St. Paul's Covent-garden, at the west-end of the said yard, on the north side, under the wall of the said church, and under that wall which parts the yard from the common highway.' Thus concludes the biographical introduction to an 1805 edition of Samuel Butler's 'Hudibras', a satrical poem originally published in two parts between 1662 and 1663 and responsible for such well-known phrases as 'Look a gift horse in the mouth', 'Make the fur fly' and 'Spare the rod and spoil the child'.

RIGHT:

A portrait of Samuel Butler from a 1715 edition of *Posthumous Works in Prose and Verse* – many of which are spurious.

Butler gives full vent to his Royalist sympathies in what is a bitterly satirical masterpiece of the Civil War period. The poem's eponymous anti-hero is comically cast in the shape of a self-serving and foolish Cromwellian colonel. The character's literary debt is to Cervantes's *Don Quixote*, but Butler draws more specific inspiration from the unfortunate puritan Sir Samuel Luke, one of a number of influential figures with whom he found employment as a clerk or attendant.

Butler's somewhat pathetic fate is perhaps ironic given that his most famous work found favour not only among the public, but with those powerful members of the Restoration establishment it set out to please. Although King Charles II himself – who, in the poet's own words 'never ate, nor drank, nor slept,/But Hudibras still near him kept;/Nor would he go to church or so,/But 'Hudibras' must with him go' – rewarded him with various grants of money, these were evidently not enough to compensate for a disastrous financial situation. His wife's fortune was lost through poor investments and he failed to profit properly from his literary success owing to numerous piracies.

BELOW:

The volume of Butler's literary remains held by The British Library contains two draft letters. In this one he thanks the unidentified recipient for remembering him.

Butler lived the latter part of his life in obscurity and relative poverty, but could rely, at least, upon one good friend: in addition to making proper arrangements for his funeral, so the lawyer William Longueville supported the author in these last years, which found him dwelling in Covent Garden's Rose Street – a place deemed fit, by one near contemporary, 'for mechanics only and persons of meane quality'. In return for his kindness, Butler appointed Longueville his heir and inheritor of all his worldly possessions. These amounted to no more than his literary remains, described by Roger North as 'loose Papers and indigested'.

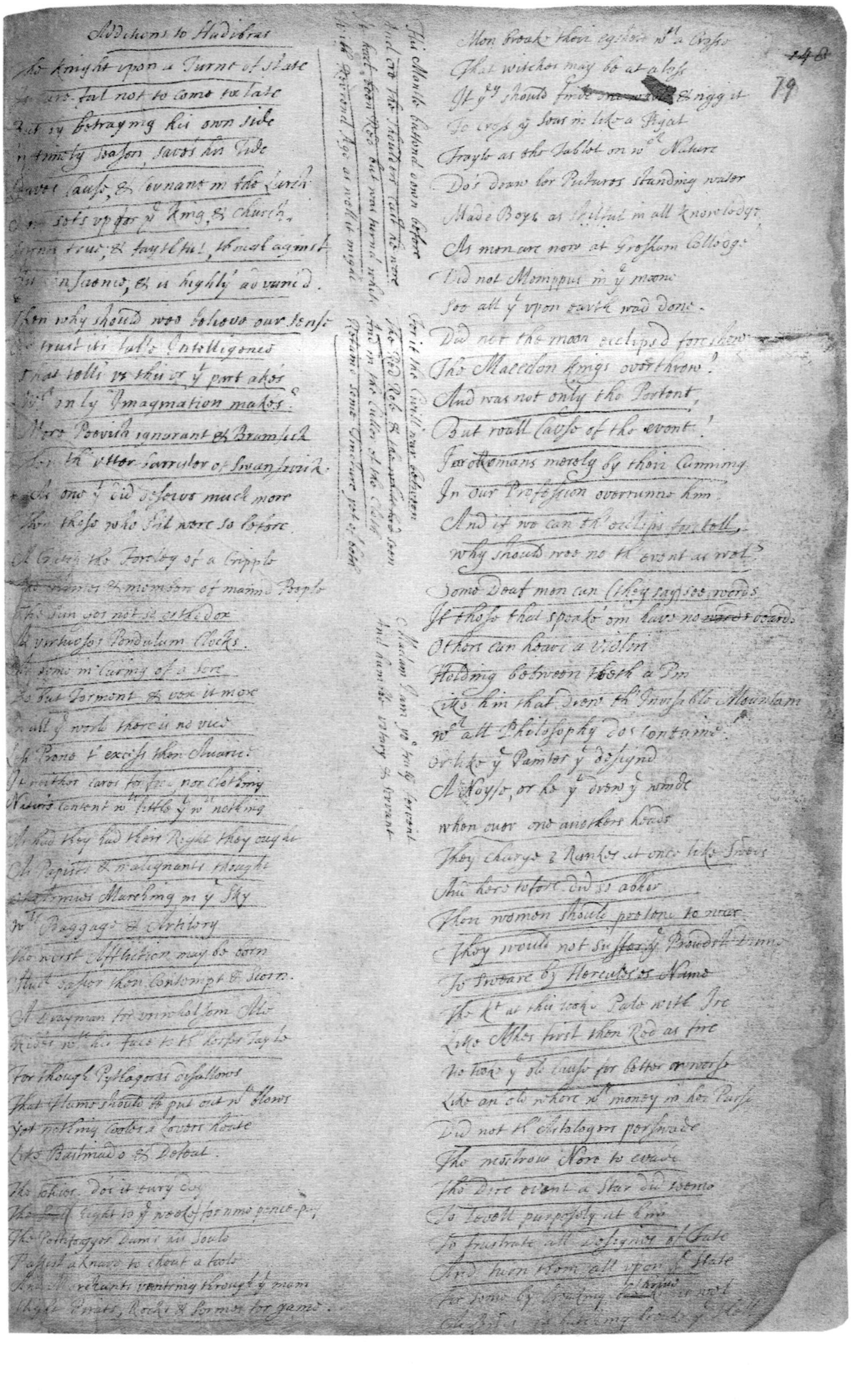

RIGHT:

The volume which includes the page shown here is thought to represent about half of the manuscripts Butler left to his friend Longueville; the whereabouts of the rest of the 'loose Papers', if they survive, remains a mystery. This manuscript is almost entirely in Butler's own hand, the rarity of which is demonstrated by the fact that only one other autograph document (four lines in Britain's Public Record Office), has been hitherto identified. Among the many lines of verse and prose passages which make up this volume can be found these 'Additions to Hudibras'.

Although later observers have liked to view the early eighteenth century as the Age of Reason, the major writers of the period would have been hard-pressed to agree with this notion, for it was the manifestations of unreason that often occupied them in their stinging commentaries on contemporary life. There is only a small step from the great satirical writing of Alexander Pope or Jonathan Swift to the lacerating treatment in paint by William Hogarth of vice, neglect, cruelty and other extremes of appalling inhumanity.

The evidence is that writers of this period needed to retreat sometimes from the world to maintain their equilibrium. This is reflected in a number of manuscripts selected here from The British Library's eighteenth-century holdings, and Pope's translation of *The Iliad* (1719–26) is a case in point. His savage pen laid aside, he immersed himself for many years in the perfecting of Augustan measures, a literary undertaking complemented by his painstaking efforts to fashion a neo-classical retreat from the grounds of his riverside house in Twickenham.

Lady Mary Wortley Montagu's poem is on the very subject of retreat and marks her abandonment of 'mankind's detested ways' for such calm rural pleasures as her 'rose and jessamin trees'. Robert Burns's celebrated poem 'The Cotter's Saturday Night' goes even further, being a paean to the virtues of domestic comfort and family piety. Perhaps in a similar vein, the gentle William Cowper's expression of friendship towards William Hayley sprang from a sense of gratitude for the homely and the familiar in what he saw as an otherwise bleak world.

Indeed, the quiet pleasure of friendship runs like a thread through the writing of the period. The ideals of order and control made the passions highly suspect and their expression ill-bred; we find none of that in the manuscripts here illustrated. Swift's somewhat cool treatment of Esther Vanhomrigh, Samuel Richardson's gentle words to Anna Meades, Johnson's affectionately shared experiences with Hester and Henry Thrale, Thomas Gray's decorous words to James Dodsley – all the voices in these pieces are far different from the public oratory of John Dryden's 'Heroique Stanzas' on one side and the earnest tone of Percy Shelley's 'Mask of Anarchy' on the other. It is as if we have reached a plateau of rest in our literature. Even Daniel Defoe, a somewhat shadowy personality, speaks as a family man here, while

Laurence Sterne's irony is muted, self-deprecating and amused. These manuscripts have the hushed quality of the parlour about them.

Sentiment, often associated only with the latter end of the century, actually informs, in varying degrees, much of the whole period's offerings here but, of course, we move into new and startling realms with William Blake. We may like to consider the domestic scene of Blake and his wife Kate working together on his prints – or, to the amazement of their neighbours, walking together naked in their back garden – but the areas of the imagination opened up by this writer's noble and yet humble vision seem to have emerged from no earthly parlour.

Whatever fearful alarms came from France in 1789, it may have been a comfort to many an Englishman to know that King George III and Queen Charlotte took joy in simple family evenings round the spinet in their little house at Kew and that this country presented no more alarming a tricoteuse than William Cowper's beloved companion Mrs Unwin.

Jonathan Swift 1667–1745

ABOVE:

This engraving of a melancholy Swift, after a painting by Benjamin Wilson, is found in a commentary on Swift's life and writings published in 1752.

Swift's letter to 'Vanessa', dated 12 August 1714 and illustrated here, was written at a time of great political ferment in the country. Queen Anne had died eleven days before and George I had been proclaimed King. The Whigs had been assured of continued supremacy in Parliament and Swift, a committed Tory journalist and apologist since 1710, had vowed to quit England for Ireland. He was to return to English soil only twice after that.

Born in Dublin into a Protestant Herefordshire family who had only just settled in Ireland, he had embraced the new order when William and Mary ascended the throne in 1688 and had moved to England where he entered the service of Sir William Temple, a retired diplomat. In Temple's enlightened and rather precious household he learned at first hand the machinations of government and the trappings of society, a good grounding for the trenchant lampoons and biting satires he was later to produce.

His writings, of which a number survive in autograph manuscripts, are the product of an acutely solipsistic mind and one wonders how romantic involvements could be accommodated into his world. Indeed, his masterpiece of 1726, *Gulliver's Travels*, is notable not only for its strong misanthropic vein in general, but for the revulsion with which it treats sexuality and sexual relations in particular. The nearest we come to a manuscript of this work is a printed edition of the text bearing Swift's own annotations (in Armagh Public Library). Considerable vagueness surrounds his attachment to Esther Johnson, known to him as 'Stella', another member of Temple's household. She was dear to him, dear enough for his remains to be laid eventually next to hers in St Patrick's Cathedral, Dublin. But did they ever marry?

Similarly, what was the nature of his relationship with 'Vanessa'? She was actually called Esther Vanhomrigh and he met her in about 1707. Childlike, passionate and self-willed, she can be seen in Swift's clandestine replies to her letters as an embarrassment, even a danger. He ultimately pushed her out of his life. She died in 1723.

The letter shown here is one of forty-four (covering the period 1711 to 1722), gathered into a volume which for many years disappeared. Sir Walter Scott published them in 1814, but only from inaccurate copies, and they did not appear in print in their original form until 1923, having been bought by the Library in 1919. Their earlier history has never been fully established.

[24]

It pierc'd the feeble Volume thro'
And deep transfix'd her Bosom too.
Some Lines, more moving than the rest,
Stuck to the Point that pierc'd her Breast,
And born directly to her Heart,
With Pains unknown increas'd her Smart.

Vanessa, not in Years a Score,
Doats on a Gown of forty-four;
Imaginary Charms can find,
In Eyes with reading almost blind;
Cadenus now no more appears
Declin'd in Health, advanc'd in Years,
She fancies Musick in his Tongue,
Nor further looks, but thinks him young.
What Mariner is not afraid,
To venture in a Ship decay'd?
What Planter will attempt to yoke,
A Sapling with a falling Oak?
As Years increase she brighter shines,
Cadenus with each Day declines,
And he must fall a Prey to Time,
While she is blooming in her Prime.

Strange that a Nymph by *Pallas* nurs'd,
In Love shou'd make Advances first.
Cadenus, common Forms apart,
In every Sense had kept his Heart,
Had sigh'd and languish'd, vow'd and writ,
For Pastime, or to shew his Wit;

But

LEFT:

This shows part of Swift's poem 'Cadenus and Vanessa', from the first edition published in London in 1726. Swift ('Cadenus') wrote it probably in late 1713. It was not written for publication but for 'Vanessa' alone. No copies were made of it until after her death.

OPPOSITE:

Swift's letter to 'Vanessa' was sent from Wantage four days before he left for Ireland, in 1714, and addressed to her 'at Mr Handcock's in Little Rider Street, near St James's Street, London'. Written in Swift's small neat script, the letter urges discretion and is left deliberately unsigned.

Aug. 12ᵗʰ 1714   21.

I had yr Letter last Post, and before you can send me another, I
shall set out for Ireld: I must go and take the Oaths, and the sooner
the better. I think since I have known you I have drawn an old house
upon my Head. You should not have come by Wantage for a thousand
Pound. you used to brag you were very discreet; where is it gone? It is
probable I may not stey in Ireland long, but be back by the beginning
of Winter. when I am there I will write to you as soon as I can
conveniently. but it shall be allways under a Cover; and if you write to
me, let some other direct it. and I beg you will write nothing that is
particular, but which may be seen, for I apprehend Letters will be opened
and Inconveniences will happen. If you are in Irel⁴ while I am there,
I shall see you very seldom. It is not a Place for any Freedom, but
where every thing is known in a Week, and magnifyed a hundred Degrees.
These are rigorous Laws that must be passed through: but it is
probable we we meet in London in Winter. or if not, leave all to
Fate, that seldom cares to humor our Inclinations.. I say all this out of
the perfect Esteem and Friendship I have for you. These Publick
Misfortunes have altered all my Measures, and broke my Spirits. God
Almighty bless you; I shall, I hope be on horseback in a Day after
this comes to yr Head. I would not answer your Questions for a
Million; nor can I think of them with any Ease of Mind. adieu,

Alexander Pope 1688–1744

With the establishment of the Protestant succession under William and Mary in the very year of Pope's birth, Catholic families such as his were certainly faced with severe disadvantages. They were denied admission to university, forbidden to hold public office and to own land and even to live within ten miles of London. Add to these privations Pope's own physical disablement and we can understand the compensatory mechanisms at work in his proud and sensitive nature: his immense ambition, his alliance with established literary and political coteries, his lacerating treatment of adversaries in his writing.

But he also sought peace. The classical studies of his youth bred in him an appreciation of Arcadian pleasures, most apparent in his early *Pastorals* of 1709 and in the celebration of the Thames in his *Windsor Forest* of 1713, but equally evident in his choice of rural Twickenham, fifteen miles to the West of London, for a home in late 1718. He was to remain here for the rest of his days and his final resting place can be found in the Parish church marked by a small slab bearing the letter 'P'.

RIGHT:
Pope's keenly intelligent features are well represented in this engraved portrait from his *Works* of 1720.

By 1718 Pope was famous and to consolidate his position he had started a kind of scholastic sabbatical – lasting ten years – in which he translated Homer's 'Iliad' and 'Odyssey', published in parts between 1715 and 1726. Surprisingly for such an august and awesome literary endeavour, the manuscript drafts of the works are really rather homely, for Pope seized scraps of paper of any size and put even the blank sides of old letters to good use.

Illustrated opposite is an extract from Book 16 of the 'Iliad' written on the reverse of a letter addressed to him from the Duchess of Hamilton, complete with wax seal. The circle in a square among the lines of Homer points to a third use to which these sheets were put: as scribbling pads, repositories for his designs, made between 1718 and 1720, for his villa and for his five-acre garden facing the Thames. Plans for serpentine paths, parterres and architectural elevations all add an endearing humanity to this most heroic of literary creations.

BELOW:
A drawing from the 'Iliad' (1719–26), showing Pope's design for the trellis at the end of his garden. Although nothing remains of his villa, vestiges of Pope's garden survive to this day. These include the remains of a tunnel under the road which separated his villa in Twickenham from his riverside gardens, and parts of his famous shell grotto.

Statue Prospect Statue
Well. Seats

Front of ye Treillis, facing ye River, 14 foot long, 8 high.

OPPOSITE:
A page from Pope's translation of the 'Iliad', Book 16, lines 426–463. Pope's numerous manuscript drafts for his translations of the 'Iliad' and the 'Odyssey' (making up three large bound volumes), which he bequeathed to a friend, were eventually presented to the British Museum Library, then in its infancy, in 1766.

great at Hector godlike ajax
[But still godlike ajax at your Hector aimd,
Still pointed toward his breast, his Javlin flamd:
The Trojan Chief experienced in the field
Oer his broad shoulders spread the massy shield,
Observed the Storm of Darts the Grecians pour,
& on his buckler caught the ringing showr.
He sees for Greece the Scale of Conquest rise,
Yet stopps & turns, & saves his lord & flies.

As when the hand of Jove a Tempest forms,
Dark oer ye field th' ascending Vapour flies, Rolls the Cloud, ye
& shades ye Sun, and blots ye golden skies, blackens heav'n wth
So from the ships along the duskey Plain, Storms
Dire Flight & Terror drove the Trojan Train:
Ev'n the Steeds of Hector fled; thro Heaps of disarray—
the fiery Coursers forcd away.
While far behind, his Trojans fall confusd:
Wedg'd in the Trench, in one vast Carnage bruisd.
Chariots on Chariots rowl, clashing Spokes
Fly diverse,
In vain they labour up the steepy Mound their
& Kings oerturnd foaming on ye Ground.
Fierce on the Rear, with Shouts, Patroclus flies;
Tumultuous clamor fills ye Fields & Skies,
Thick Drifts of Dust involve their rapid flight,
The Plains are lost, and Heavn is snatchd from sight
Clouds roll on clouds their dying lords down,
Th' affrighted Horse
& thunder towrd ye Town.
Loud the Rout was heard the Victor's cry,
Where your war bleeds, & where the thickest die.
Where Horse & arms, & chariots lye oerthrown
& bleeding Heroes under ax & Peleus Groan.
No stop, no check, the Steeds of Peleus knew;
From Bank to Bank th' Immortal Coursers flew,
High-bounding oer ye Fosse; the whirling Car
Smoaks thro ye plain, war
& thunders after Hector Hector flies;
Patroclus pois his Lance; but Fate denies.

Allan Ramsay 1686–1758

ABOVE:

A somewhat whimsical portrait of
Allan Ramsay from a 1758 edition
of his pastoral comedy *The Gentle
Shepherd*, published in Glasgow.

ABOVE:

Ramsay was also a tireless
doodler, as witnessed in this cari-
cature of a Scot, complete with
woollen bonnet.

Allan Ramsay set himself a mission to liberate the spirit of Scots poetry in an age dominated by the strictures of the Kirk. His effort is epitomized in this lively attack upon the corruption of the clergy (opposite). His early ambitions, however, were not entirely of the bookish sort. Born in Leadhills, Dumfriesshire, he moved to Edinburgh where he was apprenticed to a wigmaker, a trade in which he subsequently established himself in the city's Grassmarket. The great intellectual bustle of the capital at the time – one wonders whether he dressed the head of the philosopher Hume, later painted by his famous son, Allan Ramsay the younger – began to seduce him into pursuing his love of the literary.

In 1713 Ramsay helped to found the Easy Club, a Jacobite literary society, and by 1718 he was a bookseller, with successive premises throughout the city; his influential periodical, *The Tea Table Miscellany*, begun in 1724 and continuing until 1737, published traditional ballads and songs which might otherwise have been lost and proved an inspiration to Robert Burns among others. In 1728 he established Scotland's first circulating library and he opened a playhouse in 1736, losing a substantial amount of money when licensing regulations banning the performing of plays outside Westminster forced it to close the following year.

The Library has two full manuscript volumes of Ramsay's work, one comprising the original manuscript of his great gathering of early Scottish texts, *The Ever Green, being a collection of Scots Poems, wrote by the Ingenious before 1600*. This collection, published in 1724, reveals Ramsay's own interest in original literary remains: he worked upon the famous Bannatyne Manuscript to bring to light the works of medieval poets such as Robert Henryson and William Dunbar. In addition to selling, lending and editing books (sometimes rather too freely according to many critics), Ramsay also published his own work, much of which is collected together in the Library's second manuscript volume. *Poems* (1728) is regarded as his best collection of verse and he also turned his hand to drama in *The Gentle Shepherd* of 1725, a pastoral work which brought him much acclaim. In later years he wrote little, observing that 'the coolness of fancy that attends advanced years should make me risk the reputation I had acquired'.

Ramsay was fiercely devoted to Scotland and adored Edinburgh which, as he made clear in one typically provocative and lively poem, he considered a far better city than Rome, Paris or London. He died aged seventy-two at his home near the Castle and was buried in the churchyard of Greyfriars where there is a monument to his memory.

OPPOSITE:

The Library owns two substantial volumes of manuscript verse by Allan Ramsay. One comprises his great gathering of early Scottish poems 'wrote by the Ingenious before 1600' which he published in 1724. The other volume contains drafts and fair copies of Ramsay's own work. Ramsay enjoyed writing provocative poetry and illustrated here is a neatly satirical attack upon the corruption of the clergy.

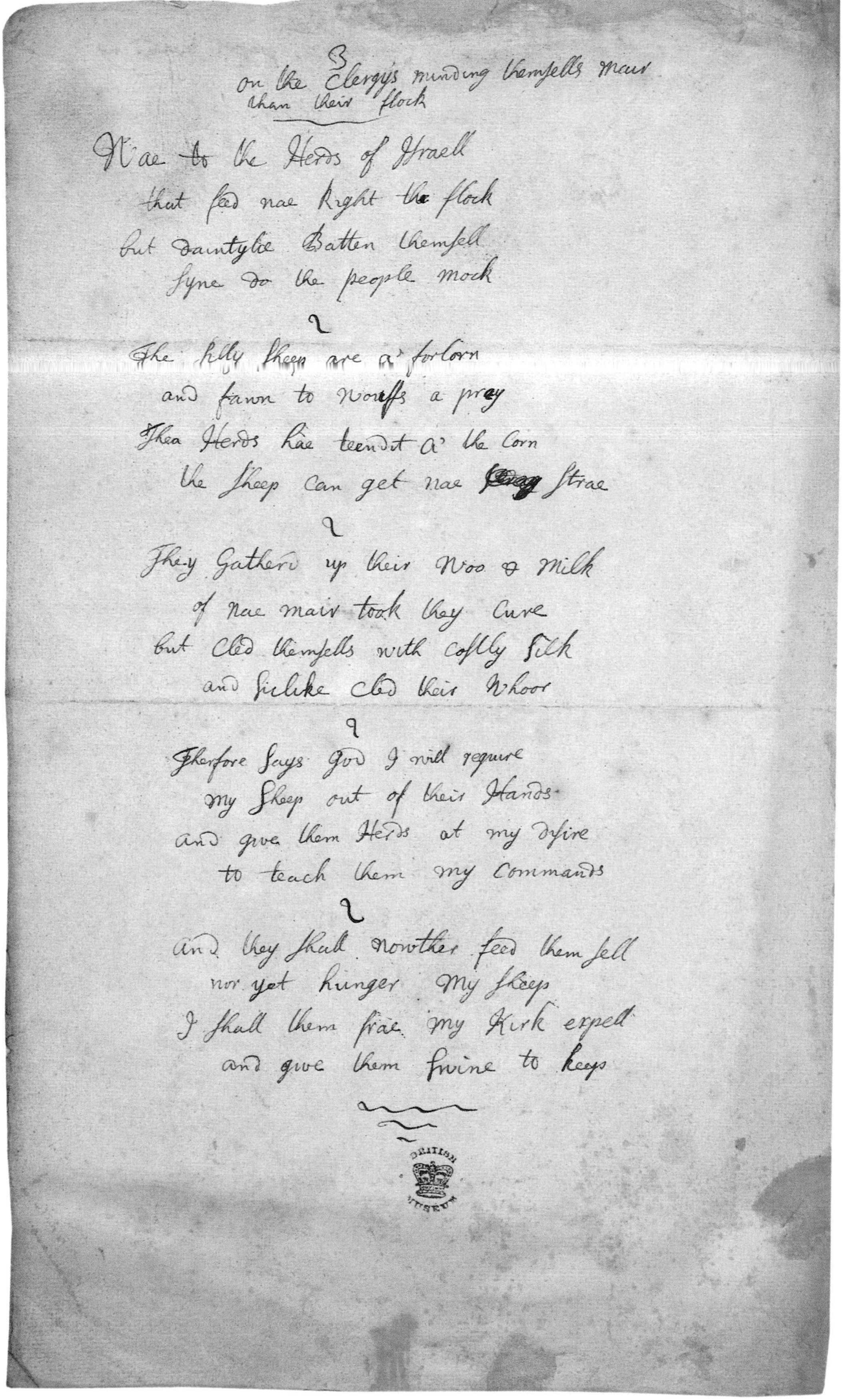

on the Clergys minding themsells mair
than their flock

Wae to the Herds of Israell
that feed nae Right the flock
but dayntylie Batten themsell
syne do the people mock

~

The silly sheep are a forlorn
and fawn to woress a prey
Thea Herds hae teendit a the Corn
the sheep can get nae Strae

~

They Gatherd up their Woo & Milk
of nae mair took they Cure
but Cled themsells with costly Silk
and siclike Cled their whoor

~

Therfore says God I will require
My Sheep out of their Hands
and give them Herds at my dysire
to teach them my Commands

~

and they shall nowther feed themsell
nor yet hunger My sheeps
I shall them frae my Kirk expell
and give them swine to keeps

~~~

Daniel Defoe 1660–1731

ABOVE:

This rare engraved portrait of Defoe appears in a collection of his *Works* which he saw through the press in 1705. Defoe's posture seems painfully strange.

Much of Defoe's life was passed in the shadows. He was at various times a tradesman whose Tilbury brickyard helped build the walls of St Paul's Cathedral, a spy whose work played a part in forging the 1707 Union of Scotland and England under Queen Anne, a soldier, a bankrupt, a political satirist pilloried and imprisoned (twice) for his views, and a journeyman writer – a kind of early hack. Shining radiantly among his achievements, nevertheless, are his great works, *Robinson Crusoe*, *Moll Flanders* and the *Tour through Great Britain*, all published between 1719 and 1726 and all revealing his close knowledge of contemporary *mores* and of humanity in general.

Defoe was a committed dissenter born at the Restoration into a family loyal to the memory of Cromwell and was thus an outsider, often on the run and little known to his contemporaries. He avoided portraiture and the accompanying image is rare indeed; one wonders whether it is even his true likeness. His real name was actually Daniel Foe and he often disguised his handwriting.

The manuscript illustrated here, however, replete with elisions and shorthand code, is in his own natural hand and shows the facility of his method of composition. It is an unfinished tract, written in 1729, and is the last of a series of four manuals giving advice on family life and morals. One was a pioneering tract on a happy sex life.

Defoe sent the work off to the printers and shown here is a corresponding page-proof, preserved with the manuscript and bearing his autograph emendations. The original manuscript bears the title 'The Compleat English Gentleman' yet he nowhere corrects its title *The Compleat Gentleman* at proof stage to include the word 'English' and the abbreviated title may have been his preferred choice. He died before the work could be published and the manuscript remained in the family until 1831. It was purchased by the British Museum Library in 1885 and first published in 1890.

Defoe, born and educated in Stoke Newington, which was then on the northern outskirts of London, lies near John Bunyan, William Blake and Isaac Watts, in the Dissenters' cemetery at Bunhill Fields in London. The memorial placed there in 1870 was almost immediately stolen only to emerge in 1940 among the rubble of a Southampton air raid.

LEFT:

This page proof from *The Compleat Gentleman* bears Defoe's own corrections and – most likely – ink smudges. He died before it could be published.

OPPOSITE:

Defoe's treatise *The Compleat Gentleman* (in manuscript entitled 'The Compleat English Gentleman'), one of five autograph prose works by the author in the Library's collections, defies easy reading. The handwriting is crabbed and idiosyncratic and is laced with abbreviations and shorthand symbols – as befits a man with a highly secretive nature.

that there seems to be an Implacable Animosity between them — they will hardly Re:
:cite One another or at least not for a time

Now this comes Exactly within . Compass of I am passing so much justice upon
the times. If the antient Nobility had either any Superiour Personal Merit upon of their
Own upon . foot of . they could justly rate themselves above . other . or if .
Modern Nobility lay under any Scandal upon . foot of . they could be reproach'd
as Unqualify'd for . Nobility . they had no Merit but their Money or were really
Personally Unworthy being Ennobled . this w'd in either Case justify . Contempt .
will . they treat them

But if Suppose now . . Noble Venetian of . antient Creation Suppose a Con:
:tarini the Bragadini . Boccalini . Cornari or . Morosini Suppose
him a Bully a Rake a B...... or a W...... or an E...... a man Useless to .
Common wealth Degenerate Vitious Unworthy of . Honour . Titles & he bears
— & he inherits but knows not how to Deserve Suppose him Dishonouring his Glori:
:ous Ancestors by his Deficiency of . Vertue Courage learning — fidelity to his
Country & justly said his ancestors to . Dignity of Counsellors — Rank them
among . Nobility

Suppose on . Contrary a Nobleman of . Modern Creation, — allow him to be
a person of Merit Wise, Prudent learning able for Council for Embassy for Conf:
Dence; a man of Conduct in . field Brave Enterprising Experience'd — faithful
— Worthily Honour'd — Ennobled on all those acco'. besides . advancing so much
money for . Public Service in a time of Exigence

Now . Case is this . . . . . Extremes of . shall Condemn . Case for . Moor .
antiquity of these Creation; How absurd is pride of . . . how Contrary to . Nature of the
thing ? . First say nothing . value himself upon low . Remote Vertues of his forgotten
Ancestors, & Weigh no more in . Scale of his personal Merit than . Yenelested . of his
Arms painted upon Silk w'd weigh against . other man's 100 Thousand Duchat

In a word . say say . Merit . first . antiquity, pray . has not . best Claim to other
owe . . say Family w'd one Vertues; . last says Virtues to Build a family; . first
last . it Ought to be . Case of his . Nobleman . as . Case is . first Nobleman of his
race there is . at Venice . antient Nobility look upon . Modern Nobility w . utt
:most Contempt, so as they will hardly keep Company . or give them . Civilitys of their rank
if they meet . in . street, let us bring . Case nearer home

In Poland this vanity of Birth is still worse; his three Carry'd to such a monstrous Ex:
:travagance . Name of G . Title of a Starost a Palatin or a Castellan gives . man a
Superiority Over all the Vassals or Common people infinitely greater than . of . or . an
:peror . & give them . Absolute power — make them more miserable
than either . Grand Seignior or . Cham of Tartary in so much . they frequently
Murther them . themselves on them as . Dogs — frequently . . when they do are accountable to
no body nor are call'd . . . So much as . . give a Reason for . . Wow

Lady Mary Wortley Montagu 1689–1762

Let Men who glory in their better sense,
Read, hear, and learn Humility from hence;
No more let them Superior Wisdom boast,
They can but equal M-nt-g-e at most.

This wonderful portrait of Lady Mary Wortley Montagu, taken from an edition of her letters published in 1764, depicts her exotically dressed and bearing what looks like a folded folio sheet. The couplets at the bottom of the page speak for themselves.

The early family papers of the Dukes of Marlborough were allotted to the Library in 1978. Among the papers of Sarah, wife of the 1st Duke, was discovered this autograph poem by Lady Mary Wortley Montagu. The 'Lady' of its title may have been Sarah herself, for Mary refers in her letters to 'a long intimacy' between them.

She was born Mary Pierrepont, a daughter of the Duke of Kingston, as he became later, and thanks to a liberal upbringing, she emerged a gifted woman, independent, eccentric, vigorous and volatile. She found friendship in kindred spirits like the Duchess and Mary Astell, the defender of women's rights in her day. Mary's husband Edward Wortley Montagu was a Member of Parliament and, on George I's accession in 1714, a Commissioner in the Treasury. She herself was often at court and a particular friend of the Princess of Wales. The poem illustrated here refers to Mary's court life and was certainly written before she left England (and even her husband) in 1739 for twenty-three years of self-imposed exile. Her literary circle in this country had been glittering: she was a friend of Alexander Pope, was admired by Richard Steele, editor of *The Tatler* magazine, and she was a second cousin of the novelist Henry Fielding. An enigmatic quarrel with Pope, however, ended their relationship and she certainly brought the odium of others upon herself by the sheer force of her personality. The poem glances at this factor in her life.

Mary's courage in the face of adversity and danger had been reflected in her wonderful letters from Turkey in 1717 and 1718. It was there that she encountered inoculation against smallpox and had her own son take advantage of the discovery, encouraging the practice in a sceptical England. Was it rumour and 'mankind's' detested ways' that drove her out of England in 1739? Her later years were spent in decaying Italian *palazzi*, where she found some simple satisfactions and solaces: 'I have mix'd in my espaliers as many Rose and jessamin Trees as I can cram in'. Only the thought of her daughter, Lady Bute, and of the newly opened British Museum, she said, would lure her back. She did return in 1762 but by then was terminally ill. She died in London and was buried in the Grosvenor Chapel in Mayfair.

A portrait of Sarah, Duchess of Marlborough, taken from a contemporary pamphlet. For some unknown reason, she appears to have been wilfully disfigured by the printer.

This manuscript of the autograph poem 'To a Lady advising me to Retirement' has all the appearance of a fair presentation copy, an observation which suggests that it may well have been composed and written down specially for Sarah, Duchess of Marlborough, in whose papers it was discovered.

To a Lady advising me to Retirement

You little know ye Heart that you advise
I view this various scene wth equal Eyes
In crouded Court I find my selfe alone
& pay my Homage to a Nobler Throne

Long since ye value of this World I know
pity ye Madness, & despise the Show
Well as I can my tedious part I bear
& wait Dismission without painfull fear

Seldom I mark Mankinds detested ways
Not hearing Censure or affecting Praise
And unconcernd my Future Fate I trust
To that sole Being, Mercifull & Just.

Samuel Richardson 1689–1761

ABOVE:

An engraved portrait of Samuel Richardson, inserted in a 1751 edition of *Clarissa*.

The autograph letter illustrated here is addressed to Anna Meades, a writer and one of Richardson's 'Songbirds', young lady admirers, often Bluestockings, whose company he cultivated. It was written very near the end of his life when, it has been suggested, he suffered from a form of Parkinson's Disease, but his beautifully controlled hand betrays none of that. The fastidious attention to details of punctuation, paragraphing and calligraphy reflects not only Richardson's literary practice but also his business practice.

As a model of superlative careerism, Richardson's life is distinguished. The son of a London joiner, he was largely self-taught. He was apprenticed to a printer when he was seventeen and became a freeman of the Stationers' Company nine years later. Within six years he established a business of his own, both printing and publishing and, by dint of sheer industry, eventually obtained the lucrative commission of printing the House of Commons journals. By 1754 he was Master of the Stationers' Company.

That a man with such a background should suddenly produce a work like *Pamela*, written in the space of two months in 1739–40 and printed, as with all his works, by himself has been the object of amazement. In this novel his perceptive delineation of the moral growth of his heroine is remarkable and the book was wildly and widely acclaimed, achieving six editions within a year. *Clarissa* (published in 1747–48) is a study of even greater intensity, and established Richardson, we can now see, as one of the chief founders of the modern English novel.

Although a good number of his letters survive, nothing has been traced of the manuscripts of Richardson's three novels, excepting an autograph transcript of a series of passages from *Clarissa* (at the Victoria and Albert Museum, London) and fragments from his long, last novel *Sir Charles Grandison* of 1753 (at the Victoria and Albert Museum and the Pierpont Morgan Library, New York).

Richardson died of apoplexy on 4 July 1761. One may find his memorial slab attached to the outside wall of St Bride's Church, off Fleet Street, but the precise location of his remains is unclear.

LEFT:

This letter written by Catherine Talbot in 1756 to a friend describes a visit to Richardson's villa in Parson's Green, to the west of London. 'One always sees there', she notes, 'a succession of young women & exceedingly elegant well behaved sensible young women... & every one (in the book style again) calls him Papa'.

OPPOSITE:

All of Richardson's novels are epistolary. He had much practice in the form, for he wrote love-letters for girls in the neighbourhood when he was a boy, and in this late manuscript of an autograph letter to Anna Meades, of 1757, purchased by the British Museum Library in 1869, we can still see his deft handling, manipulation even, of an admiring correspondent.

Sept. 5th 1757.

Dear Madam,

I mentioned to your Rev'd Friend an important Reason, why, at
this Time, my Daughters could not embrace, as they wished to do, your
kind Offer of corresponding with one of them. The Affair is not yet quite
settled; but soon will; and perhaps an Opportunity will be given, on
your Return to Town of beginning the desired Correspondence by a Personal
Acquaintance on both Sides. Mean time, my dear Anna must not think
so highly, as she seems to do, by her unmerited Compliments, of her admiring
Friend.

Admiring Friend I justly call myself, on having attentively perused
the Manuscript you put into my Hands. How so young a Lady arrived
at a Knowlege of Men and Manners so extensive, is matter of agreeable
Surprize to me; and I congratulate you on the Felicity of your Pen.

I made some few Observations, as I read; which cannot be so well
understood, as by a personal Explanation; and I hope for the Pleasure of another Interview on your coming to Town, for that purpose.

It is a Custom with my Wife and Daughters in long Evenings to sit
round a Table employ'd in Needleworks; while some one of them, in Turn, reads
to the rest. The Summer, and the concerning Affair I mentioned to your
worthy Friend, have not, since I had the Favour of your Papers, allowed of this
agreeable Amusement; and therefore they have not yet read the MS. Soon
will this Custom be resumed; a Personal Acquaintance will perhaps facilitate
the kindly desired Correspondence, between you; and in the Interim, I shall be
highly obliged to you, if you will at your Leisure, give me your pretty Hist.
brief; and your Progress in Knowlege, Step by Step, by which you arrived so
early at so much easy and natural Excellence.

Do not, dear Madam, charge with impertinent Curiosity, in this
Request.
                                        Your sincere Friend, and
                                           Humble Serv.t
                                            S. Richardson.
London,
Sept. 5. 1757.

Laurence Sterne 1713–1768

Sterne, born the son of an army subaltern serving in Ireland and educated at Cambridge University, became a country parson in Stillington, Yorkshire. He owed his position, at least in part, to the connections of his wife Elizabeth, whom he drove to distraction with his philandering. In 1760 he published, at his own expense, the first two volumes of the whimsical yet stylistically innovative *Life and Opinions of Tristram Shandy, Gentleman,* and was immediately lionised by London society.

His *Sentimental Journey*, which followed in 1768, owes something to his travels in France in 1765–1766, but it is far from being mere reportage. On one level it is a response to Smollett's *Travels through France and Italy* published in 1766, but even more it is a highly imaginative and ironic presentation of a man of high moral values (himself, no less, in the form of Parson Yorick). It lays bare, through the most commonplace of events, his susceptibility to self-delusion and in its comic vision anticipates Jane Austen. Depending on the reader's viewpoint, one may be moved by the book either to tears or to hilarity.

The work was originally intended as four volumes, but only two were completed before Sterne died, insolvent, in London's Old Bond Street. The manuscript, which was purchased by the British Museum Library in 1853, covers the first volume (that for the second survives at the Pierpont Morgan Library, New York, in what is believed to be a transcript made from the lost original). It is an autograph draft with quite a number of emendations, as prepared for the press, and is highly legible and fluid in form. An earlier owner has interleaved the folios with illustrations cut from early editions and one such quirky example is shown here.

There was something oddly Shandean about Sterne's end which came shortly after *A Sentimental Journey* was seen through the press. His newly buried corpse was seized by body-snatchers and sold to Cambridge University, before being recognised during actual anatomy-classes and returned to London. In 1969 the remains were again disinterred, Yorick-like, and laid finally to rest in the parish at Coxwold in Yorkshire, to which he had been appointed perpetual curate in 1760.

ABOVE:

A quizzical looking Sterne, taken from a Dutch edition of the writer's works of 1779.

BELOW:

An illustration inserted in the manuscript of *A Sentimental Journey*. A Désobligeant, the hero Yorick's chosen method of travel, was a carriage large enough to accommodate one person only.

OPPOSITE:

The manuscript of volume one of *A Sentimental Journey* is possibly the earliest surviving example of a novel written in the author's hand. It served as a printer's copy, as is suggested by its polished state. Here a young woman inspires in the hero Yorick a state of emotion intense enough to lead him to exclaim (over the page), 'Good God! how a man might lead such a creature as this round the world with him!'

The Remise Door
Calais.

When I told the Reader that
I did not care to get out of the Desobligeant
because I saw the monk in close conference
with a Lady just arrived at the inn —— I
told him the truth; but I did not tell
him the whole truth; for I was full as much
restrain'd by the appearance and figure
of the Lady he was talking to. Suspicion
cross'd my brain, and said, he was telling her
what had pass'd: something jar'd upon it
with in me —— I wish'd him at his convent.

When the heart flies out before the un —
—derstanding, it saves the judgment a world

Thomas Gray 1716–1771

Apart from a two-year sojourn in London to be near the British Museum, newly opened in 1759, 'with all its manuscripts and rarities by the cart-load', as he put it, Gray spent most of his adult life in Cambridge. He entered Peterhouse College in 1734, later transferring to Pembroke and in 1768 becoming Professor of Modern History.

His singularly uneventful and retiring life was in fact consumed by an indefatigable quest for knowledge, so that he became, in one friend's estimation, perhaps 'the most learned man in Europe'. Thoroughly versed in this country's literature, he was at the same time an antiquary and a botanist, a musician and a classical scholar, an entomologist and an expert on painting and architecture. This background of vast, eclectic learning is only partially reflected in the manuscript presented here.

The manuscript, which comprises seven folios, is a list of instructions to James Dodsley, his publisher, for a new edition of his poems appearing in July 1768. Gray's fastidiousness is most evident in his handwriting, meticulous punctuation, literary citations and in his careful distribution of copies. The edition was to contain republications of past work including the 'Elegy written in a country churchyard' and three new poems including 'The triumphs of Owen' whose last stanza appears at the head of the folio shown. The volume was also in the press of Robert Foulis, a Scottish publisher, coming out two months later. Gray accepted no money from either Dodsley or Foulis.

RIGHT:

Thomas Gray, an engraving taken from an original portrait painted by J.G. Eckhardt for Horace Walpole in 1747.

BELOW:

Three autograph copies of Gray's 'Elegy' survive, one at Eton College, another at Pembroke College, Cambridge and the third at The British Library. The epitaph from the Library's manuscript is shown here. Gray enclosed the poem in a letter of 1750 to his friend Thomas Warton.

OPPOSITE:

Gray's manuscript instructions to his publisher for the new edition of his poems appearing in 1768 bespeaks the quietness of his study or the gentle domesticity of his mother's home at Stoke Poges, Buckinghamshire, in whose churchyard they are both buried. It was bought for one guinea by James Bindley, a book-collector, in 1807 and was later acquired by Samuel Rogers, the poet, for eighteen guineas. Rogers's great-niece, Laetitia Sharpe, presented it to the British Museum Library in 1912.

Talymalfra's rocky shore
Echoing to the battle's roar.
✝ Where his glowing eye-balls turn,
Thousand banners round him burn.
Where he points his purple spear,
Hasty, hasty Rout is there;
Marking with indignant eye
Fear to stop & shame to fly.
There Confusion, Terror's child,
Conflict fierce, & Ruin wild;
Agony, that pants for breath,
Despair, & honourable Death.

*   *   *

Note. — The Dragon-Son) The red Dragon is the device of Cad:
=wallader, w.ch all his Descendents bore on their banner —

10.

l. 1. ——————————— the knell of parting day.
——— squilla di lontano,
Che paia 'l giorno pianger, che si muore. Dante.
(Purgat: L: 8.

l: 92. Even in our ashes live &c:
Ch' i' veggio nel pensier, dolce mio fuoco,
Fredda una lingua & due begli occhi chiusi
Rimaner doppo noi pien di favilla. Petrarch: Son: 169.

l: penult: There they alike &c:
——— paventosa speme. Petrarch: Son: 114.

I hope, you have not begun to reprint: but if you have,
you must throw the notes, &c: to the end, or where you please,
omitting the ~~xxxxxxxx~~ mottoes, w.ch do not much signify.

When you have done, I shall desire you to present in
my name a copy to M.r Walpole in Arlington-street, another
to M.r Daines Barrington (he is one of the Welch Judges) in the
Inner-Temple; & a third to M.r I: Butler at Andover: whe=
=ther this latter Gentleman be living or not, or in that neigh=
=bourhood, I am ignorant: but you will oblige me in making
the enquiry. if you have no better means of knowing, a
line directed to the Post-mistress at Andover will bring
you information. after this you may (if you please) bes=
=tow another copy or two on me. I am

P.S: It is M.r Foulis of Glasgow,   Your obed.t humble Servant
that prints them in Scotland: he has-
been told, that you are doing —   Gray.
the same. I have desired, he would-
not print a great number, & could-
wish the same of you.

Samuel Johnson 1709–1784

Dr Johnson was the son of a Lichfield bookseller. Poverty, melancholia and illness beset his early years, but on going to London in 1737 he established a living by contributing abundantly to *The Gentleman's Magazine* and later editing his own periodical, *The Rambler*, written almost entirely by himself. His great achievement, however, accomplished between 1746 and 1755, was the *Dictionary of the English Language*, a work unrivalled until the appearance of the *Oxford English Dictionary* in 1884. Almost the whole of Johnson's magnificent enterprise was carried off in his house – which may still be visited – in Gough Square, off Fleet Street.

RIGHT:

A study for the head of Johnson in a mural painting 'The Distribution of Premiums' by James Barry, *c.* 1778.

Domestic life and travel vied in his affections. His Hebridean and Scottish tours are well known from his own descriptions and from those of his biographer, James Boswell. But he was famously happy being in London with his companions, his wife, his cats or, between 1766 and 1783, with Henry and Hester Thrale, his friends in Streatham where he had his own room.

The manuscript illustrated here is from Johnson's diary of a tour in north Wales made with the Thrales in 1774. The right-hand column is particularly interesting: at Holywell the party visit a copper-foundry where Johnson's characteristic demand for truth and exactitude is manifest. It is a kind of bridging moment in our literature, for here, in effect, he tries to 'peep', as he puts it, into the early workings of the Industrial Revolution. Boswell, who did not know of the manuscript's existence, barely comments on the tour.

BELOW:

The furnace seen by Johnson (and described in his diary entry opposite) would have been of a similar type to the Dovey furnace, Cardiganshire, depicted here in an engraving of 1813 from John Wood's work *The Principal Rivers of Wales*. The furnace, built around 1755, had ceased functioning some while before the artist's picturesque interpretation.

Sadly, Johnson's connection with Streatham collapsed after Henry Thrale's death in 1781 and Hester Thrale's subsequent marriage to Gabriele Piozzi in July 1784 (which wounded Johnson deeply). Five months later, having destroyed a mass of private papers, Johnson himself was dead. He was granted burial in Westminster Abbey. The manuscript was inherited by his servant, Frank Barber and, after passing through a variety of hands, was acquired by the British Museum Library in 1839.

OPPOSITE:

The entry for 3 August 1774 in Dr Johnson's diary of a tour in north Wales. For some reason (perhaps practical, perhaps cosmetic), Johnson has folded his sheets of writing paper vertically down the middle creating two columns of script. Despite the fact that the manuscript accompanied its author *en route*, it is remarkably well preserved. Neither does Johnson's neat regular hand appear to have suffered from whatever makeshift studies (tavern tables?) he used to set down his observations.

August 3. We went in the coach to Holywel. I talk with Mistress about Sea—very — Holywel is a Market town neither very small nor mean. The Spring called Winifreds Well is very clear, and so copious that it yields one hundred tuns of water in a minute. It is all at once a very great stream which... perhaps this— by yards of the... has a mill five, and before in a... of two miles eighteen mills more. Its descent is very quick. It then falls into the Sea The Well is covered by a... circular arch supported by pillars, and over this arch is an old Chapel, now a School. The Chapel is separated by a wall. The Bath is completely and indecently open. A Woman bathed while we all looked on. In the Church which makes a good appearance, and is surrounded by galleries to receive a

numerous congregation, we were present while a child was christened in Welsh. We went down by the stream to see a prospect in which I had no part. We then saw a brass work where the... is gathered, broken, washed from the earth and the lead, though... the lead was separated I did not see, then calcined, afterwards ground five, and then mixed by fire with the copper. We saw several... with melting pots, but the construction of the fireplaces I did not learn. At a copper work which receives its... of copper, I think, from Warrington, we saw a plate of copper put between steel rollers, and spread thin. I know not whether another copper roller was set to a certain distance, as I suppose, or acted only by its weight. In the... iron work I saw round bars formed by a... hammer and anvil. The... I saw a bar of about half an inch, or more

Robert Burns 1759–1796

ABOVE:

A portrait of Burns taken from the *Collected Works* of 1834.

In 1815 a marble group was commissioned for Burns's mausoleum, newly built above the poet's grave in St Michael's Churchyard, Dumfries, Scotland. It was to portray the Muse of Poetry discovering Burns at the plough. The image of the 'Ploughman Poet', though well established by this time, was to be thus encouraged and nurtured throughout the nineteenth century.

It is not, of course, an entirely accurate image. His childhood was indeed spent among the rural retreats of Alloway where his father was head gardener to a local estate, but his father also had his own small plot and built the cottage, which survives to this day, with his own hands. One dominie who taught the boys said, 'In this mean cottage I really believe there dwelt a larger portion of content than in any place in Europe'.

It is this picture of content which infuses Burns's poem 'The Cotter's Saturday Night' and illustrated here we have the first of three folios of an autograph fair copy of the poem. The poem was the centre-piece of his first volume, *Poems, chiefly in the Scottish Dialect*, published in Kilmarnock in 1786. It is addressed to Robert Aitken, a successful lawyer of Ayr whose sound criticism Burns valued and whose industry in gathering the names of about a quarter of the subscribers ensured the volume's publication.

The poem bespeaks the study as much as the field. The verse style owes much to earlier models and the content recalls Fergusson's 'The Farmer's Ingle'. The Scots dialect is modified with a canny eye on an English market and in truth we have here the product of a sophisticated literary awareness. This is not to decry it. The poem has worn well through its annual recitations at Burns Night suppers.

Despite his erudition and the great favour he found among the cultured citizens of Edinburgh, Burns was never really able to make financial capital from his verse and, employing the skills learned helping his father, continued to work the land, at a leased farm in Dumfriesshire, until 1792. For the remaining three years of his life, married and with four children, he worked in the excise office in Dumfries.

LEFT:

'The Birth Place of Burns', a picturesque engraving from the *Collected Works* edited by Allan Cunningham in 1834.

OPPOSITE:

This manuscript, the first page of an autograph fair copy of Burns's poem, 'The Cotter's Saturday Night', was bought by the Library from Peter Cunningham in 1855. His father, Allan, had edited Burns's works in 1834 and had actually walked in the poet's funeral procession. In the nineteenth century Burns's distinctive bold slanting hand invited the attention of the forger Alexander Howland 'Antique' Smith, whose natural tendency (unlike Burns) to dot his 'i's too far to the right contributed to his undoing.

16/ The Cotter's Saturday-night. — A Scotch Poem,
inscribed to Robt. Aitken Esq. in Ayr. —

My lov'd, my honour'd, much respected friend,
　No mercenary Bard his homage pays;
With honest pride I scorn each selfish end,
　My dearest meed, a friend's esteem and praise:
To you I sing, in simple Scottish lays,
　The lowly train in life's sequester'd scene;
The native feelings strong, the guileless ways,
　What Aitken in a Cottage would have been,
Ah! tho his worth unknown, far happier there I ween!

November chill blaws loud wi' angry sugh,
　The short'ning winter day is near a close,
The miry beasts retreating frae the pleugh,
　The blackning flocks o' craws to their repose;
The toil-worn Cotter frae his labor goes,
　This night his weekly moil is at an end,
Collects his spades, his mattocks, an' his hoes,
　Hoping the MORN in ease an' rest to spend,
And weary o'er the moor his course does hameward bend.

At length his lonely Cot appears in view,
　Beneath the shelter of an aged tree;
Th' expectant wee-things, toddlin, stacher through
　To meet their Dad, with flichterin noise an' glee.
His wee-bit ingle blinking bonilie,
　His clean hearth stane, his thrifty wifie's smile,
The lisping infant prattling on his knee,
　Does a' his weary kiaugh an' care beguile,
And make him quite forget his labor an' his toil.

Lot 146.

William Cowper 1731–1800

ABOVE:

A profile of Cowper taken from James Storer's *The Rural Walks of Cowper*, a text of 1825 drawing upon 'scenery exemplified in his poems'. The portrait was drawn from Cowper's shadow.

Cowper's first volume of poems was not published until he was fifty-one. By then he had passed through three periods of intense melancholia and had twice tried to commit suicide. He had also embraced evangelical Christianity – and had shaken it off. A childhood marred by the very early death of his mother and by vicious bullying at school left their mark in the form of acute anxiety and fear of personal commitment. By 1782 he had arrived at a plateau of security in his troubled life, finding solace and comfort in the friendship of the widowed Mary Unwin with whom he lived first at Olney and then at nearby Weston in Buckinghamshire. We find Mrs Unwin in a letter he wrote in 1783 sitting 'knitting my stockings at my elbow with an industry worthy of Penelope herself'.

The poem illustrated here was written in 1792 at Weston soon after he met William Hayley, a cheerful and congenial man and a poet successful enough to be offered the laureateship (which he declined), but conservative enough to be reviled by Byron. Hayley, like Mrs Unwin, was a source of security and in fact obtained a government pension for Cowper shortly after the poem was written. Cowper addresses him as 'my dear Brother' in letters sent at this time. For all its genuine warmth, the poem, as seen here in this draft, is consciously crafted. The sonnet form needs scrupulous care and we can see the labour involved in the creation of the last six lines. It is a decorous warmth. The finely tuned artifice of Pope is nowhere to be found but we are some way off naturalness of tone.

Immediately after Cowper's death – he was buried near Mrs Unwin in East Dereham Church in Norfolk – Hayley wrote a biography of his friend, published in 1803. The manuscript of Cowper's poem went into the possession of George III's physician, Dr Edward Ash, and came to the Library from a descendant. The Ash family, according to a note appended to the manuscript, once possessed Mrs Unwin's knitting needles.

LEFT:

Cowper's Buckinghamshire home, Weston Lodge, drawn by John Greig, engraved by James Storer and published in *Cowper illustrated by a series of views...* (1803).

OPPOSITE:

Cowper's sonnet of friendship addressed to the poet William Hayley survives in two autograph versions. One, the finished 'presentation' copy, is to be found in a letter from Cowper to Hayley probably written on 3 June 1792, and is in the Library of Princeton University. The other, at The British Library and shown here, reveals Cowper working towards this final fair copy, and is dated 2 June 1792. It forms part of a manuscript volume containing some sixty-two autograph poems (and translations of poems) by the author.

Sonnet

Address'd to William Hayley Esqr. June 2. 1792.

—

Hayley – thy tenderness fraternal shown

    In our first interview, delightful guest!

    To Mary and me for her dear sake distress'd,

Such as it is has made my heart thy own,

Still Though ~~heedless now~~ *somewhat shy* of new engagements grown;

    For threescore winters make a wintry breast,

    And I had purpos'd ne'er to go in quest

Of Friendship more, except with God alone.

But Thou hast won me; nor is God my Foe,

Who e'er this last afflictive scene began

    ~~That he might sent Thee to~~ *dreadful*

    ~~Sent Thee before~~ to mitigate the *blow*

    ~~Where kind~~ My Brother, by whose sympathy I know

    ~~By true participation of my woe~~,

~~Has~~ Thy true deserts ~~justly thy deserts~~ *infallibly*

~~And taught me all thy worth at once~~ to scan,

Not more t'admire the Bard than love the Man.

—

William Blake 1757–1827

ABOVE:

A portrait of William Blake taken from the frontispiece to the 1893 edition of his *Collected Poems*, edited by W.B. Yeats.

William Blake, now recognised as one of the most visionary of literary and artistic figures, found no fame in his lifetime. It seems extraordinary to think that the man who gave us the words for 'Jerusalem' and 'The Tyger' and whose radiantly beautiful paintings and engravings are so instantly recognisable, should have experienced such a sad lack of interest when he presented his work before the public in his one-man exhibition of 1809. Yet the neglect of Blake by his contemporaries is perhaps not really so surprising. At odds with a world in which he saw the forces of science and materialism triumphing over the spirit, he stood, intellectually and politically, out of his own time.

Sent to a drawing school on the Strand at ten and apprenticed to an engraver at fourteen, Blake lived almost his entire life in London, whose exterior and interior landscapes haunt his work. The sinuous neo-gothicism which flexes and bounds through his art took its cue from the monuments in Westminster Abbey which he spent hours studying in his youth, and he once claimed to have seen angels on Peckham Rye. Blake married Catherine Boucher in 1782, having wooed her with some of the poems which were to appear in his first volume, *Poetical Sketches*, of 1783. He taught 'Kate' to read and she assisted him in their print-shop in Soho – as did William's brother, Robert, for one short year before succumbing to tuberculosis in 1787.

Commissioned as an engraver and illustrator by others more commercially successful than himself, Blake gradually developed his own innovative printing techniques which he used to publish, in tiny numbers, his own beautiful 'illuminated' editions. Most famous among these are his *Songs of Innocence* (1789) and *Songs of Experience* (1793). His work progressed in conditions of poverty, with the couple moving first to Poland Street, in Soho, and subsequently to Lambeth, just south of the Thames. Blake's one long sojourn outside London, in Felpham on the South Coast, included an incident which epitomised his relationship with the hated forces of authority. Blake came to blows with a soldier who had ventured into his garden. The intruder, manhandled back to his lodgings by an adversary renowned for his strength, subsequently accused Blake of sedition – a capital offence eventually rejected in court. In the closing years of his life, Blake's brilliance was recognised and protected by a dedicated coterie, including Samuel Palmer and George Richmond. The patronage of the artist John Linnell ensured Blake's ability to continue working. When he died, aged seventy, it was apparently while singing 'Hallelujahs and songs of joy and triumph'.

LEFT:

Blake began 'The Four Zoas' around 1797 while working on a commission to engrave illustrations for the poet Edward Young's 'Night Thoughts'. The complicated manuscript is composed partly on proofs for these illustrations; it also includes – as shown here – original pen and watercolour compositions, in various stages of completeness, decorating Blake's densely reworked text. The poem was first published in 1893 as 'Vala', the title which Blake himself had originally intended until a last-minute inspiration saw him alter the name to 'The Four Zoas'.

A B O V E :

This notebook of poems, prose and sketches was kept by William Blake from about 1787-1818. It was at one time owned by the painter and poet, Dante Gabriel Rossetti and is sometimes referred to as the 'Rossetti notebook'. The notebook contains over fifty poems from which Blake selected just eighteen for his *Songs of Experience* (1793). Included on one of the manuscript's most fascinatingly complex pages are versions of 'London' and 'The Tyger', the latter certainly among the most famous of English lyrics.

'In Xanadu did Kubla Khan a stately pleasure dome decree'. What could better illustrate the imaginative spirit of the early nineteenth century than Samuel Taylor Coleridge's poem 'Kubla Khan', which opens with these famous words? And what might better call into question that spirit than the re-discovered manuscript upon which his 'verse fragment' was written? The discrepancy between artistic claim and historical evidence in this instance warns us against taking too defined a view about any epoch, and encourages us to take good account of detail.

The nineteenth century, whose authors are all too often gathered up by commentators as 'Romantic' or 'Realist' repays the setting aside of literary critical generalisations in favour of the close scrutiny of its manuscript remains. William Wordsworth, we gather from his intensely subjective vision, 'wandered lonely as a cloud' in his quest for inspiration. Yet the manuscript of his *Poems, in Two Volumes* (1807) bears witness to a far from isolated effort in getting his ethereal words into print. Here we see the everyday evidence of postage, transit parcel and stray pieces of stitching; the industry not only of the poet himself, but his family. Even the famous record of his lonely wanderings comes down to us (as it came to his printer) in the hand of his wife Mary, complete with bodged first line.

Did Keats's poetry come, as he thought all poetry should, 'as naturally as the leaves to a tree'? The manuscript of 'Hyperion', abandoned after several pages of deletions, reworkings and additions would suggest that, in this case, it certainly did not. Bearing this in mind, it seems ironic that one of the most perfect 'finished' of all literary manuscripts, Lewis Carroll's 'Alice's Adventures under Ground', was never intended for publication as *Alice's Adventures in Wonderland* (1865), one of the world's best-loved children's books. The novels of George Eliot may indeed be praised for their magnificent sweeping portrayals of contemporary society – her realism, even. But those who have studied the manuscripts would learn of a more intimate significance, each completed work bearing a special dedication to her beloved George Henry Lewes.

Certainly well into the seventeenth century the circulation of poems by means of manuscript copies rivalled their dissemination in print. By the early nineteenth century there had been a complete reversal of this position, with the published rather than the manuscript record now the means by which

works were read. Perhaps it was for this reason that the period saw an unparalleled interest in the collecting and preserving of authors' manuscripts as prized (rather than merely useful) cultural artefacts. It is due to the perspicacity of the foreman of Dickens' publishers, Bradbury and Evans, that a manuscript fragment of *Nicholas Nickleby* (*c*.1839–40) has survived. The descendants of Jane Austen long treasured the gifts she made of her manuscripts, while the poet and anthologist F. T. Palgrave tipped his collection of Tennyson autographs into his copy of the great man's *Works* (1894). We know that the staff of the asylum to which John Clare was committed took care to preserve his remarkable verses, and posterity has Robert Ross to thank for the survival of a number of important manuscripts by his gifted friend, Oscar Wilde.

Nothing better exemplifies the nineteenth-century cult of collecting than the sad story surrounding the death of the poet Percy Bysshe Shelley. After his drowned corpse was recovered from the sea off the Italian coast (a copy of Keats's poems in his pocket), his body was cremated. In a macabre ceremony, which many would regard as the very apotheosis of Romanticism, those gathered around participated in their own grotesque form of souvenir hunt. Byron's request that the poet's skull be kept for him was denied when it crumbled away. The same fate did not befall the heart, however, which 'although bedded in fire – would not burn'. The words are those of another member of the circle, Edward Trelawny, who recovered the mysterious prize. It was next begged from him by Leigh Hunt who at first refused Byron's demand that it be passed to the poet's widow. He eventually relented and, on Mary's death, it was dicovered, shrivelled with age, enclosed in a copy of Percy's *Adonais*. There, however, the story does not end. Secure within the extensive, climate-controlled storage facilities of The British Library, further entombed in what might be better described as a mausoleum than a binding, and sharing space with a long letter from Mary recalling her husband's last days, rests a morbid trophy somehow won many years later by the great forger, book thief, bibliophile and inspired collector of nineteenth- and early-twentieth-century literary manuscripts, T. J. Wise. The trophy? Fragments of the ashes of Percy Bysshe Shelley.

Samuel Taylor Coleridge 1772–1834

ABOVE:

A fine engraving of Coleridge taken from an edition of *The Complete Poetical Works* dating from 1870.

A clergyman's son, Samuel Taylor Coleridge was educated at Christ's Hospital School, London and Jesus College, Cambridge, which he left without a degree, having enlisted in the 15th Light Dragoons after an unhappy love affair. Rescued from the army by his brother, he married Sara Fricker and planned, unsuccessfully, with Robert Southey to establish a utopian farming community in New England: just one example of the radicalism which characterised his entire life. Coleridge moved, instead, to the West Country, where he walked, preached and wrote some of his most powerful and moving lyrics. Here he met William Wordsworth, with whom he forged a deep and creative friendship, the first fruits of which appeared as *Lyrical Ballads*, which they published together in 1798. After a period in Germany, Coleridge moved with Wordsworth and his sister Dorothy to the Lake District, helping forever to associate its dramatic and beautiful landscape with the Romantic movement.

Although he continued to immerse himself in literary ventures, publishing widely in the sphere of journalism, criticism, poetry and philosophy and editing an influential periodical, *The Friend*, Coleridge was disastrously addicted to opium from about 1803. At Keswick, in 1802, he wrote 'Ode to Dejection' which has been described as possibly his last great poem and which laments the waning of his imaginative powers. Estranged from Wordsworth and destined never to recapture the intense creative vision of earlier days, he suffered his darkest suicidal years in London between 1811 and 1814. Nevertheless, the support of the Morgan family of Wiltshire and, from April 1816, the surgeon James Gillman of Highgate (who offered him lodgings for the remainder of his life), helped to effect a remarkable process of recovery, in which Coleridge grappled with his demons to emerge a sage-like figure whose influence upon English thought and letters remains strong to this day.

'Kubla Khan' is a monument to English Romanticism. For a century after Coleridge's death, the only clear authority for both the verse 'fragment', shown here, and the story of its remarkable inspiration was the author's preface in *Christabel and Other Poems*, where it was first published in 1816:

LEFT:

An engraving (1913) of Coleridge's cottage in Nether Stowey, by Edmund H. New.

OPPOSITE:

Coleridge's unique manuscript of 'Kubla Khan' does not look, on the evidence of the first page shown here, like the hastily written recollection which he claimed the poem to be. It is probably a fair copy, perhaps written up from the original 'inspired' draft. The presence of minor corrections to the text do rather invite the question as to why one should wish to meddle with a vision!

In Xanadu did Cubla Khan
A stately Pleasure-Dome decree;
Where Alph, the sacred River, ran
Thro' Caverns measureless to Man
Down to a sunless Sea.
So twice six miles of fertile ground
With Walls and Towers were compass'd round:
And here were Gardens bright with sinuous Rills
Where blossom'd many an incense-bearing Tree,
And here were Forests ancient as the Hills
Enfolding sunny Spots of Greenery.
But o! that deep romantic Chasm, that slanted
Down a green Hill athwart a cedarn Cover,
A savage Place, as holy and inchanted
As e'er beneath a waning Moon was haunted
By Woman wailing for her Dæmon-Lover:
From forth
And from this Chasm with hideous Turmoil seething,
As if this Earth in fast thick Pants were breathing,
A mighty Fountain momently was forc'd,
Amid whose swift half-intermitted Burst
Huge Fragments vaulted like rebounding Hail,
Or chaffy Grain beneath the Thresher's Flail:
And mid these dancing Rocks at once & ever
It flung up momently the sacred River.
Five miles meandring with a mazy Motion
Thro' Wood and Dale the sacred River ran,
Then reach'd the Caverns measureless to Man
And sank in Tumult to a lifeless Ocean;
And mid this Tumult Cubla heard from far
Ancestral Voices prophesying War.

    The Shadow of the Dome of Pleasure
      Floated midway on the Wave
      Where was heard the mingled Measure
      From the Fountain and the Cave.
    It was a miracle of rare Device
    A sunny Pleasure-Dome with Caves of Ice!

    A Damsel with a Dulcimer

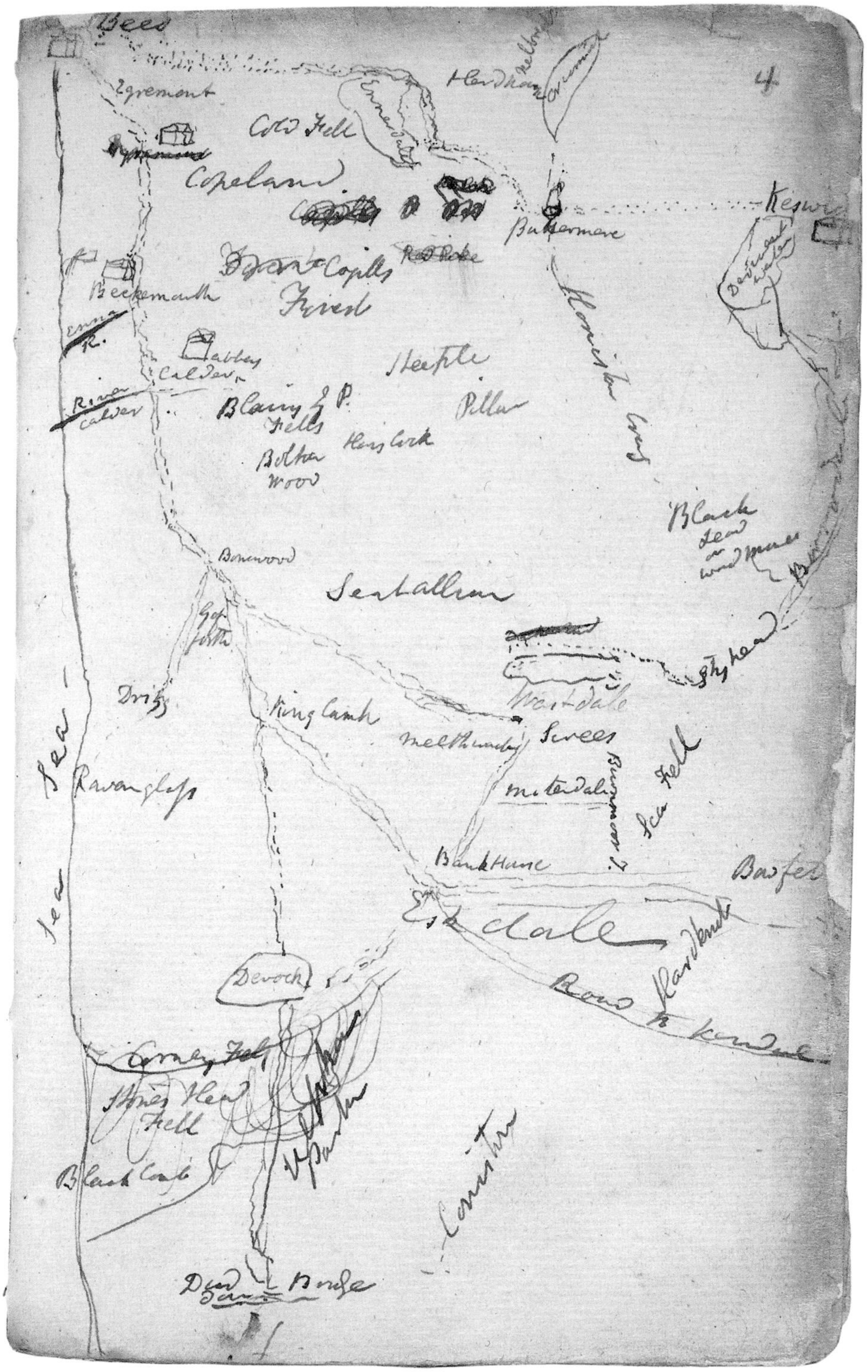

RIGHT:

In 1951 The Pilgrim Trust presented the British Museum Library with a substantial collection of manuscripts by, or relating to, Coleridge and his family, including some fifty-five notebooks kept by the poet. Shown here is a map (which occasionally confuses left and right) from notebook 'No 2', entitled 'Lakes'. Kept between July and September 1802, the notebook records Coleridge's energetic, solitary and often daring exploration of the mountainous landscape of the Lake District which seemed to him infused with the sublime. His description of Scafell, which he climbed, is somewhat reminiscent of 'Kubla Khan': 'O Scafell, they enormous Precipices – Just by the hollow stones are two enormous Columns. I am no measurer – they were vaster than any that I have ever seen, & were each a stone Mountain they could not be less than 250 yards high.'

In the summer of the year 1797, the Author, then in ill health, had retired to a lonely farmhouse between Porlock and Linton, on the Exmoor confines of Somerset and Devonshire. In consequence of a slight indisposition, an anodyne had been prescribed, from the effects of which he fell asleep in his chair at the moment he was reading the following sentence, or words of the same substance, in 'Purchas's Pilgrimage': 'Here the Khan Kubla commanded a palace to be built, and a stately garden thereunto. And thus ten miles of fertile ground were inclosed with a wall.'

The author continued for about three hours in a profound sleep, at least of the external senses, during which time he has the most vivid confidence, that he could not have composed less than from two to three hundred lines; if that can indeed be called composition in which all the images rose up before him as things, with a parallel production of the correspondent expressions, without any sensation or consciousness of effort.

On awaking he appeared to himself to have a distinct recollection of the whole, and taking his pen, ink, and paper, instantly and eagerly wrote down the lines that are here preserved. At this moment he was unfortunately called out by a person on business from Porlock, and detained by him above an hour, and on his return to his room, found to his no small surprise and mortification, that though he still retained some vague and dim recollection of the general purpose of the vision, yet, with the exception of some eight or ten scattered lines and images, all the rest had passed away.

In 1934 the unique autograph manuscript of the poem came to light. At the end of what is, in fact, a rather undistinguished document, Coleridge writes and signs the following note:

This fragment with a good deal more, not recoverable, composed, in a sort of Reverie brought on by two grains of Opium, taken to check a dysentery, at a Farm House between Porlock & Linton, a quarter of a mile from Culbone Church, in the fall of the year, 1797.

The rather prosaic account of poetic creation differs in several respects from the famous published version. In the latter, the date is given as summer 1797; the author's poor health is described; it is noted that he has retired to the farmhouse (which is more exactly located); it describes the opium as an 'anodyne', and his dysentry as a 'slight indisposition'; he has been reading 'Purchas's Pilgrimage' and, rather than a 'Reverie', falls into a profound sleep; the length of the poem as originally conceived in the vision is given as no less than 'two to three hundred lines'. Perhaps most interestingly of all, the celebrated 'man from Porlock' is nowhere mentioned in the manuscript account.

The discrepancy may perhaps be attributed to mere abbreviation on the part of Coleridge. But there is an irresistible suspicion of embellishment on his part, which, whether by design or not, has certainly enhanced the Romantic conception of the poet's unique apprehension of imaginative forces far beyond the understanding of mere mortals – such as, for instance, the 'nuisancesome' man from Porlock.

William Wordsworth 1770–1850

ABOVE:

A study of Wordsworth by
Benjamin Robert Haydon, 1819.
Tennyson, who first met
Wordsworth in 1845, described
him as 'swarthy and brown – had
very little chin', a fact disguised by
Haydon's portrait. Tennyson, it
should be said, greatly admired
Wordsworth.

Three major episodes in Wordsworth's life had a profound effect upon his development as a poet. First there was the loss of both his parents before he reached the age of fourteen which threw him upon his own resources and made him turn for solace and strength to the beauty and grandeur of the Cumbrian landscape in which he grew up. The second was his series of visits to France beginning in 1790 which nurtured in him republican principles and a respect for the outsider in society, the humble, the unregarded, the rejected. The third was his momentous meeting with Coleridge which led him to examine the growth of his own imagination.

The sum of his thinking was to be put into his vast poem 'The Recluse', begun in 1798 and worked on for years. He saw this poem in the form of a Gothic church: a part of it, *The Prelude*, published posthumously in 1850, was the 'ante-chapel' while another, *The Excursion*, published in 1814, was the 'body'. He considered the smaller poems as 'little cells, or oratories…ordinarily included in those edifices'. One such little cell is his poem 'November 1806' illustrated here in Wordsworth's hand, which refers to the overthrow of Prussia by Napoleon's forces at the Battle of Jena on 14 October 1806. It is the last of the twenty-six sonnets 'dedicated to Liberty' published in his *Poems, in Two Volumes* in April 1807.

The poem is to be found on one leaf from the extraordinary manuscript of this collection of poems, acquired by the British Museum Library in 1952. The volume is a gathering together of poems transcribed in 1806 and early 1807 by Wordsworth himself, by his wife, his sister and his sister-in-law while they were all staying, the guests of Sir George Beaumont, at Coleorton in Leicestershire. Coleridge visited at the time and his own scribal contributions are evident. He appears to have brought his own paper, otherwise anything to hand would do, including the blank sides of old letters.

Family responsibilities increasingly diminished Wordsworth's radical views until he became an establishment figure, succeeding Robert Southey as Poet Laureate in 1843. Rydal Mount, his home near Grasmere, became almost a shrine for visiting admirers and today the large number of tourists seeking out his grave in the churchyard there is testimony to his abiding stature in English Literature.

LEFT:

Wordsworth's poem 'I wandered lonely as
a cloud' was written in 1804. This particular poem was transcribed by his wife
Mary, who makes an intriguing false start.
No manuscript of the text survives in the
poet's own hand. Interestingly, the 1802
journal of Wordsworth's sister, Dorothy,
contains expressions which prefigure
William's descriptions of the daffodils,
suggesting that their minds worked in a
mutually inspirational way.

OPPOSITE:

Wordsworth's 'November 1806' is written
on a white octavo sheet countermarked
with the date 1798. The bundle of variously shaped and sized manuscripts to
which it belongs was sewn together in
sections by the Wordworth household.
Portions were intermittently sent off to
the publishers in London from the nearby
post offices.

26

November 1806

Another year! — another deadly blow!
Another mighty Empire overthrown!
And we are left, or shall be left, alone;
The last that dares to struggle with the Foe.
'Tis well! from this day forward we shall know
That in ourselves our safety must be sought;
That by our own right hands it must —
be wrought,
That we must stand unpropp'd, or be laid low.
O Dastard whom such foretaste doth not chear!
We shall exult, if they who rule the land
Be Men who hold its many blessings dear,
Wise, upright, valiant; not a venal Band
Who are to judge of danger which they fear,
And honour which they do not understand.

Jane Austen 1775–1817

Jane Austen was born into a large and affectionate Hampshire family. As a child she was an avid reader and her earliest surviving writings date from her teenage years. A delightful example, pictured here, is her parody of contemporary history textbooks, 'The History of England', written in 1790 by 'a Partial, Prejudiced and ignorant historian', as she describes herself. The illustrations were done by her sister, Cassandra.

RIGHT:

A steel engraving of Jane Austen after a watercolour sketch by her sister Cassandra of 1810.

Though leading the circumscribed life of a country clergyman's daughter, Austen developed a sharply perceptive view of the follies of mankind. She limited herself to what she knew of her age and society but what she created is a microcosm of the whole world's frailties. Self-delusion, self-aggrandisement and hypocrisy are but a few of the more distasteful traits of humanity to fall under her scrutiny; her ironic detachment and humour, nevertheless, make them joyfully palatable. *Pride and Prejudice* (1813), *Emma* (1815) and *Persuasion* (1818) are among the very greatest of English literary achievements.

It is ultimately Austen's craftsmanship that carries the day. She worked assiduously at shaping her novels, something quite apparent in the manuscript of part of *Persuasion*, also illustrated here. It constitutes what were then – in July 1816 – the two final chapters, numbers ten and eleven. The posthumously published work retains the final chapter, re-numbered as twelve, but discards the other in favour of a new chapter ten and has part of the old chapter ten embedded into a reworked chapter eleven. We can see her structuring processes clearly.

The minute size of the sheets (165 x 92 mm), deliberately cut down from foolscap size, reflects Austen's working practice: she would hide them away when her household or social duties made demands upon her. A slip attached to one of the folios reads 'The contents of this Drawer for Anna' (her niece, Anna Lefroy), a sad reminder of her last days. She died of Addison's disease in Winchester and was worthily granted a resting-place in the cathedral there.

LEFT:

Two pages of Austen's 'The History of England' (1790) from what she called 'Volume the Second'. The coloured illustrations were painted by her sister Cassandra. The manuscript also includes two brief epistolary novels ('Love and Friendship' and 'Lesley Castle'), and 'A Collection of Letters' dedicated to a niece, Fanny Austen, born in 1793. The British Library also holds the last of the three surviving volumes of juvenilia, 'Volume the Third'. 'Volume the First' is in the Bodleian Library, Oxford.

RIGHT:
This manuscript, comprising two
cancelled chapters of *Persuasion*,
was acquired by the British
Museum Library in 1925 (having
passed to Austen's sister
Cassandra after her death).
It shows the complexity of
Austen's editorial method and
represents all that survives of
the original manuscript.

John Keats 1795–1821

ABOVE:
An engraving of a wistful-looking Keats based on the original miniature by his friend Joseph Severn.

BELOW:
Keats composed this short letter to his sister Fanny on 30 November 1818, the day before their brother, Tom, died of consumption. He actually posted the letter immediately after Tom's death, to prepare his sister for the sad news.

Keats first appeared in print with a sonnet published on 5 May 1816 in Leigh Hunt's periodical *The Examiner*. His death in Rome on 23 February 1821 and his burial in the Protestant cemetery there curtailed a public poetic working life which spanned barely five years, but the legacy of that intense period is an astonishingly rich one. Although derided by many contemporaries (Byron threatened to skin him), subsequent poets have acknowledged him as one of the finest talents of the nineteenth century and his influence has been far-reaching.

The son of a livery stable-manager – not a humble profession, as has been commonly supposed – he was born in London. He lived in and around the city throughout his life and has come to be closely associated with Hampstead, where his house can still be visited. He originally chose medicine as a profession and began his working life as a dresser at Guy's Hospital. His deeper calling, however, was to poetry, and encouraged and influenced by the poet and liberal journalist Leigh Hunt, he read widely in Elizabethan literature and absorbed the colour of Italian romances.

'Hyperion' was written in late 1818 and abandoned, unfinished, in early 1819. It was a time of considerable personal distress for Keats. Symptoms of consumption began in August 1818 (recognizable to his expert eye) and through the latter months of this year he was nursing his brother Tom, whose early death from the same disease cruelly anticipated his own. Savage reviews of his work had appeared in August and September and in December Keats met Fanny Brawne for whom he developed a tormented passion.

The autograph manuscript of 'Hyperion', shown here, comprises twenty-seven very large folios and is watermarked '1810'. It was evidently intended as a fair copy of the poem but Keats had further assaults on it, often creating improvements which have a Miltonic ring. However, Keats's evident struggle with the text leading to its final abandonment perhaps bears out his famous remark, made only shortly before he began the work, that 'if poetry comes not as naturally as the leaves to a tree, it had better not come at all'.

As for the manuscript's history, it lay unrecognised through much of the nineteenth century. It was probably in Hunt's possession on Keats's death, for his son, Thornton Hunt, gave it to Miss Alice Bird, the sister of Hunt's physician, in about 1862. Only at the turn of the century did she discover that it was in Keats's own hand. It was acquired by the British Museum Library in 1904.

OPPOSITE:
Keats's dramatic manuscript of his unfinished epic poem 'Hyperion' is written, as befits its grand theme, on oversized sheets of high-quality paper. The opening page is shown here. Keats has taken considerable care to write in his best – at times almost calligraphic – hand.

Hyperion Book 1st

Deep in the shady sadness of a Vale,
Far sunken from the healthy breath of Morn,
Far from the fiery noon, and ~~evening's~~ Eve's one star,
Sat grey hair'd Saturn quiet as a Stone,
Still as the silence round about his Lair.
Forest on forest hung above his head
~~Like Clouds that whose bosoms thunderous bosoms~~
Like Cloud on Cloud. No stir of air was there;
~~Not so much life as what an eagle's wing~~
~~Might spread upon a field of green ear'd corn~~
But where the dead leaf fell there did it rest.
A Stream went voiceless by, still deadened more
By reason of his fallen divinity
~~Spreading a shade~~
Spreading a shade: the Naiad mid her reeds
Pres'd her cold finger closer to her lips.

Along the margin sand large foot marks went
No further than to where his feet had stay'd so often
And slept ~~there since~~ ~~without a motion: since that time~~ ~~where the~~ ground
His old right hand lay nerveless ~~on the ground~~ listless, dead
Unsceptr'd; and his ~~realmless~~ eyes were clos'd;
While his ~~bow'd~~ head seem'd list'ning to the Earth
His Ancient Mother for some comfort yet.

Thus the old Eagle drowsy with ~~his~~ great ~~grief~~
Sat moulting his weak Plumage never more.
To be restored or soar against the Sun,
While his three Sons upon Olympus stood—

It seem'd no force could wake him from his place.
But there came one who, with a kindred hand
Touch'd his wide Shoulders, after bending low
With reverence, though to one who knew it not.
She was a Goddess of the infant world;
~~By her~~ ~~Plac'd by her side the~~ tallest Amazon
Had stood a ~~little child~~ ~~Pigmy's height~~: she would have ta'en
Achilles by the hair and bent his neck,
Or with a ~~finger~~ ~~case~~ Ixion's toil

Percy Bysshe Shelley 1792–1822

ABOVE:
Shelley, an engraving from the original painting by Amelia Curran, a friend of the Shelleys.

The decade 1810 to 1820 was, in Coleridge's words, 'an age of anxiety from the crown to the hovel, from the cradle to the coffin'. The English victory at Waterloo did nothing to resolve deep-seated problems at home and the agents of reform clashed hopelessly with an entrenched and intransigent Tory government. Shelley's little tract 'Proposal for Putting Reform to the Vote', an argument favouring an extension of the franchise, was but one of the many dismissed out of hand, but when on 16 August 1819 a crowd of some 60,000 people gathered – peacefully, it should be said – at St Peter's Fields, Manchester, to press for the franchise, the authorities took fright. The local magistrates called in the cavalry, who hacked down over 400 people with their sabres, killing eleven. The magistracy was congratulated by the government.

This, the 'Peterloo Massacre', is what prompted Percy Bysshe Shelley's poem, 'The Mask of Anarchy', a powerful piece of invective written in a popular ballad form. The autograph draft of the poem, whose untitled opening is illustrated here, dates from the autumn of 1819. The manuscript's twelve folios appear to have been torn out of a notebook and its text varies in many places from that printed in the first edition of 1832. The voice is unmistakably Shelley's. Strikingly independent of spirit, he had been a problem to his parents, to his university (from which he was sent down) and indeed to society whose conventions he ignored. His abandonment of his first wife, Harriet, his flight to the continent in 1814 with Mary Godwin, and their liaisons with Byron and his circle all conspired to shock conventional notions of respectability.

Shelley's death shocked too. He was drowned in the Gulf of Spezia, near Leghorn, in his thirtieth year. His remains were cremated on the beach. Although most of Shelley's ashes were buried in the Protestant Cemetery in Rome (also the final resting place of Keats, a copy of whose poems was discovered on Shelley's corpse), a small phial, shown here, came to the British Museum Library in 1938, preserved in the binding of a manuscript containing a moving letter from his widow describing his last days.

RIGHT:
The collector T. J. Wise treasured the Shelley manuscripts he acquired for his Ashley collection. In one special binding, sumptuous to the point of excess, he gathered together not only an important letter from Mary Shelley describing her husband's last days, but also locks of their hair and, grotesquely, these fragments of the poet's ashes.

FRAGMENTS OF THE ASHES OF
P. B. SHELLEY

OPPOSITE:
The manuscript of Shelley's highly charged political poem, 'The Mask of Anarchy', is written on both sides of ten sheets of paper apparently ripped from a notebook. It contains, as well as his boldly written text, the occasional rather whimsical doodle. The opening of the poem is displayed here.

As I lay asleep in Italy
There came a voice from over the Sea
And with great power it forth led me
To walk in the visions of Poesy

I met Murder on the way —
He had a mask like Castlereagh,
Very smooth he looked, yet grim;
Seven bloodhounds followed him

All were fat, & well they might
Be in admirable plight,
For one by one & two by two
He tossed them human hearts to chew
Which from his wide cloak he drew

Next came Fraud the had on
Like Ld Eldon, an ermined gown
His big tears for he wept well

John Clare 1793–1864

ABOVE:

An engraving of Clare published in 1821, after a painting by W. Hilton.

BELOW:

John Clare's impassioned letter to the bookseller Edward Drury, in which he beseeches that no poem of which he disapproved should ever go to press against his will.

In 1841 John Clare was committed to Northampton Asylum, where he remained until his death some twenty-three years later. Here he wrote some of his most poignant and celebrated poems. Born at Helpstone, Northamptonshire to a poor farm labourer and his illiterate wife, from the age of seven Clare worked in the fields. He read widely, taking advantage of his father's enjoyment of popular poetry and chapbook (folk) literature; his discovery of Thomson's *The Seasons* at the age of thirteen inspired him to begin composing verse. Initially a private exercise affording a 'downright pleasure in giving vent to my feelings', his honest articulation of country life caught the imagination of a sophisticated reading public glad to discover, in the innocent voice of a 'peasant poet', a worthy successor to Robert Burns. Such fashionable interest, which perhaps failed to take into account the genuine depth of the writing, soon waned, however, and the success of *Poems Descriptive of Rural Life and Scenery*, published in 1820, was never matched by subsequent volumes.

Clare's drift back into literary obscurity together with his luckless attempts to establish himself as a farmer (having worked as a gardener and, for a short while, a soldier) may have played a part in the increasing fragility of his mental health, but his earlier life was not without melancholy. In particular, although he later married Martha Turner in 1820, he never overcame his childhood love for Mary Joyce, whose father forbade their courtship. In 1841, he wandered away from the private asylum in Epping Forest where he had been since 1837, sadly deluded in the belief that he could become reunited with her again. His exhausted return to Northampton was followed by his removal to the county asylum, where he found kindness and support for his writing and was allowed to go about his quiet ways. He died on 20 May 1864 and was buried in the village of his birth.

The poems written by Clare in the asylum survived largely through the good offices of its staff, in particular the House Steward W. F. Knight who began the task, later taken up by other copyists, of transcribing his manuscripts into two volumes. However, the autograph poems shown here date from 1819, a year in which Clare contemplated suicide. In a letter of the same year (which itself bears a poem on its reverse) he sternly instructs the bookseller Edward Drury, who did much to help publish his first poems, as to what he must on no account posthumously print: '...if I knew such things I disapprove of should appear in print after my death it would be the greatest torture possible'.

OPPOSITE:

This manuscript belonged, until 1967, in the National Portrait Gallery, where it was displayed with Clare's portrait. 'The Dying Snowdrop' and the sonnet nevertheless went unpublished until the scholar Eric Robinson brought them to light. The two stanzas at the foot of the page are from the poet's 'Song of Praise: Imitation of the 158th Psalm', which appeared in the *Village Minstrel* (1821).

144

1809 April

Sonnet

Hail to thee Violet sweet Earless thread
Neath each warm bush & covert budding hedge
In many a pleasing Walk have I beheld
To seek thee Promise of Springs earliest pledge
In modest bashfulness hanging down its head
In conscious hiding beautifss from the eye
As sweetly blossom'd oer its Graceful form
Shunning each vulgar gaze that saunters by
I kindly stoop prey from an April shower
As if thou startld by approaching harm
Shrinks from delusiously fake betray my hands
Each bashful look that shll endears her form
So sweeter I blossom the coy Violet stand
Tempting the plunderer with a double charm

———

119

The Dying Snowdrop

1816 April

Snow drop I mourn thee oer thy early tomb
Thy withered fragrance so untimely shed
Kills by the pride that gave thy guiltless bloom
Upon the snow bed droops thy withered head

———

So artless beauty oftentimes undone
In conscious weeping our seductions heed
Like the poor Lark the Fowlers wile have won
Falls on the spot where profferd of his reed

———

120

Praise his name his mercy bless
Ye poor like me in whelmd distress
Of hail protection given
When winter snow dies away
Our hopes his promise cant decay
Of recompensing heaven

———

Thunders that fright the trembly ground
Ye forked lightnings flashing round
As quenchd in whelming shower
Anfullys wells the sky torrent
Thunders in rolling rolling winds
While ransomy nature silent bends
To own almighty power

Sir Walter Scott 1771–1832

ABOVE:

An engraved portrait of Scott, at work (in the artist's imagination, one suspects) on the manuscript of *Waverley*.

BELOW:

Scott's influence was far-reaching as shown in this Cantata by Arthur Sullivan, published in 1864, some years before his series of famous collaborations with W.S.Gilbert.

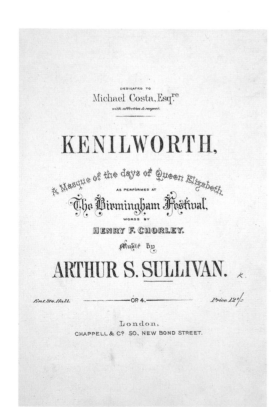

Shown here is a folio from the manuscript of Scott's novel *Kenilworth*. Vividly evident in this final draft before going to press is the massive impetus of the physical act of writing: Lockhart, his great biographer, said his handwriting reflected his legal training. He can barely stop to close and open a new paragraph and his directive 'NP' (it looks like NL) has to suffice. Interestingly, there are emendations even at this stage – Lady Paulet becomes Lady Paget.

Kenilworth was ready for publication by the end of 1820, a year which had also seen the appearance of Scott's other novels *Ivanhoe*, *The Monastery* and *The Abbot*. This breathtaking output was sustained throughout the author's working life. From childhood Scott was fascinated with his own family history. Born and educated in Edinburgh, his ancestral roots tapped deep into the beautiful Scottish border country whose literary and geographical landscapes he explored with ceaseless energy. His antiquarian enthusiasms expanded to embrace the literature and history of the Scottish people so that he became a mine of knowledge. In 1820 his immense contribution to the nation's literature was recognised by his being given a baronetcy by George IV and he was offered honorary degrees by both Oxford and Cambridge Universities.

The action of the novel is set in 1575. In that year the revels at the Earl of Leicester's Kenilworth Castle actually took place and Scott made use of contemporary accounts but historically the rest of the action is anachronistic, for Ralegh, one of the central characters in the novel, did not appear at court until 1581. Scott's tale is in fact a distillation of the Elizabethan temper but by its great attention to detail – exemplified in this fragment – it achieves the radiance of verisimilitude. Scott's evocations of a picturesque past and portrayals of wild scenery had a huge influence on the romantic sensibilities of the early nineteenth century. Equally his sense of structure and imaginative creation of individual *personae* had a major part to play in the development of the novel form.

He died worn out by his industry, by his extravagant commitment to the beauties of his prodigious home, Abbotsford, near Melrose (which he built for himself between 1817 and 1824) and by his magnificently selfless clearance of the debts he faced on the collapse in 1826 of the Ballantyne printing house in which he had a concern. In that same year his wife died, whom he had married in 1797 and with whom he had five children. He was buried in the ruins of Dryburgh Abbey in the Scottish borders, beside his ancestors, and his manuscript of *Kenilworth*, comprising 170 folios, was purchased by the British Museum Library in 1855.

OPPOSITE:

A folio from Scott's *Kenilworth*, published in early 1821. The manuscript lacks only a few folios, otherwise presenting us with a remarkable insight into Scott's fervent industry. It was prepared and corrected by Scott for the press and presumably followed a preliminary drafting process.

25

He mimicked with ready accent the manners of the affected or the clownish and made his own grace... ...of their courts, the fashions and even the dress of their ladies were equally his theme and seldom... ...to the Virgin Queen, her court and her government... ...royal person in such conversation varied by remarks upon ancient classics and modern authors and... ...mixed wisdom with the lighter talk of a female court. N.L. When they returned to the Palace Elizabeth... ...It even seemed to him (though that might arise from the flattery of his own imagination) that during this... ...by her actions and words combined to express a degree of favour which even in his proudest days he had not...

...ultimate motive of life and forget in the intoxication of the moment the perplexities and dangers of... ...his own situation. Indeed strange as it may appear he thought but at that moment of the peril arising... ...from his secret union than of the marks of grace which Elizabeth from time to time showed to young Ra-... ...leigh. They were indeed transient but they were conferred on one accomplished in mind and body with grace... ...gallantry literature and valour...

...occurred in the course of the evening which rivetted Leicester's attention to this object. N.L. The nobles and... ...courtiers who had attended the Queen on her pleasure-expedition were received with royal hospitality to... ...a splendid banquet in the hall of the palace. The table was not indeed graced by the presence of the so-... ...vereign for agreeable to her idea of what was at once modest and dignified the Queen on such... ...occasions was wont to take in private or with one or two favourite ladies her light and temperate... ...meal. After a moderate interval the court again met in the splendid gardens of the palace and... ...continued to amuse themselves with various conversation until the Queen gave the signal for departure. ...It was while thus engaged that the Queen suddenly asked a lady who was near to her both in place of favour... ...what had become of the young Squire Lack-Cloak. The Lady Paget answered she had seen Master Raleigh... ...but two or three minutes since standing at the window of a small pavilion or pleasure house which... ...looked out on the Thames and working on the glass with a diamond ring — "Keep my" said the Queen... ...a small token I gave him to make amends for his spoiled mantle — come Paget let us see what use he... ...has made of it for I can see through him already this is a marvellously sharp-witted spirit." They came... ...to the spot which but at some distance the young Cavalier still beyond as the fowler watches the... ...net while he has set. The Queen approached the window on which Mr Raleigh had used her gift to inscribe... the following lines.

Fain would I climb but that I fear to fall —   Paget

The Queen smiled, read twice over with deliberation once to Lady Paget and once again to herself. ..."It is a pretty beginning" she said after the consideration of a moment or two but methinks the Muse... ...hath deserted the young art at the very crisis of his fate — it were good natured — were it not Lady Paget to... ...employ it for him. Try your rhyming faculties" Lady Paget professes from her cradle upwards as over... ...any Lady of the bed chamber before or after her, disclaimed all possibility of assisting the young poet — "May... ...there be aught of sacrifice to the Muses" answered Elizabeth "the sacrifices of verse can be so accepted... ...hible" said Lady Paget "and your Highness will impose such obligation on the ladies of Parnassus —... "Hush Paget" said the Queen "you speak sacrilege against the immortal Nine. Yet Virgins them... ...selves they should excuse to a Virgin — and therefore — let me see how runs his verse—

Fain would I climb but that I fear to fall

Might not the answer (for fault of a better) run thus
If thy mind fail thee do not climb at all.

The duke of heaven exclaimed with joy and surprise at so happy a... ...termination and certainly a worse has been applauded coming from a less important author. The... ...Queen thus encouraged took off a diamond ring and... "we will give this gallant some cause of... ...marvel when he finds his couplet perfected without his own interference" she wrote her own line be... ...neath that of Raleigh. The Queen left the pavilion but retiring slowly and often looking back the... ...could see the young cavalier steal with the flight of a lapwing towards the place where she had been... ...seen her make a pause and leaning at the circumstance with the Lady Paget she took the way... ...slowly toward the palace. N.L. ...read with a feeling of intoxication the encou-... ...ragement thus given him by the Queen in person to follow out his ambitious career and re-... ...turned to prepare and his retinue then on the point of embarking to go up the river his heart beating... ...with gratified pride and with hope of future distinction N.L. The ...due to the person of the   Earl...

...

Mary Shelley 1797–1851

'Singularly bold, somewhat imperious, and active of mind. Her desire of knowledge is great, and her perseverence in everything she undertakes almost invincible.' Thus did William Godwin describe his fifteen-year-old daughter Mary, future wife of the poet Percy Bysshe Shelley and author of *Frankenstein* (1818). Mary's exceptional character sprang from gifted parents. Her mother, Mary Wollstonecraft, who died giving birth to her, wrote the famous *Vindication of the Rights of Woman* (1792), while William established himself as an influential philosopher and radical.

RIGHT:

An engraved portrait of Mary Shelley after the portrait by Rothwell, published in 1889.

Mary's upbringing fell in part to her stepmother, Mrs Clairmont, with whose daughter, Jane, she travelled to the continent in July 1814. With them was the poet Shelley, to whom Mary had grown increasingly close since their meeting in the Spring of that year. Their friendship developed into profound love and devotion and they married in 1816, shortly after Shelley learned of the suicide of his first, estranged wife. A competition to write a ghost story (with, among others, Lord Byron) in Italy in 1816 resulted in Mary's *Frankenstein*, a powerful gothic fable which was published two years later. It continues to exert a strong (if often misinterpreted) influence on the popular imagination.

The excitement of travel, the deepening of love, the satisfaction of literary achievement and the constant intellectual stimulation derived from the inspirational and eccentric circle of friends among whom she moved, were from this point in Mary's young life offset by a number of cruel blows. She lost two of the children she had had with Shelley: first Clara, who died in Venice in 1818, and then Willliam in 1819, in Rome. A son, Percy, was born to them in the midst of a melancholy which cast its long and ominous shadow as far as San Terenzo, on the Bay of Lerici, to which they moved in April 1822. In this remote spot, Mary suffered a dangerous miscarriage, while Shelley endured strange intimations of his own fate. On 8 July, not long after seeing the ghost of a child in the sea, he drowned while sailing off the coast, leaving Mary to fall upon the support of Byron and his circle in Genoa before her return to England.

BELOW:

In this sad list, drawn up after Shelley's death, Mary records the items of furniture she intends to send to Leigh Hunt, staying at Byron's sixteenth-century Pisan villa, Casa Lanfranchia. Hunt was charged with the task of arranging for the furniture to be forwarded on to her at Genoa.

Although for the remainder of her years Mary enjoyed a measure of success as a novelist, contributor to periodicals and literary editor, she never surpassed the achievement of her first work. 'Torn by memory', she did her best to keep alive Shelley's literary flame, and to guarantee her son's welfare. If legend is to be believed, she kept with her at all times the remains of her husband's heart, which had failed to burn during his dramatic cremation on the beach. She herself died in London and is buried in the churchyard of St Peter's, Bournemouth, together with her husband's heart and her parents – who were removed there from St Pancras Churchyard shortly after her death.

OPPOSITE:

Mary endured a terrible period of deepening fear between Shelley's embarkation on 8 July for Lerici in the small boat the *Don Juan* and the discovery ten days later of his body on the shore near Via Reggio. This undated manuscript sets out in fair copy a short poem which explores the themes of loss and hope through the vivid use of night and day imagery.

Ah! he is gone – and I alone;
How dark and dreary seems the time!
'Tis thus when the glad sun is flown,
Night rushes o'er the Indian clime.

Is there no star to cheer this night –
No soothing twilight for the breast?
Yes – Memory sheds her fairy light,
Beaming as sunsets golden West.

And hope of dawn – Oh brighter far
Than clouds that in the orient burn,
More welcome than the morning star,
Is the dear thought – he will return!

Mary W. Shelley

George Gordon, Lord Byron 1788–1824

ABOVE:

Byron, aged twenty-six, at the
height of his popularity, in a
painting by Thomas Philips of 1814.

When Byron died of fever in Greece in 1824 the world lost perhaps its most famous modern poet. That he should die in exile as self-appointed head of a 'Byron brigade', formed to lead the Greek battle for independence against the Turks, typifies his boundlessly charismatic and unconventional life. Byron was born in London, the son of a rumbustious, philandering father and a long-suffering Scottish mother descended from the ranks of the minor nobility. Despite a painfully deformed leg, Byron was strikingly handsome, a quality he used throughout his life to seduce a great many admirers. It is probable that one such was his half-sister, Augusta Leigh. The rumours surrounding the nature of their relationship destroyed his ill-advised marriage to Annabella Milbanke and forced him in 1816 to shake the dust of England from his shoes for good. He left behind a daughter, Augusta Ada, whom, like his wife, he never saw again.

By the time of his exile, Byron – boxer, swimmer, traveller, political speaker and from 1798 6th Lord Byron of Newstead Abbey – was already a famous poet, having honed his skills at Harrow and Trinity College, Cambridge to produce, in 1812, the brilliant first cantos of *Childe Harold's Pilgrimage*. He travelled in Switzerland, where he stayed with the Shelleys and Claire Clairmont (who became his mistress and bore him a daughter, Allegra, in 1817) before moving restlessly through Italy and consolidating his literary reputation with the long poem *Don Juan*. Byron played up to his devil-may-care reputation – his mistress Caroline Lamb had declared him 'mad, bad and dangerous to know' – finding it, perhaps, a useful camouflage under which to hide a genuinely melancholy disposition. His last years, if full of resolution to dedicate himself politically, physically and financially to the cause of liberty, were nevertheless tainted with sadness. In 1822 he lost his friend Shelley and received the tragic news of Allegra's sudden death. In February 1824 he suffered a convulsive fit (referred to here in one of his last poems, 'Love and Death') and two months later, weakened by fever and medical bleeding, he died at Missolonghi on the Greek mainland. His body was finally conveyed to the family vault at Hucknall Torkard, near Newstead.

LEFT:

Byron's house in Missolonghi,
where he spent the last few
months of his life.

RIGHT:

A single manuscript sheet contains drafts of Byron's last poems. 'Love and Death', shown here, was written sometime between 21 February and 9 April 1824. Byron died on 19 April. The poem of unrequited love, which has all the appearance of a first draft, is addressed to Loukas Chalandritsanos, whom Byron cared for in Greece. The poem refers to a series of dramatic events actually experienced by Byron and Loukas.

I watched thee when the foe was at our side –
Ready to strike at him, – or thee and me –
Were safety hopeless – rather than divide
Aught with one loved – save love and liberty.

I watched thee in the breakers – when the rock
Received our prow – and all was storm and fear,
And bade thee cling to me through every shock –
This arm would be thy bark – or breast thy bier.

I watched thee when the fever glazed thine eyes –
Yielding my couch – and stretched me on the ground –
When overworn with watching – ne'er to rise
From thence – if thou an early grave hadst found.

The Earthquake came and rocked the quivering wall –
And men and Nature reeled as if with wine –
Whom did I seek around the tottering Hall –
For *thee* – whose safety first provide for – thine.

And when convulsive throes denied my breath
The faintest utterance to my fading thought –
To thee – to thee – even in the grasp of death
My spirit turned – Ah! Oftener than it ought.

Thus much and more – and yet thou lov'st me not,
And never wilt – Love dwells not in our will –
Nor can I blame thee – though it be my lot
To strongly – wrongly – vainly – love thee still. –

Elizabeth Barrett Browning 1806–1861 Robert Browning 1812–1889

In the summer of 1849, in the small Tuscan town of Bagni de Lucca which Byron had once made his home, Elizabeth Barrett Browning showed her husband Robert a sequence of sonnets secretly written thoughout their courtship. Under the last of her now famous *Sonnets from the Portuguese* is written the simple statement 'Married – September 12th/1846'. Why, at this particular point in time, did she decide to reveal her testament of love? Perhaps a period of such great emotional intensity demanded the gesture. A son, Robert Wiedemann (always known as 'Pen') had been born to Elizabeth (now forty-three), after much difficulty, on 9 March, yet barely a week later, their joy was dashed by the sudden death of Robert's mother whom he had not seen for over two years. The younger man – he was thirty-six – must have been greatly comforted by his wife's assurance, which can be read in perhaps the most famous of her sonnets (opposite), that:

> I love thee to the depth & breadth & height
> My soul can reach, when feeling out of sight
> For the ends of Being and Ideal Grace.

Robert and Elizabeth met on 20 May 1845, following a fervid correspondence which had begun early in that year with him famously declaring, that 'I do, as I say, love these Books with all my heart – and I love you too'. The romance blossomed. Elizabeth's father was opposed to her marrying and so, one week after their clandestine union in St Marylebone Church, they eloped to Italy and settled in Florence, where they made 'Casa Guidi' their home. Elizabeth's literary reputation was by now well established, with her *Poems* of 1844 leading to speculation that she might well become poet laureate. Robert, who like Elizabeth was largely self-educated, was less well known; indeed, his poem *Sordello*, published in 1840, had been poorly received by the critics.

For the next fourteen years the couple remained at 'Casa Guidi', apart from two visits to London (where conciliatory approaches to her father failed) and Paris. Elizabeth's reputation soared with a collected edition of poems (including her sonnets) appearing in 1850 to be followed a year later by *Casa Guidi Windows*, a passionate poetic defence of Italian independence. *Aurora Leigh*, her innovative 'novel in verse' about a woman writer was an immediate success and has come to be seen as an important early feminist text. Her stature was such that she easily shook off censure from the English critics for her pro-Italian, anti-English *Poems before Congress* of 1860.

RIGHT:

The American writer Nathaniel Hawthorne described Elizabeth Barrett Browning as 'a pale small person scarcely embodied at all', with eyes so bright and dark 'that there is not such another figure in the world'. This portrait of 1859 was painted by Field Talfourd.

RIGHT:

The English *Dictionary of National Biography* states that 'Browning was below the middle height, but broadly built and of great muscular strength, which he retained throughout his life in spite of his indifference to all athletic exercises'. His 'full and lustrous' hair is much in evidence in this engraved portrait by J.C. Armytage of 1844.

OPPOSITE:

The manuscript draft of perhaps the most famous of Elizabeth Barrett Browning's *Sonnets from the Portuguese*. The sequence traces her growing love for Robert Browning, who nicknamed her 'my little Portuguese', in reference to her dark complexion.

XLIII

How do I love thee ? Let me count the ways !—
I love thee to the depth & breadth & height
My soul can reach, when feeling out of sight
For the ends of Being and Ideal Grace.
I love thee to the level of everyday's
Most quiet need, by sun & candlelight—
I love thee freely, as men strive for Right,—
I love thee purely, as they turn from Praise !.
I love thee with the passion, put to use
In my old griefs ; and with my childhood's faith !
I love thee with the love I seemed to lose
With my lost Saints !— I love thee with the breath,
Smiles, tears, of all my life !— and, if God choose,
I shall but love thee better after death .

ABOVE:
This lifecast of the Browning's hands was taken by their friend Harriet Hosmer in 1853. It is a fitting permanent memorial to their deep devotion to one another.

The following year Elizabeth, always physically frail, succumbed to an affliction of the lungs and on 29 June died in her husband's arms, aged fifty-five. Shattered, Browning left Florence for London, never to return. Relentlessly applying himself to his work, he now began quickly to build upon the success he had achieved with the collection *Men and Women* of 1855, which included perhaps his most famous love poem, 'Love Among the Ruins'. Among the astonishing volume of acclaimed works which ensued (much of it tinged with melancholy and doubt), was his masterpiece *The Ring and the Book*. Browning's epic, philosophically involved poem, woven around a late-seventeenth-century account of murder and published in four monthly instalments from 1868, was inspired by a collection of documents he discovered in a 'square old yellow Book' bought from a market stall in Florence.

Accolades and awards showered down upon Browning in his later years. The founding of a society devoted to him in 1881 was an astonishing, albeit somewhat embarrassing honour. In 1878 he returned to Italy for the first time since the death of his beloved Elizabeth and it was here, in Venice, that he died on 12 December 1889. Browning had said that if he died in Italy he would wish to be buried with his wife. The closure of the Protestant cemetery in Florence prevented this and Pen therefore arranged for his father to lie among the poets in Westminster Abbey.

LEFT:
The Brownings lived in a flat in 'Casa Guidi' (pictured here), in Florence, from 1847–61.

OPPOSITE:
The first page of the manuscript of Robert Browning's epic poem 'The Ring and the Book' inspired by a 'square old yellow book' bought at a market in Florence.

1. The Ring and the Book.

Do you see this Ring?

'Tis Rome-work, made to match
(By Castellani's imitative craft)
Etrurian circlets found, some happy morn,
After a dropping April; found alive
Spark-like 'mid unearthed slope-side figtree-roots
That roof old tombs at Chiusi: soft, you see,
Yet crisp as jewel-cutting. There's one trick,
(Craftsmen instruct me) one approved device
And but one, fits such slivers of pure gold
As this was,—such mere oozings from the mine,
Virgin as oval tawny pendent tear
At beehive-edge when ripened combs o'erflow,—
To bear the file's tooth and the hammer's tap;
Since hammer needs must widen out the round,
And file emboss it fine with lily-flowers,
Ere the stuff grow a ring-thing right to wear.
That trick is, the artificer melts up wax
With honey, so to speak; he mingles gold
With gold's alloy, and, duly tempering both,
Effects a manageable mass, then works.
But his work ended, once the thing a ring,
Oh, there's repristination! Just a spirt
Of the proper fiery acid o'er its face,
And forth the alloy unfastened flies in fume;
While, self-sufficient now, the shape remains,
The rondure brave, the lilied loveliness,

Emily Brontë 1818–1848

ABOVE:
This portrait of Emily by her brother Branwell, stored away and forgotten for many years, was not discovered until 1914, eighty years after it was painted as part of a family group, the rest of which has not survived.

Emily has often been acclaimed as the most imaginative of the four Brontë children. After the death of her mother in 1821 she was raised with her brother Branwell and her two sisters Charlotte and Anne by her Irish-born father, the Anglican curate of Haworth. The cloistered life of the children in an isolated village on the edge of the Yorkshire moors brought them very close to each other. They devoured the books in their father's library and began writing stories and poems from an early age.

Eccentric, stubborn and fiercely independent, Emily attended a local school only briefly and was then educated mostly at home: her passionate attachment to the parsonage and its wild surroundings led to acute homesickness whenever she was away from it. She worked for a while as a governess near Halifax and in 1842 spent some time studying languages in Brussels with Charlotte, but seized the chance to return home as soon as she could and spent the rest of her life there, dying of tuberculosis (and refusing to see a doctor until the very end) three months after her brother Branwell, in December 1848.

Emily's only novel, *Wuthering Heights*, although criticised when it was published in 1847 for being excessively violent, morbid and histrionic, is now regarded as one of the masterpieces of nineteenth-century fiction. Virginia Woolf praised it as a work that could 'free life from a dependence on fact'. She is also recognised as one of the most original, lyrical and visionary poets of her time. The poem reproduced here, from her 'Gondal' notebook, is written in the characteristically 'microscopic' hand adopted by all the Brontë children for their imaginative writings. Their father, Patrick, was afraid that this tiny writing would ruin their eyesight and once presented Charlotte with a notebook inscribed: 'All that is written in this book must be in a good, plain and <u>legible</u> hand.' Gondal, an imaginary world created by Emily and Anne, provided the setting for many of Emily's poems; the initials and names attached to them represent characters in the great Gondal epic, of which nothing in prose remains. This world was intensely real to her: in a journal entry at the age of sixteen she interspersed descriptions of music lessons and potato peeling in the kitchen with the excited declaration that 'The Gondals are discovering the interior of Gaaldine'.

RIGHT:
A watercolour by Emily of her dog, entitled 'Keeper – from life' and dated 24 April 1838.

OPPOSITE:
Shown opposite is the first page of the manuscript volume containing Emily Brontë's 'Gondal Poems'. Emily notes that the poems were 'Transcribed Feb[r]uary 1844', presumably from her own final drafts, but she continued to make additions down to 13 May 1848. Charlotte has added pencil additions and revisions throughout the manuscript. Not a manuscript trace remains of Emily's most famous work, *Wuthering Heights*.

Emily Jane Brontë . ⁓⁓⁓ Transcribed February 2nd 1844

Gondal Poems

A.G.A. ———— March 6th 1837

There shines the moon, at noon of night,
Vision of Glory - Dream of light!
Holy as heaven - undimmed and pure,
Looking down on the lonely moor -
And lonelier still beneath her ray
That drear moor stretches far away
Till it seems strange that aught can lie
Beyond its zone of silver sky =

Bright moon - dear moon! when years have past
My weary feet return at last -
And still upon Lake Elnor's breast
Thy solemn rays serenely rest
And still the Firwoods sighing wave
Like mourners over Elbë's grave
And Earth's the same but Oh to see
How wildly Time has altered me!
Am I the being nothing long ago
Sat watching by that water side
The light of life expiring slow
From his fair cheek and brow of pride?
Not oft these mountains feel the shine
Of such a day-as fading then,
Cast from its fount of gold divine
A last smile on the loathing plain
And Kissed the forest peaks of snow
That gleaming on the horizon shine
As if in summers warmest glow
Stern winter claimed a softer throne -
And there he lay among the bloom
His rich blood dyed a deeper hue
Shuddering to feel the ghastly gloom
That coming death around him threw -

Charlotte Brontë 1816–1855

ABOVE:

A portrait of Charlotte Brontë by
George Richmond, 1850.

BELOW:

The British Library holds an excellent collection of Brontë juvenilia. This is the title and first page of a tiny manuscript (measuring three by four inches) of a short story entitled 'The Search after Hapiness' (sic), composed when Charlotte was thirteen and written in the minute hand she used in imitation of print. It is set in the children's imaginary city of 'Glass Town', and Charlotte's hero, the Duke of Wellington, plays an important part.

Of the Brontës, Charlotte's literary legacy is undoubtedly the richest, yet although her voice is distinctively her own, the source of her inspiration and the pattern of her career make it difficult to isolate her efforts from those of her siblings. Indeed, it was with them that she started to write and recite her juvenile stories, several of which survive in a stupendously small 'print' hand, bound in brown sugar paper.

While Emily and Anne wrote tales of Gondal, Charlotte and Branwell conjured up the kingdom of Angria: each imaginary world a welcome escape, no doubt, from that of the parsonage, with the overcrowded graveyard pushing up against its walls from one side and the moors exposing it to wilderness and the elements on the other. Charlotte left Haworth in 1831 to attend a school in Roe Head, and later returned to teach there before working as a governess. It was in Brussels, where she travelled with her sister Emily to study languages, that she fell in love with her Professor, M. Héger. Her letters to him, rescued from destruction by his wife (who sewed up their torn pieces) are now in the British Library.

Charlotte's unhappy return to Yorkshire was followed by a failed attempt to set up her own school. In 1846 a volume of verse entitled *Poems by Currer, Ellis and Acton Bell* (pseudonyms based on the sisters' initials) appeared, and by this time each of them had written a novel. Charlotte's, entitled *The Professor*, was rejected by her publisher, but her second (and most famous), *Jane Eyre*, appeared in 1847 under the imprint of Smith, Elder & Co., the only publishing house to write her an encouraging letter about her earlier work. *Shirley* followed in 1849, after the early deaths of her brother and sisters, and *Villette* (still under the name Currer Bell) in 1853. In the following year, having turned down three earlier suitors, she married her father's curate, Arthur Nicholls, but died only a few months later, in the early stages of pregnancy.

OPPOSITE:

This emotional passage from the manuscript of *Jane Eyre* describes the moment when Mr Rochester asks Jane, the plain and penniless governess, to marry him. She accepts the proposal with trusting alacrity. The manuscript was written out with amazing speed by Charlotte between 16 and 19 March 1847 and sent to Smith, Elder & Co. on 24 August. It is a beautiful example of what her biographer, Elizabeth Gaskell, described as her 'clear, legible, delicate traced writing'. Although essentially a fair copy transcribed from earlier drafts, Charlotte has been unable to resist the occasional alteration, as is evident here in one of the text's most crucial moments.

His face was very much agitated and very much flushed, and there were strong workings in the features and strange gleams in the eyes.

"Oh Jane, you torture me!" he exclaimed "With that searching and yet faithful and generous look — you torture me!"

"How can I do that? If you are true and your offer real, my only feeling to you must be gratitude and devotion — that cannot torture."

"Gratitude!" he ejaculated, and added wildly "Jane accept me quickly — say, Edward, give me my name, Edward, I will marry you."

"Are you in earnest? Do you truly love me? Do you sincerely wish me to be your wife ~~marry you~~?"

"I do — and if an oath is necessary to satisfy you — I swear it."

"Then Sir — I will marry you."

"Edward — my little wife!"

"Dear Edward!"

"Come to me — come to me entirely now." said he, and added in his deepest tone, speaking in my ear as his cheek was laid on mine, "Make my happiness — I will make yours."

"God, pardon me!" he subjoined erelong "And man, meddle not with me; I have her and will hold her."

"There is no one to meddle Sir; I have no kindred to interfere."

"No — that is the best of it." he said and if I had loved him less

Anne Brontë 1820–1849

RIGHT:
A watercolour of Anne by
Charlotte, dated 1834.

Anne Brontë, the youngest of the surviving Brontë children, was greatly influenced by her aunt, Elizabeth Branwell, a fervent Wesleyan who came to live at the Haworth parsonage after their mother's death. Anne was meeker and quieter than her siblings, among whom she felt perhaps the greatest affinity for Emily; together they invented the fantastic Gondal in which to set their stories and poems. Unlike Emily, however, Anne forced herself to go out into the world, first (with her sister Charlotte) to school at Roe Head, and then, in 1839, to work for two periods as a governess, the second time for the distinctly unsympathetic Robinson family at Thorp Green Hall, near York. In 1843 her volatile brother Branwell joined her there as a tutor, and became romantically – and disastrously – involved with Mrs Robinson. The episode must have been acutely painful for his sister and resulted in his returning in disgrace to Haworth, where he took to drink and opium, a combination which led to his rapid decline and death five years later.

Anne's unhappy and difficult experiences as a governess were revisited in her first novel, *Agnes Grey*, published in 1847. This appeared under the pseudonym 'Acton Bell', as did a selection of her poems, including those of her sisters, in 1846. Her second novel, *The Tenant of Wildfell Hall*, drew upon her brother's unfortunate experiences in the portrayal of its main character – a source of inspiration which much upset her sister Charlotte. Later commentators, however, have come to recognise this willingness to grapple with difficult social issues as one of Anne's great strengths as a writer. In *Agnes Grey* she broke new ground in bringing to wide attention the poverty and anxiety suffered by 'droves of spirit-broken governesses'. In this, of course, she wrote from the heart.

Charlotte was at Anne's side when she died of tuberculosis on 28 May 1849. Charlotte, who had taken her to Scarborough, on the Yorkshire coast, wrote to a friend that 'she died without severe struggle, trusting in God – thankful for release from a suffering life – deeply assured that a better existence lay before her.' She was buried in Scarborough, unlike the rest of her family who lie in their vault in Haworth.

LEFT:
A page from a letter written by Charlotte Brontë to her friend and publisher W. S. Williams, in which she sadly describes Anne's death, remarking on the doctor's surprise at her sister's 'fixed tranquillity of spirit and settled longing to be gone'.

OPPOSITE:
Reproduced here is the close of Anne's sombre, soul-searching poem 'Self-Communion', which she began in 1847, and the opening of the shorter verse 'The Narrow Way', which she wrote on 24 April 1848. The writing, although clear enough, has a rather stiff quality much in contrast to that of her sister Charlotte.

And still hast borne, and didst[47]
        not faint;—
Oh, this would be reward indeed!"

"Press forward, then, without complaint;
Labour and love — and such shall
        be thy meed."

                        April 17th 1848
333 lines.   A. B.

─────────

Believe not those who say
        upward
The heavenward path is smooth,
Lest thou shouldst stumble in the way
And faint before the truth.

It is the only road
        Unto the   perfect
That tends to realms of joy;
        he
But this who seeks that blest abode
Must all his powers employ.

Bright hopes and pure delights
Always Upon his course may beam,

Charles Dickens 1812–1870

The accession of Queen Victoria on 20 June 1837 saw also the shining star that was Dickens's career very much in the ascendant. *Oliver Twist* had begun its monthly serialization in January that year and, flushed with his success, Dickens moved with his wife and baby into the comfort of a new house in Doughty Street, London (now a delightful museum devoted to the author). In November, two days before the Queen opened her first Parliament, he signed the agreement for the writing of *Nicholas Nickleby* and the first instalment appeared the following March.

RIGHT:

Dickens in 1839, taken from a coloured version of the engraving which prefaced the first bound edition of *Nicholas Nickleby*. The original portrait was by Daniel Maclise.

For Dickens, of course, it had been no mean feat to reach this point. The son of a kindly but improvident naval clerk whose indifference to thrift brought him to a debtors' prison, the young Charles was to experience a misery that struck deep. One feels that by portraying the fearful abuse of children in his first two novels he was purging something vile from his past. The heightened social conscience he acquired from his apprenticeship as a journalist and Parliamentary reporter lies behind his reproachful reference to 'the monstrous neglect of Education in England' in his preface to the 1848 edition of the novel.

The manuscript of *Nicholas Nickleby* has survived only in fragments. Two are in the United States, one in Doughty Street and the fourth, which for a time had had an owner in Switzerland, was acquired by The British Library in 1971. It owes its early survival to the perspicacity of Charles Hicks, the foreman in the firm of Bradbury and Evans, Dickens's publishers. The manuscript comprises twenty-two leaves of the author's draft of chapter fifteen, with a number of deletions and revisions. Evident from the folio shown here is his reluctance to lose a felicitous phrase, for the crossed-out 'unexpected abstraction' is relocated to an earlier part of the sentence.

MR. SQUEERS AND MRS. SLIDERSKEW UNCONSCIOUS OF VISITORS

LEFT:

Dickens had made a preparatory foray into Yorkshire in 1838, to see for himself what conditions in certain schools were like, taking the artist Hablot Browne ('Phiz') with him. Here we have one of the resulting illustrations to *Nicholas Nickleby*.

OPPOSITE:

This page from a portion of the manuscript of *Nicholas Nickleby* is full of interest. Dickens's bold and bounding hand applies itself to the page in a manner which shows, even at this early stage in his career, a huge confidence and professionalism. The graphic way in which he marks out the epitome at the head of his page from the main body of text shows him almost urging the manuscript into print, while the reference to 'No. V' reminds us that the work first appeared in instalments.

Chapter XV.

Acquaints the reader with the cause and origin
of the interruption described in the last
chapter, and with some other matters ne=
cessary to be known.

Newman Noggs scrambled in violent
haste up stairs with the steaming beverage
which he had so unceremoniously snatched
from the table of Mr. Kenwigs, and
indeed from the very grasp of the water-
rate collector who was eyeing the contents
of the tumbler at the moment of its unexpected abstraction
with lively marks of
satisfaction visible in his countenance
and looked not a little dismayed
at the sudden abstraction and bore
his prize straight to his own back
garret, where, footsore and nearly
shoeless, wet, and dirty, jaded,
and disfigured with every mark of
fatiguing travel, sat Nicholas and
Smike, the at once the cause and
partner of his toil, both perfectly

RIGHT:

A cartoon of Dickens, portraying him as editor of *All the Year Round,* the periodical which succeeded *Household Words* in 1859.

Dickens speaks, at the beginning of the accompanying manuscript draft of his 'Proposals for a National Jest-Book', of Britain's great need over the previous two years for an official joker. They had been grim years indeed: military incompetence and government bungling had led to the disastrous campaign against Russia in the Crimea in 1854 when Balaklava became a cemetery and Scutari a pesthouse. The public mind, chastened by the experience, became possessed of a deep distrust of the military system and of many cherished institutions. But, as André Maurois observed in his lectures on Dickens, the Englishman 'has a longing to believe that all is for the best…in the best of impossible worlds. So whatever is bad ought to be denied. And this is a function admirably fulfilled by humour. It dismisses evil on to a plane of absurdity.'

Dickens, fully acquainted with the world's evils since his poverty-stricken childhood, had by 1856 achieved fame and security. Indeed he was then in the middle of writing *Little Dorrit*, the last of the three great dark novels concerned with social issues. Twelve major novels were behind him and he brought to *Household Words*, published between 1850 and 1859, his customary amazing vigour and intensity.

This manuscript, once in the vast Dickens collection of John Furber Dexter (1847–1927), was purchased by the British Museum Library in 1968. It found an apt home for, as Dickens says on the verso of the folio illustrated here, the collected facetious treasures of a National Jest-Book should be 'preserved, and (in course of time), catalogued by Signor Panizzi in the British Museum'. By the end of his life Dickens himself was a national institution and his impressive burial in Westminster Abbey expressed the national mood.

RIGHT:

Dickens's autograph draft of 'Proposals for a National Jest-Book', in which he asserts that 'it has been ascertained within the last two years, that Britannia is in want of nothing but an official joker', was published in *Household Words*, on 3 May 1856.

Alfred Lord Tennyson 1809–1892

ABOVE:
This august photographic portrait of Tennyson with eyeglass and book was taken on 28 February 1877 and included in a short-lived periodical called *The Portrait,* published in the same year.

Tennyson grew up in rural Lincolnshire, one of the twelve children of a gifted but emotionally disturbed and sometimes frighteningly erratic clergyman. In later years he said of his wife 'The peace of God came into my life before the altar when I wedded her', something not lightly uttered. With one brother long shut away in an asylum for the insane, another voluntarily seeking help in one, and with a sister-in-law ultimately dying in one after years of suffering, Tennyson had first-hand experience of the disjointed mind.

'Maud' is a complex study of a deranged mind. Of all his poems, this is the one he most frequently chose to read aloud in company – and often in tears. What nerves was it touching on? It is a rich tapestry: its 'hero' is socially displaced, as Tennyson had been in the 1840s; it revolves round a love affair redolent of one he had experienced in the 1830s; it is disturbed by the rancour of mercenary family feuds which he had known in his childhood. Tennyson, nevertheless, disavowed any autobiographical intent at work in the poem and he strongly distanced himself from his hero's idea of finding a resolution in the Crimean campaign.

The poem was published in July 1855 and the manuscript dates from the previous year. Here we have a fair copy of part of one of the lyrics in the poem and a working draft of another. It was written at Farringford on the Isle of Wight, Tennyson's home since November 1853. F. T. Palgrave visited Tennyson several times in December 1854 and it was on one such occasion that the poet gave Palgrave this manuscript. He later tipped it, together with other Tennyson manuscript poems, into his copy of the 1894 edition of Tennyson's *Works* and it eventually came to the British Museum Library in 1941.

RIGHT:
Julia Margaret Cameron's photographic image of Maud has her standing by passion flowers. The model was one of Cameron's domestic staff and the picture appeared among her illustrations to the miniature edition of Tennyson's *Idylls of the King and other poems* (1875).

Birds in the high hall-garden
    Were crying & calling to her
Where is Maud, Maud, Maud,
    One is come to woo her.

Look! a horse at the door
    And little King Charles is snarling
Go back; my lord, across the moor.
    You are not her darling.

solid ground
Let not the solid earth fail
    faith beneath
And gape under my feet
                        her friend
Before my life find out
What other have found so sweet
Then let come what come may
                what may if I go mad,
To a life that has been too sad
I shall have had my day.

                        endure
Let not the sweet Heaven fail
    not
Close & darken above me
Before I am quite quite sure
                pure in one
That Maud doth love me
                                what come may
Then let me come
What matter if I go mad
I shall have lived my day.

RIGHT:
The 'high hall garden', referred to
by Tennyson in his fair copy draft
of a lyric from 'Maud', looks back
to Harrington Hall near his home
in Lincolnshire where Rosa Baring
stayed. She is thought to be a
source for the image of Maud.
The heavily worked drafts on the
lower part of the sheet belong
to a different section of the poem
from the fair copy above.

Lewis Carroll (Charles Lutwidge Dodgson) 1832–1898

ABOVE:

Charles Dodgson from a portrait by Sir Hubert Herkomer.

Lewis Carroll was the literary pseudonym adopted by Charles Lutwidge Dodgson, a shy, stuttering and academically gifted mathematics tutor at Christ Church, Oxford University. The son of a curate in Daresbury, Cheshire, he was the third in a lively and happy family of eleven children. The magazines that he edited for their amusement reveal an early fascination with parody, word games and puzzles, all of which gloriously emerge in *Alice's Adventures in Wonderland* (1865).

What might well be regarded as the world's best known children's story began on a boating trip during a 'golden afternoon' in July 1862, with a 'fairy tale' woven from Dodgson's fertile imagination for the three young daughters of the Dean of Christ Church. Alice Liddell, its ten-year-old heroine, begged him to write it out for her (as indeed he did), but it did not appear in published form until 1865, when it was an immediate success. Its sequel, *Through the Looking-Glass, and What Alice Found There*, followed in 1871, with both books memorably illustrated by John Tenniel. Among Dodgson's other works, *The Hunting of the Snark* (1876), a long, fantastical poem, is perhaps the most successful. He was also a prolific letter writer (his register of letters sent and received ran to nearly 98,721 entries) and diarist, and a successful amateur photographer, with a particular gift for photographing his young friends. His charming, often poignant photographs of Alice Liddell are amongst the most famous and sought-after of the Victorian period.

Reproduced opposite is a page from the original manuscript of the first 'Alice' story, entitled 'Alice's Adventures under Ground'. Dodgson took two years to write it out, in a neat hand which would be easy for a child to read, adding his own charming illustrations (here Alice is shown with the 'little magic bottle', the contents of which cause her to start 'growing and growing'). The finished manuscript was bound and finally presented to Alice as an early Christmas present in November 1864. She treasured it for many years until financial difficulties compelled her to sell it at auction in 1928. It was purchased by an American collector but returned to the British people in 1946 by a group of American benefactors in recognition of their strong alliance during the Second World War.

LEFT:

Dodgson's diary entry for 4 July 1862 (written in his normal hand) describes the river outing to Godstow during which he entertained the three young Liddell sisters with the enchanting story of 'Alice's Adventures under Ground'.

OPPOSITE:

This page from Dodgson's original manuscript of 'Alice's Adventures under Ground', demonstrates the great facility with which he was able to put pen to paper. It is written in what he called his 'manuscript print' hand. Although the charming drawings are Dodgson's own (filled in after he had written the text), he didn't feel they were good enough to publish, and asked John Tenniel to undertake the task on his behalf for this and subsequent books.

than she expected; before she had drunk half the bottle, she found her head pressing against the ceiling, and she stooped to save her neck from being broken, and hastily put down the bottle, saying to herself "that's quite enough— I hope I sha'n't grow any more— I wish I hadn't drunk so much!"

Alas! it was too late: she went on growing and growing, and very soon had to kneel down: in another minute there was not room even for this, and she tried the effect of lying down, with one elbow against the door, and the other arm curled round her head. Still she went on growing, and as a last resource she put one arm out of the window, and one foot up the chimney, and said to herself "now I can do no more— what will become of me?"

Edward Lear 1812–1888

Though Edward Lear was an epileptic, a repressed homosexual and a depressive dogged by feelings of failure and loneliness, he charmed all who met him. To understand why, one need not go much beyond the 'pome' illustrated here with its accompanying self-portrait with Foss, Lear's cat.

One hundred years after his death, a memorial tablet honouring Lear was laid in Westminster Abbey, a long way from his lonely grave in San Remo, about forty kilometres east of Monte Carlo. He would have been surprised that he is commemorated in Poet's Corner, for he saw himself primarily as a painter and the five books of nonsense verse he published between 1846 and 1877 hardly matched, in his thinking, the achievement of his friend Tennyson who lies nearby in the Abbey.

Lear's earliest professional work was as an ornithological draughtsman, concentrating upon the parrot family. Three types of parrot are indeed named after him, so important was his work in this field. But in 1837 Lear abandoned ornithology, concentrating thereafter on landscape-painting and from this point he became a restless wanderer in Europe, North Africa, the Middle East and India. His six travel-books containing his own illustrations were published between 1841 and 1870 and drew even the attention of Queen Victoria, who had Lear give her drawing lessons. Equally important are his illustrations to selected lines from Tennyson's poems.

The letter here was written from the Villa Emily where in 1871 Lear found refuge after so many years of rootlessness. It was built facing the Mediterranean Sea and he eased his solitariness by adding Foss to the household in 1872. However, even as this letter was being written (to the father of the girl who inspired the poem), Lear – who 'weeps by the side of the ocean' – was distressed by the building of a large new hotel, blocking his view completely. In 1880, therefore, he built the Villa Tennyson in an open spot nearby, an exact replica of the Villa Emily, so that Foss might not be unduly disturbed. Foss died, aged fifteen, in 1887. The letter was purchased by the British Library in 1981.

RIGHT:
Lear in 1881, from *The Later Letters of Edward Lear* (1911).

BELOW:
Lear's early work as an ornithological draughtsman, concentrating upon the parrot family, is shown in this modern reproduction of a lithographic illustration which first appeared (along with some forty-two others) in his work *Illustrations of the Family of Psittacidae* (1832). Three types of parrot are named after him.

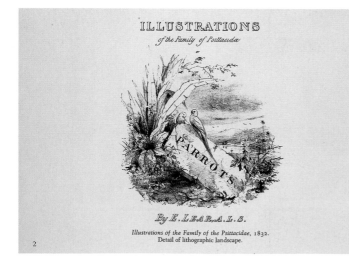

ILLUSTRATIONS
of the Family of Psittacidæ

PARROTS

By E. LEAR, A.L.S.

Illustrations of the Family of the Psittacidae, 1832.
Detail of lithographic landscape.

2

OPPOSITE:
Illustrated here is Lear's letter and 'Pome', 'How pleasant to know Mr Lear!', sent to Archdeacon Bevan and dated 14 January 1879. The poem, complete with drawing of himself – 'His beard it resembles a wig' – and Foss – 'His body is perfectly spherical' – varies in several ways from the text as published in 1895.

"How pleasant to know Mr. Lear!"

[From a Photograph.

1

"How pleasant to know Mr. Lear!"
Who has written such volumes of stuff!
Some think him ill-tempered & queer, —
But a few think him pleasant enough.

2

His mind is concrete & fastidious; —
His nose is remarkably big; —
His visage is more or less hideous; —
His beard it resembles a wig.

3

He has ears, & 2 eyes, & 10 fingers, —
(Leastways if you reckon 2 thumbs;)
Long ago he was one of the singers,
But now he is one of the dumms.

4

He sits in a beautiful parlour,
With hundreds of books on the wall;
He drinks a great deal of Marsala,
But never gets tipsy at all.

5

He has many friends, laymen & clerical;
Foss is the name of his cat;
His body is perfectly spherical; —
He wears a brown runcible hat.

6

When he walks in a waterproof white
The children run after him so!
Calling out, — "He's come out in his night-
=gown, that crazy old Englishman, — O!"

7

He weeps by the side of the ocean,
He weeps on the top of the hill;
He purchases pancakes & lotion,
And shrimps, from the Chocolate mill.

8

He reads, but he cannot speak, Spanish;
He cannot abide Ginger-beer —
Ere the days of his pilgrimage vanish, —
"How pleasant to know Mr. Lear!"

George Eliot (Mary Anne Evans) 1819–1880

ABOVE:

An engraved portrait of George Eliot aged thirty, by G. J. Stodart from a painting by M. D'Albert-Durade. The engraving is inserted in a counterfeit pamphlet edition of her poem 'Agatha' from the collection of the sometime forger T. J. Wise.

George Eliot's *Middlemarch* has been described as one of the greatest works of realism in the English language. Indeed, as an author whose rich and multi-layered narratives are intimately connected with British history and national life, perhaps only Dickens stands as her equal among novelists of the nineteenth century. The very subtitle of *Middlemarch* – 'A study of provincial life' – signals an approach in which profound moral, psychological and political questions are addressed through subtle observations of the local and the everyday. The novel was published in four volumes, 1871–72.

Born Mary Anne Evans (which she later changed to Marian Evans) to a Warwickshire land agent, she was sent to a boarding school whose headmistress inspired in her strong evangelical beliefs. Her thinking later underwent an important transformation, however, in which she held that religious belief is a condition of human rather than abstract concerns. 'One lives by faith in human goodness', she remarked in a letter of 13 March 1870 to her philanthropic friend Jane Senior, 'the only guarantee that there can be any other source of Goodness in the universe'. This very immediate philosophy, together with a deeply held conviction in the importance of duty and service, is perhaps what gives Eliot's writing, above all else, its quality of enduring relevance. Three long stories in the series *Scenes of Clerical Life* (1857–58) were her first pieces of fiction to appear in print and her standing was immediately established with her first novel, *Adam Bede* (1859), her admiring readers having no idea who she was, or indeed whether she was a man or a woman. The real identity of the mysterious George Eliot, as she had decided to call herself in print, was widely known by the time her second novel, *The Mill on the Floss*, appeared in 1860. Further acclaimed novels followed, culminating with *Daniel Deronda* (1876), although she also turned her hand to poetry. Her last work was the satirical volume of essays *Impressions of Theophrastus Such* (1879), the last chapter of which (like *Daniel Deronda*) makes clear her revulsion for anti-Semitism.

BELOW:

Eliot's inscription to George Henry Lewes, at the beginning of the first manuscript volume of *Middlemarch*. Although Eliot refers to Lewes as her husband, he remained married to another (estranged) woman throughout their unconventional union.

Most of Eliot's literary manuscripts were bound and presented by her to her beloved George Henry Lewes, a man whom she regarded as her 'husband' despite his earlier undissolved marriage to another woman. They were returned to her after his death in 1878. Eliot married John Walter Cross, some twenty years her junior, in 1880, but died only seven months later of a sudden illness. She was buried in London's Highgate cemetery, next to Lewes. Her twenty-four volumes of manuscripts, containing all but three of her novels and poems, were deposited in the British Museum Library, in accordance with her wishes, so that her manuscripts might be available to the British people.

To my dear Husband George Henry Lewes, in this nineteenth year of our blessed union December, 1872.

OPPOSITE:

Shown here is the opening chapter of *Middlemarch*, preserved in the orginal manuscript volumes sent by Eliot to the printer. Even at this late stage she was making changes to the text.

Chapter I.

"Since I can do no good because a woman,
Reach constantly at something that is near it."
                        The Maid's Tragedy: Beaumont & Fletcher

Miss Brooke had that kind of beauty which seems
to be thrown into relief by poor dress. Her hand &
wrist were so finely formed that she could wear
sleeves not less bare of style than those in which the
Blessed Virgin appeared to Italian painters, & her
profile as well as her stature & bearing seemed to
gain the more dignity from her plain garments, which by
the side of provincial fashion gave her the im-
pressiveness of a fine quotation from the Bible, or from
one of our elder poets, in a paragraph of today's
newspaper. She was usually spoken of as being
remarkably clever, but with the addition that
her sister Celia had more common sense. Nevertheless
Celia wore scarcely more trimmings; & to Miss Brooke's
plain dressing was due to mixed conditions in most
of which her sister shared. The pride of being ladies
had something to do with it: the Brooke connexions,
though not exactly aristocratic, were unquestionably
"good": if you inquired backward for a generation or
two you would not find any yard-measuring or
parcel-tying forefathers; nothing lower than an admiral
or a clergyman; & there was even an ancestor dis-
cernible as a Puritan gentleman who served under
Cromwell, but had afterwards conformed, & had
managed to come out of all political troubles as the
proprietor of a respectable family estate. Young
women of such birth, living in a quiet country house,

& it were any to close observers
that her dress differed from her
sister's, & had a shade of
coquetry in its arrangements)

Christina Rossetti 1830–1894

ABOVE:

An engraved portrait of Christina Rossetti from a drawing of 1877 by her brother the Pre-Raphaelite artist Dante Gabriel Rossetti, published in *The Family Letters of Christina Georgina Rossetti* (1908), edited by her other brother, William.

This manuscript is an autograph fair copy of a short poem given by Christina Rossetti to her mother as a Valentine on 14 February 1884. On its accompanying leaf she has addressed her mother as the Queen of Hearts and because there are traces of folds resulting from the triangular envelope-like form of the latter leaf, we can be sure that this was the copy presented on the day.

The Valentine is one of eleven she gave to her mother between 1876 and 1886, all acquired by the Library from the sale of T. J. Wise's Ashley collection in 1938. A pencil note in Christina's hand on a separate sheet declares 'These <u>Valentines</u> had their origins from my dearest Mother's remarking that she had never received one _____ I, her CGR, ever after supplied one on the day; and so far as I recollect it was a <u>surprise</u> every time, she having forgotten all about it in the interim'.

The poem is loving but it is also a sad remembrancer of the domestic events of 1883–1884. Quite typical of its author, it carries no reference beyond the circumscribed world of family experience. The year 1883 saw the centenary of Christina's father's birth and its celebration in his native Italian town but it also saw the deaths of two relatives including her brother William's baby. She also suffered the loss of Charles Bagot Cayley, to whom she had had a tender and serious attachment since 1862. She had in fact made a solitary visit to his grave in Hastings only a month before she presented her Valentine to her mother. As he bequeathed her his writing-desk, one may wonder if the poem was actually written on it.

The marking of significant moments of time was a long-established practice in the Rossetti household; Christina's earliest poem, written when she was eleven, was a birthday tribute to her mother. Mrs Rossetti died, as old as the century, in 1886 and was buried in the family plot in Highgate Cemetery, her steadfastly loyal daughter joining her there eight years later.

RIGHT:

Torrington Square, Bloomsbury, London as it is today. Christina Rossetti lived at number 30 from 1876 to 1894.

OPPOSITE:

This is one of eleven Valentine greetings given by Christina Rossetti to her mother. She alludes to the experiences of the family – some joyful, some sad – over the course of the year 1883–1884.

1884.

Another year of joy & grief,
  Another year of hope & fear:
O Mother, is life long or brief?
  We hasten while we linger here.

But since we linger, love me still
  And bless me still, O Mother mine,
While hand in hand we scale life's hill,
  You Guide, & I your Valentine.

Thomas Hardy 1840–1928

ABOVE:

A cheerful photograph of Hardy, with cane and straw hat, taken in 1921.

RIGHT:

Hardy's 'A Reconsideration on my eighty sixth Birthday', written in ink with pencil corrections. It was published in 1926 under the title 'He never expected much'. Hardy's death two years later was mourned as the passing of English literature's 'most eminent figure' in newspapers all over the world. His ashes were placed, with great pomp and ceremony, in Westminster Abbey.

Thomas Hardy's parents encouraged early on the signs of creative sensitivity in their son, teaching him the violin and encouraging him to read widely. He went to school in Dorchester and then worked as an architectural assistant, in Dorset and London, until the enthusiastic reception of his second published novel, *Under the Greenwood Tree* (1872), spurred him into becoming a full-time writer. Over the next quarter century Hardy went on to create some of the best-loved novels in English literature, whose grandeur of theme emerges from an intensely human vision; but in 1895 the controversy surrounding the last, *Jude the Obscure*, distressed and disillusioned him so much that he returned to his first love, poetry, winning huge acclaim for his distinctive lyrical style and acute observation of human emotions. His marriage to Emma Gifford, in 1874, at first idyllic, was soon overtaken by great strain and unhappiness; it did, however, produce some of his most moving poems, written after her death in 1912. Two years later Hardy married a younger woman, Florence Dugdale, who was increasingly protective of him as he became a widely revered public figure, showered with medals and honorary degrees.

Reproduced here is a page from the heavily corrected manuscript of Hardy's novel *Tess of the D'Urbervilles*, subtitled 'A Pure Woman'. Its publication in three volumes in 1891 (it first appeared as an illustrated serial in the *Graphic Magazine*) created a sensation, with Hardy pilloried for his 'pessimism' and 'immorality'. Although hurt and offended – 'I have put in it the best of me', he later said – sales surged as a result. The manuscript was presented by Hardy to the British Museum Library, along with that of his novel *The Dynasts*, in 1911. Although its policy was not to accept the manuscripts of living authors, the Library was in this instance pleased to make an exception.

OPPOSITE:

The impressive complexity of Hardy's working method is much in evidence in this page from the manuscript draft of *Tess of the D'Urbervilles*. Instructions to move text, evidence of repagination, amendments (Tess was originally to be called Rose Mary), additions and determined deletions all point to a tremendous effort on the part of the author. Elsewhere in the manuscript, Hardy has colour-coded (in blue) differences between the texts for publication in serial and book form.

Fled

Tess

Tess had never before visited this part of the country, & yet she felt akin to the landscape. Not so very far to the left of her she could discern a dark patch in the scenery, which inquiry confirmed her in supposing to be trees, marking the environs of Kings-Bere — in the church of which parish lay the bones of her ancestors — her useless ancestors — lay entombed.

She had no admiration for them: Not a single material thing of all that had been theirs did she retain but the old silver spoon / yet to diverge from the direct route in order to glance a passing courtesy to which they were entitled, and at their resting-place was no serious task for so active a walker. Tess entered the church about two in the afternoon, and beheld for the first time in her life the spot where her father had spoken or sung to painfulness ever since Parson Tringham's announcement.

Here stood the tombs of the d'Urbervilles — formed of grey Purbeck-marble; canopied, altar-shaped, & plain; their carvings defaced & broken; their brasses torn from their matrices. Of all the reminders that she had ever received that they were socially an extinct family there was none so forcible as this spoliation.

She drew near to a dark stone, on which was inscribed:

[Blank line]

[Old English] "Ostium sepulchri antiquæ familiæ D'Urberville."

[Blank line] Tess did not read Latin, but she knew that this was the door of her ancestral sepulchre, & that the tall knights of whom her father chanted in his cups lay inside it in their leaden shrouds.

"Pooh — what's the good of thinking about them!" she said, with a sudden sigh. She left the church, & resumed her course.

"I have as much of mother as father in me, & she was only a dairymaid: all my prettiness comes from her."

For Volume 3, transfer this to p. 520.

Oscar Wilde 1854–1900

ABOVE:

Wilde, as presented in a rare
Hungarian edition (1911) of his play
Vera, or the Nihilists. Concerned
with sensitive issues of revolution
in Tsarist Russia, this was Wilde's
first play, written in 1881.

Oscar Wilde, the epitome of *fin de siècle* aestheticism and the greatest wit and conversationalist of his generation, is still among the most widely read and translated authors in the English language. By turns poet, journalist, writer of short stories, novelist and playwright, he was also a prolific correspondent. Born in Dublin, the son of a distinguished Irish surgeon and a well-known writer and literary hostess who published under the name 'Speranza', he attended a Protestant school. Here he began to excel at Classics and develop a reputation as a gifted conversationalist and story-teller before entering Trinity College, Dublin University. From Trinity, where he came under the spell of a lifelong infatuation with Greek culture and literature, he won a scholarship to Magdalen College, Oxford, where he shunned sport, cultivated a flamboyant aestheticism and proclaimed himself a disciple of Pater and his creed of 'art for art's sake'. He also covered himself in academic glory by winning the Newdigate Poetry Prize and gaining a double first in Classics.

In 1882, a year after the publication of his first volume of poems, Wilde embarked on a hugely successful lecture tour of America, returning determined to conquer the London social and literary worlds. Four years after his marriage to Constance Lloyd, he published in 1888 a volume of fairy stories, *The Happy Prince and other Tales*, originally written for his two young sons. Other stories followed, and in 1890 his disturbing and macabre novel, *The Picture of Dorian Gray*, caused a scandal when it first appeared in the American *Lippincott's Magazine*. In the following year he met Lord Alfred Douglas – the great, but ill-starred romance of his life – and a year later began his rapid theatrical rise with his first successful play, *Lady Windermere's Fan*. Shortly after the triumphant opening of *The Importance of Being Earnest* in February 1895, Wilde took the fatal decision to sue Douglas's father, the violent and erratic Marquess of Queensberry, for criminal libel, and so set in train the sequence of events which led to his own two-year imprisonment for homosexual offences and descent into public disgrace, poverty and exile. His early boast that 'Somehow or other, I'll be famous, and if not famous, notorious' had sadly proved true. A mere twelve years after publishing his first work of fiction, he was dead at the age of 46, buried in a pauper's grave on the outskirts of Paris.

LEFT:

An autograph draft of an early poem by
Wilde, entitled 'In the Gold Room'. It was
published in 1881 in his first collection,
Poems, which had a mixed critical reception: one reviewer dismissed its contents
as 'Swinburne and water'. Wilde's hand,
with its sporadic Greek 'e's and 'a's is quite
unmistakable.

ABOVE:

The British Library possesses an important collection of Wilde's manuscripts, including poems, letters (among them 'De Profundis,' his long letter to Douglas written in prison), and drafts of his plays. Reproduced here is an early draft, dating from 1894, of his fourth and final West End play, *The Importance of Being Earnest* (subtitled 'A Trivial Comedy for Serious People'). Written very quickly, with many changes and corrections, it is open at the famous 'handbag scene', in which the formidable Lady Bracknell (here called 'Lady Brancaster') interrogates Jack Worthing about his family history.

In 1923 John Quinn, an American collector of books and manuscripts, sold a number of autograph works he had bought from Joseph Conrad a decade earlier. To the author's considerable irritation, Quinn made a tenfold profit. From the early part of the twentieth century, literary manuscripts began to be collected with a hitherto unknown fervour. Indeed, such was the burgeoning demand that one may wonder whether all the many signatures and inked endorsements on Conrad's typewritten dramatisation of *The Secret Agent* (1922) arose as a natural consequence of the artist at work or were deliberately concocted to satisfy the bibliographical whims of his new patron, T. J. Wise.

With drafts from James Joyce's *Ulysses* recently being purchased by the Irish government for dramatic sums and debates continuing to rage about which international institutions have a right to collect the papers of which authors (dead or alive), the considerable interest in modern literary manuscripts shows little signs of abating. And nor should it. For all the suspicion which may surround the scrivening activities of cash-strapped Conrad in his later years (he had a taste for large houses and fast cars), the modern literary manuscript can be just as intellectually rich and culturally resonant as any boasting the romantic patina of a more distant age. For this reason, The British Library continues to augment its literary holdings with letters, notebooks, drafts, diaries and an extraordinary assortment of non-print media produced by writers of the twentieth and twenty-first centuries – including, as part of large personal archives, it should be stressed, a hat worn by G. K. Chesterton and a clay bowl fashioned by Gerald Durrell.

One of the most moving and impressive group of modern manuscripts to survive anywhere, must surely be those of the soldier poet Wilfred Owen. At the time of his death by machine gunfire in 1918, just one week before the signing of the Armistice, Owen had seen only five poems into print. Yet among his papers was discovered a remarkable body of work in various states of draft, some written at the front, others worked on with the help of Siegfried Sassoon on paper supplied by Craiglockhart Hospital where both men were sent to recuperate from the shattering effects of modern warfare. A heavily worked draft preface containing one of the most powerful statements of poetic principle ever formulated revealed to those he left behind

that the winner of a Military Cross had summoned up enough literary courage to offer a book for publication.

The modern literary manuscript often seems to have a remarkably intimate, revealing quality. Philip Larkin, a librarian as well as a poet, recognized this, perhaps, when he set to work censoring the earliest of his poetic notebooks before presenting it to The British Library. Yet even those poems which remain – together with the cutting advertising military-style boots which he evidently overlooked – invite us into a privileged personal realm. We see, in 'Wedding Wind', for example, the writer's easy, fluid facility with a conversational idiom, twist, flex and tie itself in knots as he struggles to articulate a profound emotional mood towards the poem's conclusion. And to the many who justifiably stand in awe of Sylvia Plath's poetry, with all its raw super-concentrated feeling and barely controlled energy, her manuscript copy of 'Ariel' must come as a revelation, written out, as it is, in a slow, round, childish hand and finished off with a naïve flower motif.

All the manuscripts chosen have the special marks of their respective authors stamped upon them: Virginia Woolf's favoured purple ink, W.H. Auden's syllabic notations, Katherine Mansfield's near illegible scrawl, Dylan Thomas's surprisingly meticulous hand, Ted Hughes's bounding, bible-black, gothic script, Harold Pinter's bold extravagant approach. All radiate something of what Larkin called the 'magical quality of manuscripts'.

Joseph Conrad 1857–1924

ABOVE:

A photograph of Conrad taken on his voyage to America in 1923.

Joseph Conrad, born to Polish nobility, had endured, by the age of eleven, a harsh exile in the snowy wastes of Russia, the slow and painful death of his mother from tuberculosis and the imprisonment and death of his father. A patchy education under the guardianship of his long-suffering uncle was followed by a move to Marseilles and a reckless period sailing the West Indies in the company – if his later lively recollections are to be believed – of smugglers and gun runners. A half-hearted suicide attempt following heavy gambling losses marked his twenty-first year, as did a decision to reinvent himself as an English sailor. Jozef Korzeniowski became Joseph Conrad, a British citizen who sailed the world for fifteen years. Another astonishing transformation occurred in 1893 when, now a master mariner, he gave up the sea, settled in the southern English countryside with his wife Jessie and two sons, and began to write, in his third language, some of the most celebrated works in the English literary tradition.

Conrad's writing, often drawing upon the strange and disturbing experiences of his own life is, in his own words, profoundly preoccupied with the 'single-minded attempt to render the highest kind of justice to the visible universe, by bringing to light the truth, manifold and one, underlying its every aspect'. For him this truth was often far from palatable. The uncompromising bleakness of much of his writing – perhaps reaching an apotheosis with the short but shattering *Heart of Darkness* – did little to endear Conrad to a mass audience unprepared to grapple with any work of literature whose purpose ventured beyond simple entertainment or instruction. When Conrad finally attained success, chiefly with the populist *Chance* in 1914, he had long since completed his best works, among them *Lord Jim* (1900) and *Nostromo* (1904). In his later years he moved from house to house (mostly in Kent), wrote profitable film scripts and became one of the first authors to benefit from the sale of his manuscripts. He died in Bishopsbourne, Kent, and is buried in Canterbury City Cemetery.

LEFT:

Conrad's somewhat superfluous signatures and endorsements were probably added to this page of his 1922 dramatisation of *The Secret Agent* for the benefit of T. J. Wise, to whom he sold the manuscript. Although his annotations are in this instance strong and relatively fluent, at this late stage in his writing career Conrad often suffered the symptoms of gout and preferred to dictate his work to his typist, Miss Hallowes. *The Secret Agent* originally appeared as a novel in 1907.

OPPOSITE:

Conrad's intensive drafting is shown in this manuscript fragment from *Nostromo*, which appeared in 1904. The process of composition was, for Conrad, typically arduous, and beset with all sorts of difficulties. Nevertheless, he had confidence in the work, writing to his agent in 1903: 'I have never worked so hard before – with so much anxiety. But the result is good. You know I take no credit to myself for what I do – and so I may judge my own performance. There is no mistake about this. You may take up a strong position when you offer it here. It is very genuine Conrad.'

Chap VII

(in the Intendencia of Sulaco Charles Gould was assuring Pedrito Montero
who had sent a request for his presence there, that he would never let
the mine pass out of his hands for the profit of a government

threat   At about that time Charles Gould was bringing forward his expressed
~~that with his notions of devoted fidelity Don Pepe would hesitate at~~
threat, in the Intendencia of Sulaco when he had been sent for by Pedrito Montero.
"You may rest assured he had said that I shall not leave
nothing.   With Don Pepe there Charles Gould could talk of the utter
the mine behind me for the profit of a government who had robbed him of
~~and complete destruction~~ of the San Tomé mine with the perfect assurance
who had broken faith robbed him of it. The Gould Concession could not be resumed.
his father had not desired it. The son would never surrender it. He would never surrender it alive.
~~of being taken seriously.~~   capable of
~~And once dead where was the power~~ resuscitating such an enterprise
in all its vigour and wealth out out of the ashes and ruin of destruction? There was none in the
country. And where was the skill, and capital abroad that would condescend to touch such
an ill-omened corpse. Charles Gould talked in the impassive tone which had for many years
served to conceal his anger and contempt. He suffered. He was disgusted with what he had to say. It was
~~imperium in imperio were looking at each other thoughtfully in Father~~
too much like heroics. In him the strictly practical instinct was in bad accord with the almost
mystic view he took of his right. The Gould concession was symbolic of abstract justice. Let the heaven fall. But
~~Father excellency Charles~~ Gould was talking of it in the audience room of
since the San Tomé mine had developed into world wide fame his threat had enough force and effective-
ness to reach the rudimentary intelligence of Pedro Montero wrapped up as it was in the futilities of historical anecdotes
~~the Intendencia where he had been sent for by Pedro Montero.~~   A table
The Gould concession was a serious asset in the country's finance, and what was more in the private budgets
of many officials. It was known. It was said. It was credible. Every minister of interior drew a
~~a chair a wooden bedstead had been found for His Excellency who after~~
salary from the San Tomé mine. It was natural. And Pedrito intended to be minister of the interior and president
of the council. The duc de Morny had occupied those high posts during the second French Empire with conspicuous advantage to himself.
~~having had his siesta very necessary after the labours and the pomps of~~
A table, a chair, a wooden bedstead had been procured for His Excellency, who after a short siesta rendered
absolutely necessary by the labours and the pomps of his
~~His~~ entry into Sulaco had been getting hold of the administrative machine
giving orders   Alone with Charles Gould in the
by making appointments and signing proclamations.   ~~They were alone in the~~

audience
~~his~~ room ~~and~~ His Excellency managed with his well known skill to conceal his
annoyance
~~fury~~ and consternation. He had begun at first to
~~talk~~ San Tomé mine   He had talked to Charles
all proper feeling and
~~Gould~~ loftily of confiscation but the want of mobility in the Señor
ended by   adversely his power of masterful expression.
Administrador's face affecting ~~the masterful confidence of his state~~
had repeated. The government can certainly bring about the destruction of the San Tomé mine
Charles Gould ~~had said~~ "~~You can certainly destroy it if it likes~~ but
without me it can do nothing else". It was an alarming pronouncement and
~~that is all that you can do."~~   it was an amazing pronouncement.
I well calculated to offend the sensibilities of a politician whose
mind is bent upon the spoils of victory. And Charles Gould said also that the destruction
of the San Tomé mine would cause the ruin 32 of other undertakings, the withdrawal of European capital
the withholding most probably of the last instalment of the foreign loan. That field of a man
said all these things (which were accessible to his Excellency's intelligence) in a cold blooded
manner which made you shudder.

E. M. Forster 1879–1970

ABOVE:
E.M. Forster, painted by the
Bloomsbury artist Dora
Carrington in 1920.

BELOW:
This covering sheet for the manuscript of *Where Angels Fear to
Tread* reveals that Forster had
originally entitled the novel
'Monteriano'. His instructions to
his typist show his consideration
for the difficulty she might face
with unfamiliar Italian words.

In 1905 the twenty-six-year-old Edward Morgan Forster published his first
novel, *Where Angels Fear to Tread*, the first manuscript page of which is illustrated opposite. His story of a belligerent English family gradually educated
out of their prejudices while in Italy drew, like his next two novels, *The Longest
Journey* (1907) and *A Room with a View* (1908), upon his own experiences:
the miserable time he had spent at public school in Tonbridge (which became
the small-minded fictional 'Sawston') and his travels through Greece and Italy
following four happy years at King's College Cambridge where, he later recalled,
'They taught the perky boy that he was not everything, and the limp boy that
he might be something.'

Forster's early years were spent with his mother and a number of aunts at their
home 'Rooksnest' in Hertfordshire, just to the north of London. They had
moved here after the death of his father and he grew to love it deeply enough
for it to become 'Howards End' in his eponymous novel of 1910, a symbol of
the continually threatened virtues of continuity and quiet humanity. The novel,
which takes as its main theme the resolution of conflicting values, introduced
the phrase by which Forster's admired philosophy has come to be defined:
'Only connect!'.

Forster's next novel, *A Passage to India*, which he had started in 1912, did
not appear until 1924. Its picture of Empire in decline, which he himself had
observed in two visits (the last in 1921 as the private secretary to a Maharaja) was
immediately acclaimed a masterpiece. During the novel's long gestation Forster
had drafted and then returned time and again to *Maurice*, a story of homosexual
love which he circulated privately but which remained unpublished until the
year after his death; his own serious relationships began in Alexandria, where he
served in the Red Cross during the War, and in the early 1930s he found his
long term companion in a young policeman.

A Passage to India was to be Forster's last novel, yet for the remainder of his long
years he occupied a position at the very centre of British literary, intellectual and
cultural life, issuing numerous essays, biographies, lectures and broadcasts and
supporting political and social causes with such an honesty
and vigour that the British *Dictionary of National Biography* felt able to describe him as 'the sage of humanism'.
He believed perhaps above all else in the importance of
personal relations and died, as was his wish, in the
Coventry home of his closest companions Bob and May
Buckingham. His ashes were scattered in their rose garden.

OPPOSITE:
The opening page of E. M. Forster's first novel, *Where Angels
Fear to Tread*. The manuscript was found among the papers
of Nathaniel Wedd (1864–1940), one of the Fellows under
whose influence he had come while studying at King's
College Cambridge. Forster maintained close links with
King's throughout his life and the college, which presented
this manuscript to The British Library in 1971, holds the
most important collection of his papers.

They were all at Charing Cross to see Lilia off — Philip,
Harriet
~~Georgie~~, Irma, Mrs Herriton herself. Even Mrs Theobald
squired by Mr Kingcroft, had braved the journey from Yorkshire
to bid her ~~of~~ only daughter goodbye. Miss Abbott was likewise attended
by numerous relatives, and the sight of so many people talking at once
and saying such different things caused Lilia to break into ungovern-
-able peals of laughter

"Quite an ovation. she cried, ~~feeling~~ ^{sprawling} out of her 1st class carriage.
They'll take us for royalty. Oh. Mr Kingcroft. get us footwarmers."

The good natured ^{young} man hurried away, and Philip, taking his place
flooded her with a final stream of advice and injunctions, where to
stop, how to learn Italian. when to use mosquitoes ^{nets} what pictures to
look at. "Remember, he concluded. "that it is only by going off the track
that you get to know the country. See the little towns — Gubbio, Pienza,
Cortona, San Gemignano, Volterra, Monteriano. And dont let me
beg you. go with that awful tourist idea that Italy's only a museum
of antiquities & art. Italy's living. Love and understand the Italians
for the people are ~~more~~ more marvellous than the land"

"How I wish you were coming, Philip." she said, flattered at
the unwonted notice her brother in law was giving her.

"I wish I were." He could have managed ~~not~~ it without
great difficulty, for his career at the bar was not so intense as to
prevent occasional holidays. But his family disliked his continual
~~absences on~~ visits to the continent, and he himself often ~~took~~ ^{found} pleasure in the

Wilfred Owen 1893–1918

ABOVE:

A photographic portrait of
Wilfred Owen by John
Gunsten, 1916

On 4 November 1918, just one week before the signing of the armistice to end the First World War, a young officer and recipient of the Military Cross for 'conspicuous gallantry', was killed by machine gunfire at the Sambre canal in France. The soldier was Wilfred Owen, whose total of five published poems had done little to raise him from literary obscurity at the time of his death, but who has subsequently emerged as the best known of all modern British war poets. He was born at Oswestry in Shropshire and completed his education at London University, following which he travelled to France where he worked as a private tutor. He volunteered for active service in 1915.

In language and style, Owen's work owes more to the poetic idioms of the past (John Keats was a strong influence) than to the hard and fractured forms emerging from his 'modernist' contemporaries such as T. S. Eliot, Ezra Pound and T. E. Hulme. Nonetheless, he developed a high degree of technical sophistication and is credited with inventing 'pararhyme', in which consonants are matched before and after different vowels.

It is, however, the sheer visceral power of the subject matter which truly sets Owen's writing apart; the ability to bring home from the trenches the full brutality and pathos of a war whose 'actualities', as he put it, were at best unknown, at worse ignored, by the 'pulpit professionals' who sent men to their uncertain fates. It has been pointed out that after Owen no one could ever again write poetry which saw in war the possibility of romance and gallantry.

Owen's literary manuscripts, often comprising successive heavily reworked drafts of one poem, were gathered together after his death and brought to wide public attention in editions by the poet Siegfried Sassoon, helped by Edith Sitwell (1920) and Edmund Blunden (1931). Sassoon, also the winner of a Military Cross (which he later threw away in disgust), had already embraced the pacifist cause when, invalided with 'shell-shock', he met the younger soldier at Craiglockhart Hospital, near Edinburgh. It was here, under a diagnosis of 'neurasthenia', that the twenty-four-year-old Owen wrote many of his finest poems. Among them was 'Anthem for Doomed Youth' shown here in a first draft. Sassoon's suggested amendments can be seen in addition to Owen's firm and fluid hand. Despite his encouragement and help in giving the piece its final well-wrought shape, Sassoon was in no doubt as to the essential genius from which it sprang. He recognised 'that my little friend was much more than the promising minor poet I had hitherto adjudged him to be' and that the sonnet in all its 'noble naturalness and depth of meaning…was a revelation'.

LEFT:

Owen's unfinished draft preface to what was evidently an envisaged collection of poems has been described by Jon Stallworthy, the poet's biographer, as 'perhaps the most famous literary manifesto of the twentieth century'.

Anthem for Dead Youth.

What passing-bells for these who die so fast?
 — Only the {solemn monstrous anger of the guns.
Let the majestic insults of their mouths
Be as the requiem of their burials.
Of choristers and holy music, none;
 Nor any voice of mourning save the wail
The long-drawn wail of high far-sailing shells.

 What candles may we hold for these lost souls?
 — Not in the hands of boys, but in their eyes
Shall many candles shine, and flames
And Women's wide-spreaded arms shall be their wreaths,
 And pallor of girl's cheeks shall be their palls.
Their flowers, the tenderness of minds,
And Dusk, a drawing-down of blinds.

First Draft
(With Sassoon's amendments.)

ABOVE:
Wilfred Owen's first draft of 'Anthem for Doomed Youth' reveals the young poet working hard to find the final shape of the poem. The draft bears pencil amendments by Siegfried Sassoon, with whom Owen spent time at Craiglockhart Hospital in Scotland. Owen's literary manuscripts were acquired by the British Museum Library in 1934, through the good offices of the Friends of the National Libraries and other generous subscribers.

Katherine Mansfield 1888–1923

ABOVE:

Katherine Mansfield sent this postcard photograph in 1921 to her friend S. S. Koteliansky, the Russian writer and man of letters.

Although she often berated herself for laziness and was extremely critical of everything she wrote, Katherine Mansfield's literary output was considerable. Born Kathleen Mansfield Beauchamp in Wellington, New Zealand, she was sent to board at Queen's College, London from 1903 to 1906, then studied music in New Zealand before returning to London in 1908, seeking – as she wrote in her diary – 'Power, wealth and freedom'. She became part of a progressive and liberated literary and artistic set, which included Virginia Woolf and D. H. Lawrence, and began to write poems and short stories for small avant-garde magazines. Her personal life was eventful and difficult, involving an affair and pregnancy (which ended in miscarriage) and an extremely brief face-saving marriage to another man.

In 1911 Mansfield met the writer and editor John Middleton Murry; they finally married in 1918, by which time she was suffering from tuberculosis, which compelled her to spend part of every year in the South of France and Switzerland. Her first collection of short stories, *In a German Pension*, appeared in 1911, *Bliss, and Other Stories* in 1920 and *The Garden Party and Other Stories* in 1922. Two further collections, as well as various editions of her letters and journal extracts, were published after her death, in Paris, at the age of thirty-five. Murry described his wife as 'the most wonderful writer…of her time' and her influence, particularly on the form of the short story, has been considerable.

Reproduced here is a page from the manuscript draft of a story, dated 15 March 1919. Entitled 'A Suburban Fairy Tale', it appeared in the collection *Something Childish and Other Stories*, published in 1924, a year after her death.

RIGHT:

The British Library possesses a significant collection of Mansfield's letters. This sad plea for love was sent from Switzerland on 18 October 1921 to Koteliansky, who had first introduced her to Anton Chekhov, an important influence.

OPPOSITE:

Katherine Mansfield's 'A Suburban Fairy Tale' tells the strange, poignant story of a sensitive and timid little boy who is transformed into a hungry sparrow and flies away with his flock, leaving his hitherto complacent parents bereft and horrified. Although she starts relatively neatly, by the end of the story Mansfield's hand is virtually indecipherable.

A Suburban Fairy Tale.

15. xii. 1919.

Mr and Mrs B. sat a breakfast in the cosy red dining room of their 'snug little crib just under half an hour's run from the city.'

There was a good fire in the grate — for the dining room was the living room as well — the two windows overlooking the cold empty garden patch were closed, and the air smelled agreeably of bacon and eggs, toast and coffee. Now that this rationing business was near over Mr B. made a point of a thoroughly good tuck in before facing the very real perils of the day. He didn't mind who knew it — he was a true Englishman about his breakfast — he had to have it; he's lost without it and if you told him that these continental chaps could get through half the mornings work he did on a roll and a coffee of coffee — you simply didn't know what you were talking about. Mr B. was a stout

T. S. Eliot 1888–1965

ABOVE:
This portrait of T.S. Eliot was taken by Ida Kar in 1956.

Thomas Stearns Eliot is perhaps the most influential English-speaking poet of the twentieth century and certainly one of its greatest literary and cultural critics. Born in St Louis, Missouri, he was educated at Harvard, Boston, the Sorbonne, Paris, and Merton College, Oxford. Although he generally presented himself to the world with a formal gravity (the philosopher Bertrand Russell commented that his manners were 'of the finest Etonian type') he possessed a strong sense of humour and a love of practical jokes: while working in London as a publisher at Faber and Faber he once set off firecrackers at a board meeting on 4 July.

It was his poetic mentor, Ezra Pound, who encouraged Eliot to settle in England and by 1928 he was famously declaring himself 'classical in literature, royalist in politics and Anglo-Catholic in religion'. In 1915 he married for the first time, and after a brief period of teaching went to work for Lloyds Bank. From 1917, when he published *Prufrock and Other Observations*, he was also assistant editor of *The Egoist* and in 1922 he founded *The Criterion;* his great and controversial poem *The Waste Land* appeared in its first issue, and, after radical editing by Pound, was published in 1922. Eliot completed the poem in a Swiss sanitorium to which he had retreated in the aftermath of an emotional crisis triggered in part by his troubled marriage. In its abstract forms, fragmented meanings and apocalyptic tone, the poem stands as a plangent articulation of Modernism, a complicated, pervasive and avant-garde movement of the early twentieth century in which the scientific, cultural and political assumptions of the previous age were called into question. The manuscript is now in the New York Public Library.

Eliot's continuing versatility is witnessed in his sequence of highly lyrical long poems, *Four Quartets*, which appeared together in 1943, and in his acclaimed poetic dramas of the 1930s and 50s, including the moving and powerful *Murder in the Cathedral*. A classic book of comic verse for children, the delightful *Old Possum's Book of Practical Cats*, appeared in 1939. Eliot became a British subject in 1927, found happiness in a second marriage and, living and working in London for the remainder of his years, was the recipient of both the Nobel Prize for Literature and the Order of Merit. He died in 1965 and was cremated at Golders Green Crematorium.

LEFT:
Most of the poems in *Old Possum's Book of Practical Cats* were written between 1936 and 1938. They were, Eliot later wrote, 'certainly written for children, insofar as they were intended to amuse anyone but myself...'. The children of his friend Geoffrey Tandy were sent copies as he wrote them, partly for their amusement and partly to test their reactions. This charming pen-and-ink illustration was added by Eliot to one such copy.

OPPOSITE:
Reproduced here is a page from a letter of September 1921, from Eliot to his close friend and fellow writer Sydney Schiff, written at Margate during his recuperation from a severe nervous breakdown. In it Eliot describes his attempts to write what would become *The Waste Land*. He refers to his difficulties in making much progress with the third section, having so far managed only fifty lines; the whole letter has a weary, tense and desolate air which reflects his physical and mental state at that time.

But I have written only some
50 lines, and have read nothing.
Literally, — I sketch the people,
after a fashion, and practise
scales on the mandoline.

I rather dread being in town
at all — one becomes dependent,
too, on sea or mountains, which
give some sense of security in
which one relaxes — and hope to
be only a day or two. I hope
to have good news of you both
from Vivienne — She tells me
very little about her own
health, inspite of my com-
plaints. With best love to you
and Violet y{r}s aff — Tom.

32

Virginia Woolf 1882–1941

ABOVE:

A photographic portrait of
Virginia Woolf taken in 1902 by
George Charles Beresford.

Virginia Woolf, the daughter of Julia Duckworth and Leslie Stephen, scholar and editor of the *Dictionary of National Biography*, was born at Hyde Park Gate, London. Her literary talents revealed themselves at an early age, when she compiled, with her brother, Thoby, and elder sister Vanessa (destined, as Vanessa Bell, to became an important painter), the witty and inventive home-made periodical, 'Hyde Park Gate News'. By the age of twenty-three she had established herself firmly at the centre of London's literary world, writing for the *Times Literary Supplement* and forming, with her siblings, the influential 'Bloomsbury Group' of writers and artists. She married, in 1912, Leonard Woolf, a writer, journalist and political thinker, with whom she founded the Hogarth Press in 1917. Her first novel, *The Voyage Out*, appeared in 1915.

The ensuing decade saw a stream of increasingly innovative prose, leading to a highly concentrated and exhausting period of creativity in which she composed the major works by which she is best known. The first of these, *Mrs Dalloway* (1925), traces the thoughts, memories and emotions of one character through the course of a single day in London. The novel's inventive narrative technique is brilliantly assured, its evocation of isolation and loneliness moving and beautiful. Indeed, it is hard at times not to associate the heroine's sadness with that of Woolf herself, who suffered mental anguish throughout a life which she eventually took by her own hand in 1941. Woolf's novel, originally entitled 'The Hours', was published in 1925 and helped, in its adventurous treatment of narrative structure and interior monologue, to establish her as an important exponent of the Modernist style. Indeed, by limiting the events of her novel to just one day, Woolf recalls the work of another great Modernist and exact contemporary, James Joyce, whose *Ulysses* was serialized from 1918.

LEFT:

The entry for 12 September 1892 in the Stephen children's juvenile periodical, 'Hyde Parke Gate News'. Most of the contributions to the series are in the hand of Vanessa, with some – mostly later – passages in the hand of Virginia; the hand does not, however, necessarily identify the author of any particular piece, since the children took turns in copying them out. This particular entry goes on to describe a trip to a lighthouse – a theme Woolf would revisit in her adult fiction.

OPPOSITE:

The British Library has several important manuscripts by Virginia Woolf. This page is taken from one of three notebooks containing drafts for *Mrs Dalloway* (1925) and for essays published in the periodical, *The Common Reader*. Woolf here sets down, in her favoured purple ink, a wonderful account of what Mrs Dalloway sees on her visit to Mulberry's, the florists, early in the novel.

Monday

by the red faced, button faced Miss Pym, whose hands were always tight red, as if they had been stood in cold water with the flowers.

There were flowers; delphiniums, sweet peas; bunches of lilac; & carnations, masses of carnations. There were roses; there were irises & lilies. Ah yes. So she breathed in the earthy took Garden smell; talking to Miss Pym, who owed her help, & would therefore always come to her little box; & come a tayhe box always when Mr Dalloway came in; & thought her kinder kind she had been, years ago: kind she still was, standing there, turning looking older, now this year, turning her head from side to side among the irises & roses, & nodding tufts of lilac, with her eyes half closed, snuffing in the delicious scent. And then, opening her eyes, how fresh, like frilled linen clean from a laundry laid in wicker trays they looked; & dark & sniffed from, the red carnations, holding their head up; & all the sweet peas spreading in their bowls, tinged violet, snow white, pale, — & now & were the evening, Girls in muslin frocks came out to pick sweet peas & roses to hick after the superb summers day, with its almost blue-black sky, its delphiniums, its carnations, its arum lilies, was over; & was the exhausting moment between six & seven, when every flower — roses, carnations, irises, lilac, glows whatever its colour — white, violet, red, deep orange; every flower seems to burn by itself, softly purely in the misty beds; — & how she loved the grey white moths spinning over the purple cherry pie, the yellow evening primroses!

Dont you get hourfully tired, she said to Miss Pym. When standing all day — When d'you get your holiday?

George Bernard Shaw 1856–1950

ABOVE:

A strong photographic portrait of
Shaw on a postcard of 9 February
1930 sent from him to the
collector T. J. Wise and thanking
him for a 'jolly book'. Although
cordial enough with Wise, Shaw
was plagued by autograph hunters
whom he occasionally obliged
with a withering signed message.

Shaw's *Pygmalion* had its first theatrical performance in Vienna (in German) in October 1913, followed shortly afterwards by one in Berlin. Illustrated below is a prompt copy for the first English production, containing Shaw's autograph staging instructions, written while he was directing rehearsals in early 1914. It is interesting to see how he asked Mrs Patrick Campbell, who played Eliza Doolittle, to substitute 'No bloody fear!' for the immortal 'Not bloody likely!' As we know, he returned to his original wording before the first London performance on 11 April 1914.

Twenty years later he was at work on *Pygmalion* again, this time on the screenplay. A folio from the manuscript is shown opposite. It is dated 1 October 1934 (by which time Shaw was seventy-eight) and the film was released in 1938. Though unwilling to attend studio filming, he exerted a strict control, prefacing the manuscript with the injunction that 'the printed play should be carefully kept out of the studio, as it can only confuse and mislead the producer and the performers'. He brings to the scenario a sharp perception of what the camera can achieve. This is the work of an old mind quite at ease in a relatively new medium: in fact he won an Academy Award for 'Best Screenplay of 1938'. Shaw had developed an interest in photography in the 1880s and published his first articles on the subject in 1901. By 1912 he admitted to being a cinema-addict. Interestingly, both he and G. K. Chesterton played the parts of cowboys in a comic skit on the early Western genre directed by J. M. Barrie, in 1914.

Was the theme of *Pygmalion*, in which a working class cockney heroine, Eliza Doolittle, is transformed by a speech coach into a woman able to pass as a duchess, somehow rooted in Shaw's Dublin childhood? From a shabby genteel background he emerged resoundingly with an independent and influential voice – sometimes waspish, often humorous – in journalism in the London of the 1880s. A founder member of the Fabian Society, a campaigner for women's suffrage and a defender of free speech, he was a self-educated man who said he owed all to the Library of the British Museum. His bequests to the institution bespeak his gratitude. The *Pygmalion* manuscripts are among the large collection the Library acquired from his estate in 1960.

LEFT:

This prompt copy for the first English production of *Pygmalion* bears autograph instructions made by Shaw while directing rehearsals in 1914. Shaw enjoyed using different coloured inks, and his emphatic red is entirely appropriate here. It is used, in one instance, to alter (only temporarily) what has since become the play's most famous line: 'Not bloody likely!'.

OPPOSITE:

This page from George Bernard Shaw's screenplay for *Pygmalion* provides an excellent example of his idiosyncratic and easily identifiable hand, the character of which, in its combinations of tight forms and loops, lies somewhere between neat and spidery.

her hat, an old black straw with a
band of violets, indescribable.

②

3. Eliza and her next neighbor, an elderly woman.
The audience now has a better look at Eliza; but her
good looks are not yet discoverable: she is dirty and her
ill combed hair is dirty. Her shawl and skirt are
old and ugly, her boots are deplorable. The older woman, though
also dirty with London grime, and no better dressed, is slightly
more distinguished by experience. She is busy packing her
basket and covering it. Eliza is listless, discouraged,
and miserable.

OLD WOMAN. Now then, Liza; wake up: its going to rain something
chronic. You going to sit there and get soaked?

LIZA. O gawd, I avnt sold a bloody thing
since five o'clock, I avnt. Whats the good of doing anything
in this weather?

OLD WOMAN. Come now: talking like that wont elp.
Better get home dry than wet.
The old woman takes up her basket and hurries off.
Thunder, much nearer, after a flash.
Eliza looks up, and hastily stirs herself to pack
her basket. She finishes by putting her hat into the basket
and drawing her shawl over her head. Then she rushes off.

Dylan Thomas 1914–1953

ABOVE:

A portrait of Dylan Thomas, painted in oil in 1953 by Gordon Stuart.

Dylan Thomas, the son of a Swansea school teacher, spoke no Welsh and often spoke slightingly of Wales, but in his later restless years Wales became for him, as one biographer succinctly puts it, a frame of mind he settled into. The small town of Llaregyb in his *Under Milk Wood* (1954) is an imaginary spot but it takes its life from the real New Quay, and particularly from the real Laugharne.

Thomas first lived in Laugharne from 1938 until 1940. It lies to the north-west of Swansea overlooking the estuary of three rivers that run into Carmarthen Bay. In a letter sent to his friend and fellow poet Vernon Watkins in late August 1944, he said he had written 'a Laugharne poem: the first place poem I've written' and part of it is here reproduced. Although Thomas described 'Poem in October' as a 'new poem', Watkins later recalled its having been first worked on three years earlier – with a first line of 'It was my twenty-seventh year to heaven' – and it may actually have begun life earlier than that in Laugharne itself. Such re-working was characteristic of Thomas; even the title had been once used and later abandoned for another poem first published in *The Listener* in 1934. We can see how meticulously it is written out in this fair copy in a somewhat fastidious naïve hand quite at variance with his notoriously ill-disciplined everyday existence. It was first published simultaneously in *Horizon* and in *Poetry (Chicago)* in February 1945.

Thomas married Caitlin Macnamara in 1936 and worked for the BBC throughout the war years, before returning to Laugharne in May 1949. From then on 'The Boat House', generously lent him by the wife of the historian A. J. P. Taylor, became his main residence, though he never possessed a home of his own. There he wrote *Under Milk Wood* and it was in New York, where that glorious work (originally written for broadcasting) had its first performance, that he died. There were plans to have his remains buried in the garden of The Boat House but he lies not far off in Laugharne Churchyard. His letters to Watkins, written between 1936 and 1952, were acquired by the British Library in 1965.

LEFT:

The letter sent by Dylan Thomas to Vernon Watkins on 30 August 1944 enclosing 'Poem in October'. Thomas stresses the importance of the poem's sound – something often overlooked in modern poetry.

OPPOSITE:

This fair copy of Dylan Thomas's 'Poem in October' was sent by him, in 1944, to his friend and fellow poet, Vernon Watkins. Thomas's hand is fastidiously neat and, in its preference of print to cursive, curiously childish. The first five verses of seven are shown.

It was my thirtieth year to heaven
Woke to my hearing from harbour and neighbour wood
And the mussel pooled and the heron
         Priested shore
      The morning beckon
With water praying and call of sea gull and rook
And the knock of sailing boats on the net webbed wall
      Myself to set foot
         That second
In the still sleeping town and set forth.

      My birthday began with the water
Birds and the birds of the bare trees flying my name
Above the farms and the white horses
         And I rose
      In rainy autumn
And walked abroad in a shower of all my days.
High tide and the heron dived when I took the road
      Over the border
         And the gates
Of the town closed as the town awoke.

      A springful of larks in a rolling
Cloud and the roadside bushes brimming with whistling
Blackbirds and the sun of October
         Summery
      On the hill's shoulder,
Here were fond climates and sweet singers suddenly
Come in the morning where I wandered and listened
      To the rain wringing
         Wind blow cold
In the wood faraway under me.

      Pale rain over the dwindling harbour
And over the sea wet church the size of a snail
With its horns through mist and the castle
         Brown as owls
      But all the gardens
Of spring and summer were blooming in the tall tales
Beyond the border and under the lark full cloud.
      There could I marvel
         My birthday
Away but the weather turned around.

      It turned away from the blithe country
And down the other air and the blue altered sky
Streamed again a wonder of summer
         With apples
      Pears and red currants
And I saw in the turning so clearly a child's
Forgotten mornings when he walked with his mother
      Through the parables
         Of sun light
And the legends of the green chapels

Philip Larkin 1922–1985

ABOVE:

A photographic portrait of Philip Larkin at work at the Brynmor Jones Library, Hull University.

BELOW:

In this postcard Larkin informs Maeve Brennan, for many years a close friend, that he has just donated his notebook to the nation – and reassures her that it contains nothing compromising! The postcard was donated by her in 2000 after she saw the notebook exhibited at the Library and felt that the two belonged together.

Although by his death in 1985 Philip Larkin had published just four slim collections of verse (in addition to two early novels), his superb modulation of tone, technical brilliance and ability to speak of both the mundane and the marvellous had endeared him to a broad audience. Larkin's work is at its most visceral when addressing the dismal and the dull, the fear of growing old and death, while his own essential conservatism (he rarely went abroad) is reflected in accounts of contemporary England which strike a bitterly satiric tone. In some of his best poems, however, this darker vision is transcended and redeemed by moments of great lyric intensity.

Larkin was born in 1922 in Coventry where he went to school before attending St John's College, Oxford. After graduating, he began his lifelong career as a librarian, first in Wellington, Leicester, then in Belfast, and finally at the University of Hull, where he ran the Brynmor Jones Library, whose 'high windows' inspired the title of his last collection. He once commented in an interview that 'Librarianship suits me – I love the feel of libraries…And I've always thought that a regular job was no bad thing for a poet.'

Larkin's first collection, *The North Ship*, was issued in 1945, followed by *The Less Deceived* (1955) and *The Whitsun Weddings* (1964) which, with *High Windows* (1974), has proved the most enduringly popular. Less acclaimed were his two novels, *Jill* (1946) and *A Girl in Winter* (1947). Larkin was a shy man who lived an outwardly unassuming life, the routine of which was enlivened by a love of jazz and a series of occasionally outrageous correspondences with friends and fellow writers. Although he never married, he had close relationships with women who inspired some of his most tender poems.

Larkin died on 2 December 1985, his funeral in Westminster Abbey marked with a performance of the jazz he found to be so affirmative. He decreed at the end of his life that his papers should be burnt; many of his diaries indeed met that fate, but other of his manuscripts were, controversially, preserved.

Larkin's commitment to his chosen profession was clearly shown by his involvement, from 1965, in a scheme to secure contemporary literary manuscripts for British libraries. This draft of 'Wedding Wind', written at the age of twenty-four, is from a notebook which he donated to The British Library as part of that project in 1965 – having first cut from it anything he did not wish to meet the public eye. The convincingly intimate voice of the narrator as she wavers between melancholy and joy, the elemental imagery contrasted with domestic detail, the shift from the palpable contexts of the first lines to the metaphysical questionings of the last – all anticipate some of Larkin's late, great verses.

OPPOSITE:

In this draft of his poem 'Wedding Wind', Philip Larkin adopts the persona of a newly wed bride. Her voice, in all its beauty and emotional sincerity, reminds us that Larkin could be sensitive and subtle as well as acerbic and irreverent. The manuscript notebook in which it is written was kept by the poet from 5 October 1944 to 10 March 1950.

The wind blew all my wedding-day

And my wedding-night was the night of the high wind,

And a stable door was banging, again and again,

~~So~~ That he must go and shut it, leaving me

Stupid in candlelight, hearing ~~the~~ rain,

Seeing my face ~~twisted~~ in the ~~brass~~ candlestick, _twisted_

~~Yet seeing nothing ~~till~~ he came back~~

He said the horses were restless, and I was sad

That any man ~~or beast~~ that night should lack

The happiness I had.

                    Now in the morning

All's ~~restless~~ _travelled_ under the sun ~~with~~ the ~~wind still blows~~ wind's blowing.

He has gone to look at the ~~fences~~ _floods_, and I

Carry a clipped pail to the chicken-run,

~~Set~~ Set it down, and ~~stare~~. All is the wind

Hunting through cloud and forests, thrashing

My apron and the hanging ~~things~~ _clothes on the line_.

Can it be borne, this bodying-forth by wind

Of joy ~~with~~ _my_ actions turn on, ~~and like a~~ ~~thread~~

~~of the undreamed joy at the root of day and night~~,

Carrying ~~a seeds~~? ~~Shall~~ I be let to sleep,

Now this ~~With this~~ perpetual morning ~~shews~~ ~~my~~ _fills_ bed?

~~Will two death conclude~~

~~Our~~ ~~This~~ Kneeling ~~like~~ _like_ cattle among new ~~takes of faith~~?

Can

~~Will~~ ~~win~~ death dry up

These new delighted lakes, conclude

Our kneeling as cattle ~~among~~ _by_ all generous waters?

                            28 Sept

Canto

Lawrence Durrell 1912–1990

ABOVE:

This photograph of Lawrence Durrell on board his boat, the *Van Norden*, is taken from a negative discovered among his papers. The vessel is named after a character in Henry Miller's *Tropic of Cancer*.

Lawrence Durrell was born in India and, apart from his schooling in London and Canterbury, spent most of his life out of England for he felt oppressed and deadened by this country's social *mores*. His first liberation came in 1935 when the family moved to Corfu, the idyllic years there being celebrated in his book *Prospero's Cell* (1945) and in his brother Gerald's *My Family and Other Animals* (1956). By 1935 Durrell had already published some tiny volumes of verse and that year saw the publication of his first novel, *Pied Piper of Lovers*.

The great adventure of this period is encapsulated in the photograph of Durrell on board his boat, the *Van Norden*, named after a character in Henry Miller's *Tropic of Cancer* (1935). Miller's influence on Durrell was huge. They met in 1937. The Second World War saw the departure of the Durrells from Greece. Durrell himself was in Cairo and Alexandria during the conflict and it was in the rich ambiguity of Alexandrian life, its squalor, its allure, its brutishness, its lyricism, that Durrell was to find inspirational sources for the four novels known as the *Alexandria Quartet*, his most notable achievement, published between 1957 and 1960.

Durrell's drafts for the first two of these novels, *Justine* and *Balthazar*, came to the British Library by bequest in 1995 among the large collection of Durrelliana gathered by his most loyal friend, the antiquarian bookseller, Alan Thomas. Shown opposite is a folio from one of the *Justine* notebooks whose inner front cover declares that the work was begun in Venice on 21 January 1954, based on notes made in 1946–47 with some passages from 1943. In the same notebook we can also see (left) the kind of idle sketch he turned to slightly better account in his painting exhibitions under the pseudonym Oscar Epfs. Below it is the outline of his daughter Sappho's hand and one may wonder if this was the source of the cover design for the first edition in 1957.

France became Durrell's adopted home. He died in Sommières, near Nîmes, where he had lived since 1966 and his remains are in the nearby cemetery of the chapel of St Julien de Salinelles.

ABOVE:

The inside cover of the manuscript notebook used by Lawrence Durrell to draft *Justine* includes a print of his daughter Sappho's hand. The image of a hand is used on early Faber & Faber editions of the novel – a sweet paternal tribute?

ABOVE:

A bowl made around 1964 by Gerald Durrell, Lawrence's brother. On it he has drawn the family, each member accompanied by an appropriate image: himself with a squirrel; Lawrence with *Justine*; Leslie (the middle brother) with a gun; Margo, his sister, with a bottle of perfume; and their mother, who died in early 1964 but is still centrally placed, in heaven with her knitting and one of her renowned curries.

OPPOSITE:

This manuscript notebook contains one of two drafts of *Justine* acquired by the British Library as part of Lawrence Durrell's large archive in 1995. Here we can plainly see (thanks to the change of pen) Durrell returning to, correcting and continuing his work.

And Melissa? She lacked the insight of Justine into my human case. She only knew that my strength supported her where she was at her weakest — in her dealings with the world. She indeed loved me for every sign of my human weakness — disorderly habits, incapacity over money affairs, and so on. She loved my weaknesses because here she could feel of use to me; Justine brushed all this aside. I interested her only in this one particular which I could not offer her as a gift or she steal from me — my real self. This is what is meant by possession — to be passionately at war for the qualities in one another; to contend for the treasures of each others' personalities. How can such a war be anything but destructive and hopeless? The greater insight of the ~~xxxxxxxxxxxxxxxxxx~~ Justine with the more deeply divining sense of the powers had isolated what was dear to her in me; Melissa accepted everything, even the pain I caused her without criticism, unflinchingly as part of my weakness.

Yet, so entangled are human motives — it was really she (Melissa) who had driven Nessim from his refuge in the world of fantasy towards an action which he knew we would all bitterly regret. For it was she who, overmastered by the impulse of her unhappiness one night approached the table where he was sitting alone before his work of carnets of one pensively watching the cabinet, and blushing and trembling under false eyelashes, blurted out the words "You are in no longer a threat to you" — a phrase which fell and remained quivering in Nessim's heart like a thrown knife. It is true that for a long time now his dossiers had been swollen with reports of this dreaded fact, but these reports themselves seemed somehow to lack a personal application. They were like the reports one reads in a newspaper of some huge earthquake which has destroyed a country and rendered a million people homeless. The difference was now that he was face to

Stevie Smith 1902–1971

ABOVE:

A photograph of Stevie Smith.

In her essay 'Too Tired for Words', published in *Medical World* in December 1956, Stevie Smith relishes the thought that death summoned at command is 'a great relief to the tired' and, speaking of God in that same essay, she adds 'when I am dead I hope that he will eat Everything I have been and have not been'. These thoughts evidently possessed her considerably in late 1956, for we can see them again in the letter illustrated opposite, addressed to her friend Sally Chilver and sent on 20 November of that year. 'Death as end and remedy', she writes. But after she had sought such a remedy in an unbalanced moment in 1953, she was filled with remorse about the pain she had inflicted on the person she most cared about, her aunt back home in Palmers Green.

This trim suburb of north London had been Stevie Smith's home since she was three and, comfortable in its discomforts ('…the lavatory cistern floods the garden…', she writes in this letter), it remained so until her death from a brain tumour in Ashburton Hospital, near Plymouth. She was much occupied with what to her were deeply satisfying domestic duties and with caring for her aunt, but she nevertheless held down a secretarial job in Covent Garden for thirty years, published three novels between 1936 and 1949, eight volumes of poems, all illustrated with her own drawings, between 1937 and 1969, and various essays and reviews.

Though actually quite a gregarious woman (she had her home telephone number put into her entry in *Who's Who*), she found intimacies beyond friendship quite suffocating and she was aware that she was limited in her ability to portray love between couples – 'that troubled stirring world of Two's' as she puts it earlier in the letter. The two 'new' poems embedded in the letter to Chilver show her own strange – one might even say lonely – experiences of the emotion. The manuscript was given to The British Library by Sally Chilver in 1980.

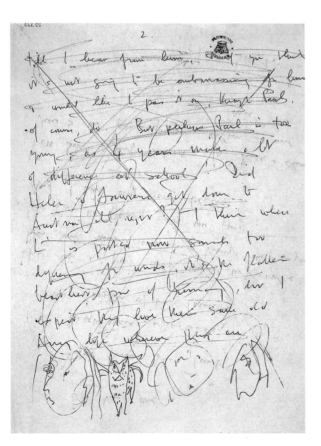

LEFT:

Stevie Smith has used this sheet for a variety of purposes. Starting off as a letter which she discarded, it turned into a vehicle for doodling, as can be seen in these images of faces and a cat. Eventually, overleaf, the paper presented a convenient space to set out, in fair copy, one of her poems.

OPPOSITE:

In this page from a letter to Sally Chilver, Stevie Smith includes two new poems, one of which, 'My Heart Goes Out' appeared in her radio play *A Turn Outside*, broadcast on 23 May 1959. Smith uses a ballpoint pen. Invented in its modern form in 1935 in Prague, and marketed in New York from 1945, it was still a relatively new instrument.

I do not quite catch it. But I know
it means a lot to some people, so I
suppose it does mean a lot. Now (of
course.) I must tell you my new
ones. (1) ~~My Heart's Out~~   It Filled My
                                    Heart with love
(When I hold in my hand a
soft & crushable animal, & feel
the fur beat for fear, & the
soft feathers, I cannot feel
unhappy.) [N.B. This is a sort of
                    introduction or sub-title.]

In his fur the animal rode & in
                    his fur he strove.
And oh it filled my heart, my heart,
          it filled my heart with love.

(2)   My Heart Goes Out.

My heart goes out to my creator in love
Who gave me Death, as end & remedy.
All living creatures come to quiet Death
For him to eat up their activity
And give them nothing, which is what
                    they want although
When they are living they do not think so.

('what I like about this, is that
it's so apt to be 'my creator-in-law')

Sylvia Plath 1932–1963

ABOVE:

A photographic portrait of
Sylvia Plath.

Sylvia Plath was born in Boston, Massachusetts. The death of her father, a German immigrant Professor and entomologist, in 1940, had a profound effect upon her and his image haunts her later poems. An excellent student – talented, clever and attractive – in 1952 she won a *Mademoiselle* magazine fiction award, and spent some time in New York as a guest editor. Despite her many shining qualities, she was troubled. When she graduated from Smith College, Massachusetts, in 1955, she had already survived severe bouts of depression, two suicide attempts, hospitalization and electro-convulsive therapy. A year later, she married the poet Ted Hughes, whom she met in England while a Fulbright scholar at Newnham College, Cambridge. After teaching together in America, they returned to England in 1959, living in London before moving to Devon in 1961. Her first volume of poetry, *The Colossus*, appeared in 1960, and her autobiographical novel, *The Bell Jar*, was published under a pseudonym (Victoria Lucas) in 1963. Less than a month after its publication, early in the morning of 11 February, during the coldest winter experienced in England for many years, she committed suicide. Tired and worn down after a severe bout of influenza, and suffering from a recurrence of her depressive illness, she had been living alone in London with her two young children after separating from Hughes.

In 1965 Plath's best known collection of poems, *Ariel*, established her reputation as one of the most powerful poets of the twentieth century with its vivid, rich, turbulent poems of fury, ecstasy and anguish; as she herself explained: 'The blood jet is poetry/There is no stopping it.' A friend, the poet Anne Sexton, wrote that 'These last poems stun me. They eat time.' The stanzas reproduced here, heavily revised in her distinctive, rather girlish hand are from a poem entitled 'Insomniac'. It was completed in May 1961 and won a prize at the Cheltenham Literary Festival that summer. On receiving the prize, Plath wrote to the judges 'I am happy to hear…that sleeplessness has its own very pleasant reward' – although 'sleeplessness' might be regarded as a rather understated way of referring to the mental anguish depicted in the poem. Always her own sternest critic, Plath was a constant discarder of her own work (which was written on any paper that came to hand – including, on occasion, the backs of her husband's early drafts). These impressive and heavily revised stanzas, signed at the top of the page, did not appear in the poem's final version.

Ariel
(for al)

Stasis in darkness.
Then the substanceless blue
Pour of tor and distances.

God's lioness!
How one we grow!
Pivot of heels and knees! The furrow

Splits and passes, sister to
The brown arc
Of the neck I cannot catch,

Nigger-eye
Berries cast dark
Hooks—

Black sweet blood mouthfuls!
Shadows!
Something else

Hauls me through air —
Thighs, hair;
Flakes from my heels.

White
Godiva, I unpeel —
Dead hands, dead stringencies!

And now I
Foam to wheat, a glitter of seas.
The child's cry

Melts in the wall.
And I
Am the arrow,

The dew that flies
Suicidal, at one with the drive
Into the red

Eye, the cauldron of morning.

—Sylvia Plath—

LEFT:

These lines, signed by Plath with her trademark pink flower, are a fair copy of one of her most famous poems, 'Ariel'. They were sent in the last months of her life as a gift to a close friend, the poet and critic Al Alvarez. The dedication, 'for Al', does not appear in the published version.

OPPOSITE:

This is the first of several pages of a draft of 'Insomniac' by Sylvia Plath, a prize-winning poem submitted to the Cheltenham Literary Festival in 1961. It shows the opening of a poem which, in its alterations, corrections and additions, seems as restless as the subject it treats.

Insomniac

The night sky is ~~only a sheet~~ only a suit of carbon paper,
Blue-black, with the much-poked periods of stars
letting in light, peephole after peephole —
A bone-white light, ~~past too,~~ like death, behind all things.
~~He his~~ under the eyes of the stars, the ~~busy~~ moon's picture
~~of a moon that carries her light into the world~~
~~of the aluminium-colored moon, he suffers~~

He suffers his desert silences; sleeplessness
Stretching ~~his~~ / irritating ~~like~~ sand in all directions
is a fine,

Over & over the old, granular movie
Exposes embarrassments, the ~~mizzling~~ days
Of childhood & adolescence, sticky with dreams,
Parental faces on tall stalks, alternately stern & tearful;
A garden of buggy roses that made him cry.
His forehead is bumpy as a sack of rocks.
~~the~~ Memories jostle each other ~~like~~ obsolete film stars.

                    for feau-room

He is immune to
             pills: a ~~these are~~, red, purple, blue —
~~they bloomed the~~   protracted
~~the sleepent pellets of oblivion~~ ~~veil~~
Those   How new ~~lit~~ the tedium of the ~~various~~ evening! With for
sugary ~~low morning~~ planets, ~~under~~ whose ~~easy~~ influence ~~part~~
        ~~And a science fiction life~~ no life ~~at all~~ for a while,
f the   ~~Again~~ sweet, drugged wakening, ~~like~~ a forgetful baby.
He ~~this is to~~ immune to ~~death~~ their rosy-cheerful colors.
                         to him no good.

W. H. Auden 1907–1973

ABOVE:

W.H. Auden on Fire Island, near New York, in 1946. The photograph was taken by his good friend, the Irish writer James Stern.

Wystan Hughes Auden gave his name to a generation of poets who, during the 1930s, sought to reconcile the chaos they perceived in the 'public' world around them with their own 'private' vision. Stephen Spender, Louis MacNeice, Cecil Day Lewis and Christopher Isherwood all formed part of a closely-knit group characterised by left-leaning principles which formed a counterpoint to the plangent and uncompromising position adopted by their Modernist predecessors. Of a solid middle-class background, Auden was educated at Gresham's School in Norfolk, and Christ Church College, Oxford University. He published his first volume of verse in 1930. His homosexuality and residence in America during the Second World War caused him some difficulty among the reading public but his return to Oxford in 1956 as Professor of Poetry signified a widening respect for his assured, distinctive voice.

In a letter of 19 August 1963 to Cecil Day Lewis, Auden wrote: 'I have no manuscripts in the ordinary sense of the word. I keep a working notebook in which poems are sketched out. For the most part, these sketches are illegible to anyone but myself: further, they are almost always incomplete, for the final revisions are made in my head or on the typewriter.' Scholars were able to judge Auden's words at first hand when, in the mid-1960s, an important notebook which he had kept since 1947 came to The British Library under a scheme initiated by Philip Larkin to preserve modern literary manuscripts.

The fascinating complexity of Auden's method is well illustrated here in one of many heavily revised drafts of the poem 'To-Night at Seven-Thirty', probably written in 1963 as part of a profound and touching sequence 'Thanksgiving for a Habitat' in which he questions where, how and, quite simply, why we live.

RIGHT:

In this notebook dating from about 1928–1935, W. H. Auden wrote out a 'Glossary of Christian and Psychological terms'. From the early 1940s Christianity became an increasingly important influence upon his work.

OPPOSITE:

Auden's poetic drafts often bear a series of dots and dashes together with alphabetic and numeric schemes, indicating the importance he attached to rhyme and metre in the process of composition.

both — a table to mood be along when to stop,
a temporal re-presentation of to interested,

visible life

The feast is a human invention. The life of a plant
Is one long meal; movements interrupt theirs,
To sleep or mate, or while predators got a bite
And bolt it when they get the chance but
the custom eat alone is even the pack-hunters
who dine en famille do not invited guests
A Greek who can fit first as above
as a them in-ig-pulse
of placement placed — place
of placement placed — place here never, into
A good who i life but
our temporal celebration awareness
of the ritual silence — I see a table

Facing a wall both	a	4
dinner table, too far you are dog eye	b	10
At which the you — a dog better present	a	4
make the eye grateful	c	12
	b	4
of Eating as	d	12
To life, speech as a representing	d	12
of the ritual silence	e	12
	e	7
	c	12
	f	10
	g	8
	f	9
	g	6

Harold Pinter 1930–

Harold Pinter, one of the world's most revered playwrights, screenwriters and theatre directors, began to publish poetry in periodicals before he was twenty, and then became a professional actor, working mainly in repertory. The son of

ABOVE:

A photographic portrait of Harold Pinter.

a tailor, he was born in East London and educated at Hackney Downs Grammar School. His first play, *The Room*, performed in Bristol in 1957, was revived in London, to great acclaim, in 2000. It was followed in 1958 by a production of *The Birthday Party*, now regarded as one of the seminal plays of the twentieth century but which, on the occasion of its London opening, was greeted with horrified incomprehension by the critics, one writing of '*non sequiturs* [sic], half-gibberish and lunatic ravings'. However, after the distinguished reviewer Harold Hobson wrote a highly appreciative piece, in which he praised Pinter's mastery of impalpable terror, the tide quickly turned and many critical and commercial successes followed. The term 'Pinteresque', with its connotations of nameless menace, erotic fantasy, obsession, jealousy and family rivalries, has now entered the English vocabulary to the extent that it is occasionally used by people who have never seen a Pinter play.

Pinter's archive of poems and playscripts is now on loan to The British Library, where it is used by literary researchers from all over the world. Reproduced here is the first page from the earliest draft of one of his most powerful and frequently acted plays, *The Homecoming*, first performed in June 1965. The play still shocks audiences with its stark portrayal of what the critic Michael Billington called 'the naked violence of family life and…the primal, atavistic power of the female'.

RIGHT:

An autograph draft, in Pinter's distinctive, strong and confident hand, of a typically spare and striking early poem entitled 'Before They Fall'. Like many of his drafts, it is written in ink on lined yellow paper.

OPPOSITE:

The first page from Harold Pinter's play *The Homecoming*. Its revisions – the letter 'p' denotes a pause – show Pinter constantly tightening, re-shaping and refining the rhythm and language of this dark drama, in which the opening dialogue between father and son immediately sets an aggressive, needling and confrontational tone.

I.

Son 3 jotting notes on sports page. Enter Father.

F.   - What have you done with the scissors ?
                p.
         I want the scissors.
3.   - What for ?
F.   - What have you done with them ?
3.   - What do you want the scissors for ?
F.   - I want to cut something out. I want to cut something
         out the bleeding paper. You bastard.
                p.
3.   -I'm reading the paper.
F.   - Not that paper. The sunday paper.
                F. sits.
F   - I think I'll have a fag.
                p.
         Theres an advertisement in the paper about flannel
         vests. Cut price. Navy wear. I could do with a few of
         them. Give me a fag.
                p.
         Give me a cigarette !   Piss It i've got enough
                                                              to do.
3.   + Why should I give you a cigarette ? I've got enough
         to do.
F.   - Look what I'm landed with. ✓ A pair of bastards. Well
         you can drown in your own blood, anyway. You can drown
         in your own blood. As far as I go. And the other one.
         All these tough boys. You and your bleeding bastard
         brother. Louzy stinking prostitutes.   Crumpled.
                           p. takes fag from pocket   whats the matter
         I'm getting old, my word of honour. You think I wasnt
         a tearaway ? I could have taken care of you, twice over.
         I'm still strong. You ask your uncle Sam what I was.
         I was a villian. At the same time I always had a kind
         heart. I used to knock about with a man called Berkowitz.
         I called him Berki. Come on Berki, where you going
         tonight ? Coming up West tonight ? Go round the back
         doubles, do a few snooker halls, run in a couple of
         tarts. I still got the scars. We used to walk back to
         back, Berki and me. The terrible twins they used to call
         us. He was six feet tall. But even his family called
         him Berki. He had a big family, mind you. But even his
         old man called him Berki. Of course the old man was a
         Berkowitz too. They were all Berkotitzs, it goes without
         saying. But he was the only one they called Berki. His
         other brothers we called Berks. Anyway, he's dead. One
         of his sisters died in prison. The other one died in
         hospital. We went to see her. She was dead when by the
         time we got there.
                        p. she   such a bad, your mother
         Mind you, your mother was a good woman, even though she
         was too honest. Even though she made me sick she wasnt
         a bad bitch. Not that you two care a fart about your
         mother. Where did you put those bastard scissors ?
3.   - Why dont you shut up ?   I gave her the best years
                                 of my bleeding life,
                                       anyway.

MacGregor

He was fond of
your mother
Berkowitz. I was
always had a
good word for
her.

Plug it, will you,
you stupid sod.
I'm trying to read the paper.

Ted Hughes 1930–1998

ABOVE:

A photographic portrait of
Ted Hughes.

BELOW:

A later draft of 'The Green Wolf'
reveals an almost entirely
different poem from that
shown opposite.

Thematically rich, aggressively rhythmic, intensely aware of the natural world but with roots tapping deeply down into realms of myth and the inchoate, Ted Hughes's verse blew away the studied indolence and urbanity which had come to define the poetic voice of the post-war generation. The dark and violent allegorical vision presented in *Crow* (1970), his most celebrated collection, couldn't be further from the urbane reflections of Sir John Betjeman, whom he succeeded as Poet Laureate in 1985.

Born in Yorkshire, whose tough unforgiving landscape remained a lasting influence in his work, Hughes emerged as a major poetic force with his first collection *The Hawk in the Rain*. This appeared in 1957, the year following his marriage to the poet Sylvia Plath whom he met at Cambridge. Fewer literary relationships have inspired such controversy. At first reckless, passionate and inspiring (Plath drew blood with her first, biting, embrace), the union collapsed under the strain of Plath's fragile mental state and Hughes's affair with a married woman, Assia Wevill. Left with their two children, Plath became increasingly depressed and, after completing her most ecstatic yet disturbing work, 'Ariel', committed suicide in 1963. The similar suicide of Assia in 1969 (in which their daughter also died), and the passing, in the same year of his mother, left Hughes, by his own admission, in a state of 'psychological meltdown'.

Finding solace in Devon, where he settled happily with his second wife, Carol, Hughes consolidated his literary reputation and entered into fruitful collaborations with artists and fellow poets such as Leonard Baskin and Seamus Heaney. Increasingly fêted by the literary establishment and public alike (working tirelessly for the cause of poetry, writing enchanting children's stories, accepting the Laureateship), Hughes maintained silence on the matter of Plath's death until the sensational publication, in early 1998 of the hitherto secret *Birthday Letters*, a series of moving and illuminating elegies written over the course of some twenty-five years.

The drafts shown are of the poem 'The Green Wolf', published in *Wodwo* (1967). In that entitled 'Mid-May' (opposite), Hughes's powerful, bounding script is written on a discarded typewritten version of Plath's 'Sleep in the Mojave Desert' – a graphic illustration, perhaps, of their close creative relationship. The later draft, now provisionally titled 'The evening star will be the morning star' (left), is dashed out on the reverse of a letter of 14 February 1962, from his publisher Peter du Sautoy, which congratulates the couple on the recent birth of Nicholas.

OPPOSITE:

This manuscript draft of 'The Green Wolf' by Ted Hughes, here
entitled 'Mid-May', bursts with energy; his almost gothic script
is among the most charismatic of post-war writers.

Mid-May

The evening star ~~the~~ dark woman of Assyria,
Wiser in with ~~her~~ ~~brimming tears~~ ~~what~~ sweetly & pure
the ~~blossom~~ blossoms ~~now~~ ~~prove~~ ~~on the bean flower~~
~~the~~ bells of ~~ring~~ ~~the bean flower~~
bridges with yet like the ear of a type

Plucking me out of the old age of childhood
because that she
And men's blood & women's blood are
One basin
Of old ~~bowels~~ old bowels, old bodies

In the slaver of dew, the wet hair of nightfall.
So it ~~it~~ the steam of many recovered
by neighbour in his bed more less & less
the old root of a right hand more — a farewell
already reap forth undid —

~~Bites~~ the left hand deepens ~~home~~
An eating cold & the left leg took its condescending into tape
And the left half-pan & the left eyelid & the words, till the
huge eyes
frozen in the ~~vein~~ the tongue cannot unfreeze
while somewhere through a dark heaven the dark bloodclot widens in.

Further Reading

M. H. Abrams and Stephen Greenblatt, eds, *The Norton Anthology of English Literature* (New York and London, 2001)

Alexandra Barratt, ed., *Women's Writing in Middle English* (London and New York, 1992)

Michelle P. Brown, *Anglo-Saxon Manuscripts* (London, 1991)

Sally Brown and Hilton Kelliher, *English Literary Manuscripts* (London, 1986)

John Burrow, ed., *English Verse 1300–1500* (London and New York, 1977)

John Burrow and Thorlac Turville-Petre, eds, *A Book of Middle English Verse* (Oxford, 1992)

P. J. Croft, *Autograph Poetry in the English Language*, two volumes (London, 1973)

Margaret Drabble, ed., *The Oxford Companion to English Literature* (Oxford, 1985)

Philip. R. Harris, *A History of the British Museum Library 1753–1973* (London, 1998)

The Index of English Literary Manuscripts 1450–1900, volumes 1–4 (London and New York, 1980–)

Location Register of Twentieth-Century English Literary Manuscripts and Letters, two volumes (London, 1988)

Location Register of Eighteenth- and Nineteenth-Century English Literary Manuscripts and Letters, two volumes (London, 1995)

Arthur F. Marotti, *Manuscript, Print and The English Renaissance Lyric* (Ithaca, 1995)

Ian Ousby, ed., *Cambridge Guide to Literature in English* (Cambridge, 1988)

Rodney Phillips, *The Hand of the Poet* (New York, 1997)

Andrew Prescott and Elizabeth Hallam, eds, *The British Inheritance: A Treasury of Historic Documents* (London, 1999)

Michael Swanton, *English Poetry before Chaucer* (Exeter, 2002)

Robert Woof, Stephen Hebron and Pamela Woof, *English Poetry 850–1850: The First Thousand Years, with some Romantic Perspectives* (Grasmere, 2000)

Acknowledgements

This book would not have been possible without the help of numerous friends and colleagues. Of those closely involved in bringing it to light I must offer particular thanks to David Way, Peter Way, Lara Speicher, Kathleen Houghton, Charlotte Lochhead, Belinda Wilkinson, Andrew Shoolbred, Natasha Kornilof and Laurence Pordes. For their encouragement and advice, I thank my colleagues Hilton Kelliher, Claire Breay, John Rhatigan, Andrew Prescott, Ann Payne, Hugh Cobbe, John Tuck, Christopher Wright, Michelle Brown, Rachel Stockdale, Jacqui Hunt, Greg Buzwell, Alixe Bovey and Jennie Patrice. The greatest debt of gratitude goes to my excellent contributors Sally Brown and, in particular, Roger Evans, who not only contributed many of the articles but also made special trips to take photographs for the book and undertook valuable picture research and careful reading of the text.

Picture Credits

All pictures are copyright The British Library except where noted otherwise. Pictures are listed in order of use from left-hand to right-hand page and from top to bottom. All effort has been made to contact copyright holders. We apologise for any omissions.

'BEOWULF': draft of Heaney's 'Beowulf' translation, Cotton MS Vitellius A XV f. 132; WULFSTAN: Stowe MS 944 f. 6: translation courtesy of The Electronic *Sermo Lupi ad Anglos*, Melissa J Bernstein, University of Rochester, Cotton MS Nero A I f. 110; 'HARLEY LYRICS': National Portrait Gallery, Royal MS App. 58 f. 5, Harley MS 2253 ff. 71v; 'SIR ORFEO': Yates Thompson MS 13 f. 62, Harley MS 3810 f. 1; LANGLAND: C99.f. 10 p. 6, Cotton MS Vespasian B XVI f. 9; 'THE GAWAIN POET': Cotton MS Nero A X ff. 42, 94v and 43; GOWER: Roger Evans (portrait by kind permission of the Dean and Chapter of Southwark Cathedral), Harley MS 7184 f. 59v; CHAUCER: Lansdowne MS 851 f. 2 detail and f. 2, Harley MS 4866 f. 88 detail, C43h.19 prologue; THE 'SLOANE LYRICS': National Portrait Gallery, Sloane MS 2593 ff. 10v–11 and f. 10v; KEMPE: Additional MS 29704 f. 192, Additional MS 61823 f. 123 and 3v; D'ORLEANS: Royal MS 16 F II f. 73, Harley MS 682 f. 88v; MALORY: G10510, Additional MS 59678 f. 35; HENRYSON: Harley MS 3865 f. 4, Additional MS 11896 f. 2, Harley MS 3865 f. 3v; WYATT: C117 aa 3, Egerton MS 2711 ff. 66 and 69v; ANDREWES: Roger Evans (by kind permission of the Dean and Chapter of Southwark Cathedral), C35.l.13, Harley MS 6994 f. 179; HARRINGTON: C70 g 1 title page and p. 146, Additional MS 18920 f. 46; PEELE: 840.i.33, Cotton MS Nero D IX f. 32v, Additional MS 21432 f. 7; SHAKESPEARE: C39.k.15, Harley MS 7368 f. 9, Egerton MS 1787, Guildhall Library Corporation of London, Sloane MS 2596 f. 52*; RALEGH: 9005.h.2, Additional MS 57555 ff. 23 and 172v; JONSON: G11630, C116.g.2 p. 4, Royal MS 18 A XLV f. 2v; GREVILLE: 1765.c.17 Vol. 1, G11602 p. 224–5, Additional MS 54570 f. 56; HERRICK: 11630.ee.38, 11607.i.4 p. 126, Harley MS 367 f. 154; MASSINGER: 628.b.18 Vol. 1, Egerton MS 2428 ff. 27v and 20; MILTON: Additional MS 34816 f. 353, Additional MS 36357 f. 258v, Additional MS 36354 f. 55v; BROWNE: C118.g.1, X100/787 opp. 80 and opp. 89, Sloane MS 1862 f. 48; DRYDEN: 11771.aaa.4, Seal XXXIX.30, Lansdowne MS 1045 f. 101; PHILIPS: 83.l.3 frontispiece and p. 122, Additional MS 78234; TRAHERNE: Chris Fletcher, Additional MS 63054 ff. 2 and 164v; BUTLER: 12270.a.10, Additional MS 32625 ff. 1 and 79; SWIFT: 1509/1192 frontispiece, C71.h.10 p. 24, Additional MS 39839 f. 35; POPE: 11630.aa.46, Additional MS 4808 ff. 116v and 16; RAMSAY: Hirsch III 1003, Egerton MS 2023 ff. 40 and 66v; DEFOE: G13274 Vol. 1, Additional MS 32555 ff. 150v and 10; MONTAGU: 1568/5378 frontispiece, Cup 408.k.41, Additional MS 61479 f. 127; RICHARDSON: 12614.h.13, Additional MS 39311 f. 84v, Additional MS 28097 f. 15; STERNE: 1180.a.34 Vol. 1, Egerton MS 1610 ff. 32v and 60; GRAY: Additional MS 38511 f. 1v, Egerton 2400 f. 46, Additional MS 38511 f. 7; JOHNSON: National Portrait Gallery, 1782.c.32, Additional MS 12070 f. 8; BURNS: 991.b.1 Vol. 1 frontispiece and title page, Egerton MS 1656 f. 30; COWPER: 11643.k.1, 186.b.5 opp. p. 42, Additional MS 37059 f. 51; BLAKE: 2290b, Additional MS 39764 f. 2, Additional MS 49460 f. 56; COLERIDGE: C126.c.10, 010826.i.12, Additional MS 50847r, Additional MS 47497 f. 4; WORDSWORTH: The Wordsworth Trust, Additional MS 47864 ff. 80 and 46v; AUSTEN: 10855.e.8 frontispiece, Additional MS 59874 ff. 77v–8, Egerton MS 3038 ff. 9v; KEATS: Ashley MS 4869 f. 11v, Additional MS 34019 f. 15, Additional MS 37000 f. 1; SHELLEY (Percy): Ashley MS 5249 f. ii, Ashley MS 5022 back cover, Ashley MS 4086 f. 1; CLARE: 993.b.8 Vol. 1, Additional MS 54224 ff. 143 and 144; SCOTT: 1765.c.17 Vol. 4, H1389.a, Egerton MS 1661 f. 68; SHELLEY (Mary): 2408.d.3 Vol. 1, Additional MS 46878 f. 10, Ashley MS A 4023 f. 114; BYRON: Newstead Abbey, 841 m.20 Vol. 3, Ashley MS 4754r; BROWNINGS: National Portrait Gallery, 1203.G.3, Additional MS 43487 f. 49, National Portrait Gallery, Chris Fletcher, Additional MS 43485 f. 1; BRONTE (Emily): National Portrait Gallery, The Brontë Society, Additional MS 43483 f. 1; BRONTE (Charlotte): National Portrait Gallery, Ashley MS 156 ff. 2v–3, Additional MS 43475 f. 179; BRONTE (Anne): The Brontë Society, Ashley MS 172 f. 1v, Ashley MS 154 f. 9; DICKENS: 012612i.8 frontispiece and opp. 872, Additional MS 57493 f. 1, cartoon by permission of the Trustees of Dickens' House, Additional MS 56083 f. 1; TENNYSON: PP 1931pcg, Julia Margaret Cameron photograph from the Tennyson Research Centre by permission of Lincolnshire County Council, Additional MS 45741 f. 279; CARROLL: portrait by permission of the Governing Body of Christ Church, Oxford, Additional MS 54343 f. 15, Additional MS 46700 f. 19v; LEAR: 01092ff opp. 232, LR 410.n.6(2), Additional MS 61891 f. 110; ELIOT (George): Ashley MS 712, Additional MS 34034 ff. 1 and 5; ROSSETTI: 010920 f. 20, Roger Evans, Ashley MS 1376 f. 16; HARDY: Ashley MS 5523, Additional MS 59878, Additional MS 38182 f. 107; WILDE: X909/12111 frontispiece, Zweig MS 199 f. 1, Additional MS 37948 ff. 109v–110; CONRAD: Ashley MS 2953 f. 83, Ashley MS 2946 f. 54, Ashley MS A463 Vol. II f. 10v; FORSTER: National Portrait Gallery, Additional MS 57472 ff. 1 and 2 (courtesy The Provost and Scholars of King's College, Cambridge, and The Society of Authors as the literary representatives of the E.M. Forster Estate); OWEN: National Portrait Gallery, Additional MS 43720 f. 1, Additional MS 43721 f. 54; MANSFIELD: Additional MS 48970 f. 228 and 227, Additional MS 62128 f. 1; ELIOT (T.S.): National Portrait Gallery, Additional MS 71004 f. 151, Additional MS 52918 f. 32 (copyright © Mrs Valerie Eliot, published in her edition of her husband's letters 1898–1922 and reproduced here by kind permission); WOOLF: National Portrait Gallery, Additional 70725 f. 71, Additional MS 51045 f. 136 (courtesy of The Society of Authors as the Literary Representative of the Estate of Virginia Woolf); SHAW: Ashley B1529 f. 15v, Additional MS 50629 f. 26v, Additional MS 50628 f. 7 (by courtesy of The Society of Authors on behalf of the Bernard Shaw Estate); THOMAS: National Portrait Gallery , Additional MS 52612 ff. 152 (first published by MacMillan) and 153 (first published by Dent); LARKIN: The Philip Larkin papers, Additional MS 74734NNv, Additional MS 52619 f. 50 (by kind permission of the Estate of Philip Larkin); DURRELL: Additional MS 73131A f. 70, Additional MS 73099C f. 1v, Additional 73130A, Additional MS 73099C f. 21 (by kind permission of Curtis Brown for the Lawrence and Gerald Durrell Estates); SMITH: The Stevie Smith papers, Additional MS 53732 f. 4v, Additional MS 60753H f. 38; PLATH: portrait, 'Ariel' poem and Additional MS 52617 f. 78 from The Alvarez Papers; AUDEN: portrait, Additional MS 52430 f. 44 and Additional 53772 f. 79 copyright the Estate of W.H. Auden; PINTER: The Harold Pinter loan. By kind permission of Judy Daish Associates Ltd; HUGHES: The Ted Hughes papers, Additional MS 53784 ff. 39 and 35 (copyright the Estate of Ted Hughes)

Index

Page numbers in italics refer to illustrations

Text © Contributors as named 2003

All texts by Chris Fletcher except:
By Roger Evans: Launcelot Andrewes, Ben Jonson, John Milton, John Dryden,
Thomas Traherne, Introduction to the Eighteenth Century, Jonathan Swift,
Alexander Pope, Daniel Defoe, Lady Mary Wortley Montagu, Samuel Richardson,
Laurence Sterne, Thomas Gray, Samuel Johnson, Robert Burns, William Cowper,
William Wordsworth, Jane Austen, John Keats, P.B. Shelley, Sir Walter Scott,
Charles Dickens, Alfred Lord Tennyson, Edward Lear, Christina Rossetti,
George Bernard Shaw, Lawrence Durrell, Dylan Thomas and Stevie Smith
By Sally Brown: Emily Brontë, Charlotte Brontë, Anne Brontë, Lewis Carroll,
Thomas Hardy, Oscar Wilde, Katherine Mansfield, T.S. Eliot, Virginia Woolf,
Sylvia Plath and Harold Pinter

Illustrations © The British Library Board 2003 and other named copyright owners
Designed and typeset by Andrew Shoolbred and Gregory Taylor

Library of Congress Control Number: 2003109927
ISBN: 0–8109–4606–8

Published in the USA 2003 by Harry N. Abrams, Incorporated, New York. All rights
reserved. No part of the contents of this book may be reproduced without written permission
of the publisher.
First published in Great Britain in 2003 by The British Library
Printed and bound in Hong Kong by South Sea International Press

10 9 8 7 6 5 4 3 2 1

Harry N. Abrams, Inc.
100 Fifth Avenue
New York, N.Y. 10011
www.abramsbooks.com

Abrams is a subsidiary of